ALL ABOUT
INVESTING

OTHER TITLES IN THE "ALL ABOUT..." SERIES

All About Stocks, 2nd edition
by Esmé Faerber

All About Bonds and Bond Mutual Funds, 2nd edition
by Esmé Faerber

All About Options, 2nd edition
by Thomas McCafferty

All About Futures, 2nd edition
by Russell Wasendorf

All About Real Estate Investing, 2nd edition
by William Benke and Joseph M. Fowler

All About DRIPs and DSPs
by George C. Fisher

All About Mutual Funds, 2nd edition
by Bruce Jacobs

All About Stock Market Strategies
by David Brown and Kassandra Bentley

All About Index Funds
by Richard Ferri

All About Hedge Funds
by Robert Jaeger

All About Technical Analysis
by Constance Brown

All About Exchange-Traded funds
by Archie Richards

All About Retirement Funds
by Ellie Williams and Diane Pearl

All About Dividend Investing
by Don Schreiber, Jr., and Gary E. Stroik

All About Market Timing
by Leslie N. Masonson

All About Asset Allocation
by Richard Ferri

All About Derivatives
by Michael Durbin

All About Six Sigma
by Warren Brussee

ALL ABOUT INVESTING

The Easy Way to Get Started

ESMÉ FAERBER

McGraw-Hill

New York Chicago San Francisco Lisbon London
Madrid Mexico City Milan New Delhi San Juan
Seoul Singapore Sydney Toronto

1 2 3 4 5 6 7 8 9 0 DOC/DOC 0 9 8 7 6

ISBN 0-07-145752-6

McGraw-Hill books are available at special discounts to use as premiums and sales promotions, or for use in corporate training programs. For more information, please write to the Director of Special Sales, McGraw-Hill, Two Penn Plaza, New York, NY 10121-2298. Or contact your local bookstore.

This publication is designed to provide accurate and authoritative information in regard to the subject matter covered. It is sold with the understanding that the publisher is not engaged in rendering legal, accounting or other professional service. If legal advice or other expert assistance is required, the services of a competent professional person should be sought.

> —*From a Declaration of Principles Jointly Adopted by a Committee of the American Bar Association and a Committee of Publishers.*

All investing concepts, ideas, strategies, methods, etc. in this book are intended for educational purposes only. They are not meant to recommend or promote any investing strategy or philosophy. You are advised to consult a financial professional before investing.

This book is printed on recycled, acid-free paper containing a minimum of 50% recycled de-inked paper.

Investing is not easy, and this book attempts to make the investing process less difficult for both beginning and more sophisticated investors. This book was written to provide the necessary knowledge for investing in stocks, bonds, options, futures, real estate, and precious metals. The early chapters discuss the components of constructing an investment portfolio based on each investor's needs, objectives, and constraints, providing a blueprint for which investments to invest in.

A chapter on how the stock and bond markets work provides investors with the insights and knowledge to avoid the typical mistakes made in buying and selling financial securities.

In the mutual fund chapter, exchange-traded-funds (ETFs), the popular alternative to open-end funds, are highlighted and compared to real estate investment trusts (REITs), closed-end and open-end funds. A chapter follows with a discussion of the different money market securities with attention paid to investing in individual money market securities, such as Treasury bills and bankers' acceptances.

A chapter is devoted to the different types of common stocks with attention paid to the development of a diversified stock portfolio, along with a discussion of the different characteristics of preferred stock.

Three chapters are devoted to bonds, beginning with a discussion of the basic characteristics, a presentation of the types of bonds and their key differences, which provides an understanding of how to assemble a bond portfolio (Treasury notes and bonds, Treasury inflation protected securities, corporate bonds, junk bonds, Government agency bonds, GNMA and FNMA securities, and municipal bonds). Zero-coupon bonds and convertible bonds are discussed in a separate chapter.

An understanding of these individual securities provides investors with the tools and knowledge to increase their returns without significantly increasing their risks.

The chapters on options and futures contracts provide sophisticated investors with the tools and strategies to take on more risk to magnify their returns.

The last chapter focuses on alternative investments such as real estate, precious metals, and collectibles, and provides the fundamental principles for investors interested in these investments.

By understanding the different types of investments you can apply the principles discussed to develop a diversified portfolio, which can lead to financial independence and the achievement of your personal objectives.

ALL ABOUT
INVESTING

CHAPTER 1

Introduction to Investing

KEY CONCEPTS

- Saving, investing or speculating?
- Reasons for investing
- Investment process
- Types of investments

SAVING, INVESTING OR SPECULATING?

Is investing similar to gambling? You might think so if you had invested monthly amounts to purchase the stock of Enron Corporation for five years before it filed for bankruptcy in November 2001. Instead of investing your money in Enron stock, if you had put your money in a savings account, you would have earned on average 1 to 2 percent per year during that time frame. Yet, during the same period of time, the Dow Jones Industrial Average, a measure of the stock market, had doubled. Average real estate prices of homes in some large major cities in the United States had increased by about 7 to 9 percent during that same period. Bonds earned on average around 5 percent per year. Perhaps your odds of success would be better by playing roulette in Atlantic City or Las Vegas? All that is needed is some luck at the tables, and you can double your money in a few minutes, although there is also the potential to lose the entire amount.

Investing in stocks, bonds, and real estate is not the same as gambling, despite the volatility of stock, bond, and real estate prices.

1

Neither is investing the same as putting money under the mattress. The differences are attributed to the following concepts: *Saving* is preserving the value of money not spent, whereas *investing* involves taking on more risk with regard to the different types of investments in the hopes of earning greater returns. Investing is allocating money into financial or real assets to increase future value. Examples of investment assets include stocks, bonds, real estate, options, and futures contracts; an example of a savings vehicle is a bank account. *Speculating* is allocating money to an investment in which the odds of receiving positive returns over a period of time are stacked against the investor. Investing and speculating are not the same. With investing, the probabilities of receiving positive returns over a long period of time are high. Speculating is similar to gambling, where the odds of losing are greater than the odds of winning.

Speculative investments involve a high degree of risk, in which the odds of positive returns are stacked against the investor. The risk of loss from investing in futures contracts is high. For every dollar gained in trading futures contracts, there is a dollar lost. So why do investors invest in speculative securities? The answer is simple. If these investments work as intended, investors realize excessively high returns.

Success in investing requires knowledge of both the investment assets and their risks. Investment options are numerous, and the plethora of information on the Internet can help to make you more knowledgeable about your investment options. The downside to Internet technology is that it is so quick and easy to invest that investment mistakes are made easily. Without discussing your investment ideas with a broker, you could invest in poor-quality stocks or bonds with higher levels of tolerable risk. Investment advice is disseminated easily on the Internet, but you need to be aware of the saying, "There are no free lunches on Wall Street." Had you followed some of the advice of research analysts with regard to which stocks to buy and sell during the 2000–2002 period, you could have lost most of your invested principal. Many analysts had buy recommendations on stocks with poor fundamentals that were falling in price. For example, the sell recommendations on the stocks of Enron, WorldCom, and Global Crossing came only when they were close to bankruptcy.

By understanding how to construct a portfolio of investments, you can insulate against potential losses such as holding the likes of Enron, WorldCom, and Global Crossing stocks.

REASONS FOR INVESTING

Of the many compelling reasons to invest, perhaps the most important is that we will need more money to fund our retirement because we are living longer. Today's investments form the basis for future purchasing power. Poor investments can lead to negative returns and reduce future purchasing power.

You are faced with two options regarding your money. You can spend it or save and invest it. According the Bureau of Economic Analysis, the personal savings of Americans are low compared with people in other developed nations. A low savings rate indicates that Americans are not accumulating enough savings to fund emergencies and sustain their standard of living during retirement. Table 1-1 lists some of the reasons why it is more important to save and invest than to spend.

Other than winning the lottery, you *can* accumulate a large retirement fund in the future without having a large amount of money at your disposal. It is easier than you think. All you need is time, money to deposit at regular intervals, and a rate of return on your investments. Table 1-2 shows how these three elements interact to accumulate $1 million.

You can make the following overriding conclusions from Table 1-2:

- The longer the time horizon, the greater are the effects of compounding, which reduces the initial single-sum deposit or the amounts of the series of deposits.
- The higher the rate of return, the greater are the effects of compounding, which reduces the initial single-sum deposit or the amounts of the series of deposits.

TABLE 1-1

Why It Is More Important to Save and Invest than to Spend

- People are living longer and need more money to live on.
- Medical costs and education and insurance costs are rising.
- The more that you save now, the greater is your future purchasing power owing to compounding.
- By investing wisely, you can improve your standard of living and increase your future wealth.

TABLE 1-2

How to Accumulate a Million Dollars

The following investment scenarios show how the three elements time, amount deposited, and rate of return interact to accumulate $1 million.

For example:

A deposit of $231,377 invested for 30 years at 5 percent per annum has a future value of $1 million.

If the rate of return increases from 5 to 8 percent, the initial amount needed is reduced to $99,377:

A deposit of $99,377 invested for 30 years at 8 percent per annum has a future value of $1 million.

If you make a series of regular deposits instead of investing a single lump sum, the deposit amounts are reduced significantly:

$15, 051 deposited every year for 30 years earning 5 percent per annum has a future value of $1 million.

Earning a greater return reduces the amount of the yearly deposits:

$8,827 deposited every year for 30 years earning 8 percent per annum has a future value of $1 million.

If you make the deposits monthly instead of yearly, the amount of each deposit is reduced further:

$1,202 deposited every month for 30 years at 5 percent per annum has a future value of $1 million.

If you make the deposits weekly instead of monthly, the deposit amounts are reduced further by significant amounts:

$276 deposited every week for 30 years at 5 percent per annum has a future value of $1 million.

If the rate of return increases from 5 to 8 percent, the deposit amount is as follows:

$154 invested every week earning 8 percent per annum for 30 years has a future value of $1 million.

If we extend the time horizon from 30 to 40 years and retain the 8 percent rate of return, the weekly deposit is reduced to a mere $66:

$66 invested every week earning 8 percent per annum for 40 years has a future value of $1 million.

- The longer the time horizon and the greater the rate of return, the lower is the initial single-sum deposit or are the series of deposits.

The key to successful financial planning is to set aside more for saving and to invest it wisely using a long time horizon. The rate of return on investments should exceed the rate of inflation and cover taxes paid, as well as earning an excess amount related to the intrinsic risk of the investment. Savings accounts and low-rate-of-return money-market accounts do not contribute significantly to large future accumulations of interest. The higher rates of return come from stocks, bonds, and other investment-class assets such as real estate. However, these investments are not without risk, so you should understand the types of risks associated with each of these investments before you invest. Risk and return are discussed in Chapter 2.

History provides a good example of the risk of loss from investing in investment classes without an understanding of their characteristics. The record appreciation of stock market prices from 1998 to 2000 enticed many investors who had never previously invested in stocks to jump into the market. This enthusiasm of investors to invest in Internet stocks, initial public offerings (IPOs), and other risky stocks, which defied gravity in their meteoric ascent to dangerously high valuations, became apparent. The incredibly high returns earned by these stocks in relatively short periods of time prompted many investors to disregard the risk of investing in these expensive stocks. The rapid and steep declines in the stock market in March 2000 emphasize the volatility of stock prices, which drove many investors back to the safety of their low-yielding bank accounts and money-market funds. This lack of understanding how stocks perform perpetuates this myopic view of investing in the stock market (jumping in when valuations are high and selling when valuations are low). Understanding the characteristics of the different types of investments can help you to determine which investments are right for your needs.

INVESTMENT PROCESS

Many types of investments are available, but some might not be suitable for you. The process of buying and selling securities is relatively easy, but knowing what to buy and when to sell is more difficult. In essence, the types of investments you choose are determined by your objectives and personal characteristics. The investment process begins with an *investment plan* that lists your objectives and includes a written strategic plan for achieving those objectives. Before committing money to investments in your plan, you should have enough money saved in an *emergency fund*, which provides for contingent expenses, such as medical emergencies, loss of a job, damage to property, or loss of personal assets. Investing your emergency funds in stocks is never a good idea because stock markets are volatile, and emergency funds might need to be withdrawn at unpredictable times. If the stock market declines, you might not have enough money to cover your emergency needs. Thus you should invest emergency funds in *liquid investments*, which can be converted to cash on demand with no loss of principal. All money-market investments and bank accounts are liquid investments.

After you create an emergency fund, you should begin following an investment plan for the near and long-term future. Even if you have a modest salary, consistently setting aside and investing small amounts of money can make a difference. Table 1-3 illustrates the power of paying yourself first, which is the key to accumulating financial wealth.

The result of increasing the length of time of your investments is an acceleration of earnings owing to the power of compounding. You should write a check to your investment account at the beginning of each month rather than waiting until the end of the month to see what remains for savings. This is so because the temptation to spend money is far greater than the desire to save money, and often there is not much money left to save at the end of the month because it has been spent.

TABLE 1-3

The Results of Frequent Investments
of Small Amounts of Money

Suppose that you save $50 at the beginning of the month and earn 6 percent per annum. By the time you reach age 65, your earning would be

Begin investing at age 25: ⟶ $100,072

Begin investing at age 35: ⟶ $50,476

Begin investing at age 45: ⟶ $23,217

Begin investing at age 55: ⟶ $8,234

How do you know where to invest your funds? A discussion of the following five steps can help you to build and maintain a portfolio of investments:

1. Determine your financial objectives.
2. Allocate your assets.
3. Prepare your investment strategy.
4. Select your investments.
5. Evaluate your portfolio.

1. Determine Your Financial Objectives

Financial objectives are the financial milestones that you would like to achieve through investing. Listing your objectives is the first step in an investment plan. Possible objectives might include the following:

- Accumulating an emergency fund within six months
- Buying a car in the next two years
- Saving for a down payment on a house in five years
- Funding a college education in 10 years
- Building a retirement fund over the next 25 years

Funding Your Objectives

All these objectives have time horizons so that you can determine how much you will need to fund each investment. After listing your objectives, you determine the amount of money you will need to fund each objective. For example, suppose that you want to buy a $25,000 car within the next two years. Table 1-4 illustrates the savings options, given an estimated rate of return of 5 percent per year. In the first option, you invest $22, 675 now, which will equal $25,000 in two years. In the second option, you invest $12,195 at the end of each year to equal $25,000. In the third option, you invest $11,614 at the beginning of years 1 and 2 to equal $25,000.

Noting the time frame and the amount you need to fund your objectives gives you a better sense of how much to invest for each of the options. Asking the following questions can help you to formulate which objectives you want to fund first:

- What will I use the money or savings for?
- Am I committed to making sacrifices to fund my objectives?

TABLE 1-4

How to Fund Your Objectives

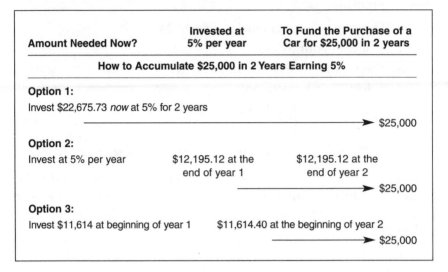

Amount Needed Now?	Invested at 5% per year	To Fund the Purchase of a Car for $25,000 in 2 years
How to Accumulate $25,000 in 2 Years Earning 5%		

Option 1:
Invest $22,675.73 *now* at 5% for 2 years
———————————————————————————————➤ $25,000

Option 2:
Invest at 5% per year $12,195.12 at the $12,195.12 at the
                             end of year 1   end of year 2
                                        ———————————————————➤ $25,000

Option 3:
Invest $11,614 at beginning of year 1 $11,614.40 at the beginning of year 2
                                        ———————————————————➤ $25,000

- What are the consequences if I cannot fund my objectives?
- What do I need to do to increase my savings to fund my objectives?

To answer these questions, you must quantify the amount of money you will need every year to fund your objectives. Assuming that the objectives in Table 1-5 are yours, you would need to fund many of these objectives simultaneously. In this example, you need to save $58,321 in the first year to begin funding all your objectives.

Time Horizon and Risk. The investments you choose are geared to the time horizons of the objectives and your tolerable levels of risk. The first two objectives listed in Table 1-5 have short time horizons, which mean that the investments for those objectives should focus on capital preservation. For instance, you would not invest money set aside for a car purchase in stocks because the risk of losing money in the stock market over a two-year period is quite high.

Determining Your Assets and Liabilities

Your investment plan should be tailored to suit your financial circumstances (assets and liabilities), which are unique. To determine your financial assets and liabilities, you need to create a *balance sheet*, which lists your assets (everything of value that you own) and your

TABLE 1-5

List and Quantify Dollar Amounts for Objectives

Objective	Time Horizon	Future Amount Needed	Rate of Return	Yearly Investments to Fund Objectives
Short term (2 years or less)				
Establish an emergency fund	1 year	$10,000	>1%	$10,000 in year 1
Buy a car	2 years	$25,000	5%	$12,195 in years 1 and 2
Medium term (2 to 7 years)				
Make a down payment on a house	5 years	$40,000	5.5%	$ 6,793 in years 1 through 5
Long term (7 plus years)				
Fund a college education	10 years	$120,000	8%	$ 7,670 in years 1 through 10
Save for retirement	25 years	$2,000,000	9%	$21,663 in years 1 through 25
Total amount needed to fund objectives				**$58,321**

liabilities (what you owe). The difference between your assets and liabilities is your *net worth*. By comparing balance sheets you have compiled at different points in time, you can determine whether you have

- Accumulated or drawn down assets
- Paid down or increased liabilities
- Increased or decreased your net worth

If you do not have the income or net worth to fund your objectives, you can prioritize your objectives and allocate funding to the most important objectives first. To determine the level of risk that you can assume in your portfolio, you should evaluate your personal circumstances, that is, your marital status, income, and job (Table 1-6).

The Financial Life Cycle

By working through your responses in Table 1-6, you build a profile that determines your acceptable level of risk, the stage you are at in your financial life cycle, and the size of your portfolio. For example,

TABLE 1-6

Evaluate Your Circumstances

Circle the answer that applies	
Marital status	Single, married, divorcee, widower
Family	No children, young children, teenage children, empty nest
Age	Under 25, 25–39 years, 40–60 years, over 60
Education	High school graduate, college degree, graduate degree
Income	Stable and level, good future growth prospects
Income, spouse	Stable and level, good future growth prospects, not applicable
Job/profession	Skills and expertise, ability to improve level of earnings
Net worth	Level of income: _____; assets and net worth _____ _____
Size of portfolio	_____

if you are a single person in your twenties with an MBA degree, no dependents, and a growing income, you can absorb far more risk than if you are in your twenties, married, and the sole breadwinner with three small children. Similarly, a widow who depends on the income generated from investment assets cannot assume much risk in the choice of investments as compared with a wealthy 65-year-old who has other sources of income outside of investment assets.

Your age, income, and net worth generally guide the direction of your investment plan. Your age typically determines in which of the following three stages of the financial life cycle you reside:

- *Accumulation stage.* During the early years of your career when your income is rising, you will accumulate investments, mainly in the form of pension and retirement plans. Usually, your debt load increases owing to a mortgage, car loan, or other borrowing. However, in this stage you incur debt to purchase assets, which over time you pay down. The investment emphasis here is on capital growth.

- *Preservation stage.* In this stage your investment assets are growing, and generally, income exceeds expenditures. Here the investment emphasis includes both capital growth and income generation.

- *Depletion-of-wealth stage.* This stage begins with retirement, in which income from pensions (retirement plans), Social Security, and investments replaces your salary. Your priorities in this stage are to make your investment assets last throughout your retirement and to earn enough income to support a comfortable lifestyle. In this stage your investment emphasis is primarily on the preservation of capital and income generation. However, to provide for longer life expectancies, you should commit some of your investment assets to capital growth.

In summary, the key to accumulating wealth is twofold: Save money, and invest your money wisely. This is especially true in your early years owing to the effects of compounding, which produces greater appreciation for longer time periods, as illustrated in Table 1-3. *Compounding* is defined as the adding of interest to principal for the current and previous periods in order to calculate the interest for the next period.

Your personal circumstances often determine the level of risk that you can assume in your investment choices. Generally, younger investors can withstand greater risk owing to their longer-term outlook of at least 20 years or more before retirement.

2. Allocate Your Assets

After determining your objectives, the second step in the investment process is to determine how to allocate your funds among the different types of investments (money-market securities, bonds, stocks, options, futures, real estate, and collectibles). Funds that you need on demand should be invested in money-market securities. Funds with longer time horizons can be invested in bonds, stocks, and other assets such as real estate, options, futures, or collectibles. Figure 1-1 shows an example of an asset allocation plan.

FIGURE 1-1

Asset Allocation Plan

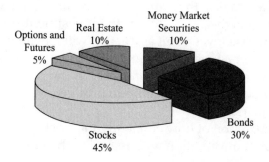

Asset allocation is the assignment of funds to different categories of investments, such as money-market securities, bonds, stocks, options, futures contracts, real estate, and collectibles. For example, if you had all your money in savings accounts, you would decide how much of it to allocate to money-market securities (for immediate and short-term needs), bonds, stocks, options, futures, real estate, and any other investment-class assets. Money-market securities generally earn the least, but they provide instant access to the funds should you need them. Bonds are investments that provide regular payments of income and earn more than money-market securities. Bonds have maturity dates, and the risk of loss of principal invested is greater should you need to liquidate your bonds before maturity. Stocks provide the greatest returns of financial securities over long periods of time (10-year or greater period). However, because stock prices are volatile, the risk of loss may be large if you need to liquidate stocks when prices are down. This is why investments in stocks require a long time horizon so that you can sell stocks when they have appreciated rather than having to sell them at an inopportune time.

Investors with long time horizons (30 years or more to retirement) generally should allocate their investment assets to stocks and other appreciating investment asset classes such as real estate to grow funds for funding long-term future objectives. Investors close to retirement should have the greatest portion of their investments allocated to money-market securities and bonds, which provide income for living expenses, and a smaller portion allocated to investments such as stocks to provide portfolio growth. Asset allocation plans are revisited and changed from time to time as financial circumstances change.

3. Identify Your Investment Strategy

Developing a strategy that conforms to your objectives and asset allocation plan is the third step in the investment process. If you intend to purchase investment assets that will remain in your investment portfolio for a long time, you are following a *passive investment strategy*. An *active investment strategy* involves active trading of the investment assets in your portfolio to produce greater returns than those of the market.

Your perception of how efficiently the stock and bond markets process relevant information with regard to the pricing of securities determines whether you will pursue an active or passive portfolio strategy. If you believe that the stock and bond markets are *efficient*, meaning that all current and new information is reflected quickly and efficiently in stock and bond prices, you would pursue a passive investment strategy. This is so because when there are underpriced stocks (or bonds), they will be bought immediately, driving their prices up to their fair values. Consequently, there will be very few underpriced stocks or overpriced stocks in an efficient market. An efficient market means that few investors will be able to consistently beat the market returns on a risk-adjusted basis (seeking returns that are greater than the market by investing in securities with the same level of risk). Investors who believe that markets are efficient would hope to do as well as the market averages, seeing that they cannot beat the market averages. They would buy and hold investments resembling the market average, which is a passive investment strategy.

If investors believe that markets are *inefficient* (slow to reflect pricing information), there will be many undervalued stocks. Consequently, an investor will use many different financial tools and techniques to look for underpriced stocks and bonds to earn higher returns than those of the market averages. This involves an active strategy of buying investments when they are underpriced and selling them when they have appreciated.

4. Select Your Investments

After you formulate your objectives, asset allocation plan, and investment strategy, it is time to select your investments. Passive investors choose diversified assets in each class of investments. A *diversified stock portfolio*, for example, consists of securities of companies whose returns are not directly related. In other words, a diversified portfolio includes stocks from different sectors of the economy, such as the technology, energy, health care, consumer, industrial, auto, basic materials, manufacturing, and financial sectors. An active investor assembles a portfolio by evaluating the fundamental strengths of companies in different economic sectors to find undervalued securities and then selling the securities when they become overpriced. A diversified bond portfolio would include bonds from different issuers with different maturities. Diversification is not as important with money-market securities because of their short maturities (less than one year) and their relative safety.

Liquid investments can be converted to cash without losing much of their principal in the conversion. Examples of liquid investments are U.S. Treasury bills, commercial paper, bankers' acceptances, money-market mutual funds, short-term certificates of deposit, money-market bank and deposits, and savings and checking accounts. These are ideal investments for an emergency fund.

Investing for short and medium-term time horizons should produce higher yields than money-market investments. Investments in two- and five-year U.S. Treasury notes, for example, provide current income with virtually no risk of default on the interest and principal amount invested. Other options for these shorter maturities are U.S. government agency notes, U.S. Treasury bonds (with maturities of five years or less), and short-term bond mutual funds.

If you want to fund an education in 10 years, you have more investment options, such as a mix of common stock and long-term bonds. With a time horizon of 25 years, you can weigh the mix of investments more heavily toward stocks than bonds because stocks generally outperform bonds and most other financial investments over long periods of time. If the past is a reflection of the future, you can expect average yearly returns of 7 percent for stocks versus 4 to 5 percent for bonds. Investors who are nervous about stock market corrections or crashes might consider investing some of their funds in real estate and 30-year bonds. However, bonds and real estate also can be risky because they also react to changes in interest rates and economic policies.

5. Evaluate Your Portfolio

You should evaluate your portfolio periodically because a change in your circumstances might necessitate a change in your asset allocation plan. Also, fluctuating economic and market conditions might affect your asset allocation plan. Similarly, a change in a company's business will have a direct bearing on the valuation of that company's securities in your investment portfolio.

TYPES OF INVESTMENTS

The most common investment alternatives are financial investments, although investments in real assets (nonfinancial) such as real estate and collectibles also can be found in many investment portfolios. See Figure 1-2 for a classification of investment securities.

FIGURE 1-2

Classification of Investments

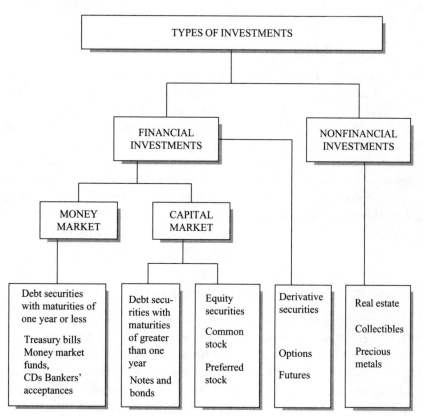

Financial investments are grouped into four categories:

1. *Money-market securities,* which are short-term securities with maturities of one year or less
2. *Debt securities,* which are fixed income securities with maturities of greater than one year
3. *Equity securities,* which are long-term securities that do not mature
4. *Derivative securities,* which are securities that derive their value from other securities and involve transactions that are completed at a future date

Nonfinancial investments include real estate, collectibles (art, antiques, baseball cards, stamps, and other collections as a store of value), precious metals, and physical resources. Besides the special-ized knowledge required for investing in these nonfinancial invest-ments, there are many similarities to investing in financial assets.

Money-Market Securities

Money-market securities are debt or fixed-income securities with maturities of one year or less. They are generally liquid, safe investments that investors use for emergency funds and short-term invest-ments. These securities are used as temporary parking places for funds. Idle cash can be invested in money-market securities to earn a return. These securities are lower-risk investments than stocks and bonds. However, over long periods of time, the returns on money-market securities are much lower than those of stocks and bonds. Examples of money-market securities are Treasury bills, commercial paper, bankers' acceptances, certificates of deposit (CDs), repur-chase agreements, and money-market mutual funds.

Debt Securities

Debt securities are similar to IOUs or promissory notes. A debt secu-rity is created when funds are borrowed, which are then repaid at some point in the future along with the payment of interest at regu-lar intervals of time. The maturities of debt securities vary widely. Debt securities with maturities of longer than one year trade in the capital market, whereas debt securities with maturities of less than a year trade in the money-market.

Bonds are debt securities issued by governments and corpora-tions with different maturities. Medium-term bonds have maturities of 1 to 10 years, and long-term bonds mature 10 to 50 years after issuance. Both types of bonds are referred to as *capital market secu-rities*. Long-term securities that make regular payments are U.S. Treasury notes and bonds, U.S. agency debt, municipal bond issues, and corporate issues. Zero-coupon bonds and convertible bonds are hybrid debt securities that have different characteristics, but they are also considered to be capital market securities. They are consid-ered to be hybrid securities because zero-coupon bonds do not pay fixed amounts of interest like regular bonds, and convertible bonds may be exchanged for common stock at the discretion of the holder instead of maturing like a regular bond.

Equity Securities

Equity securities come in two forms; common stock and preferred stock. Both types of securities are traded in the capital markets. *Common stock* represents ownership or an equity interest in a company. For example, if you bought 1,000 shares of Microsoft Corporation, you would be a fractional owner of the company. If a company has 100,000 shares outstanding and you bought 1,000 shares, you would have a 1 percent (1/100) ownership stake in the company. Returns from common stock come in two forms: dividends and capital gains. Some companies pay dividends on their common stock, although they are not obligated to do so. These companies try to maintain regular payments and increase them over time.

Dividends are payments to stockholders out of the company's net profits, usually in cash but possibly in stock or property. Exxon Mobil, for example, paid a dividend of $1.16 per share in four quarterly payments of $0.29 per share in 2005. Cisco Systems, Inc., does not pay dividends. Instead, investors buy Cisco stock for the potential capital gains. If you bought Cisco stock at $14 per share and sold the stock at $20 per share, you realized a capital gain of $6 per share. *Capital gains* are the excess proceeds over the cost basis of a stock when the stock is sold.

Preferred stock also represents equity ownership in a company, and it gives the preferred stockholder a claim before the common stockholder to the company's earnings and assets in the event of liquidation. Unlike common stock, a preferred stock's dividend rate generally is fixed. The receipt of regular payments makes preferred stock similar to bonds. However, the difference between preferred stocks and bonds is that companies are not obligated to pay dividends on their preferred stock unless the board of directors declares the dividend. Other features of preferred stock are discussed in detail in Chapter 6.

Derivative Securities

Derivative securities derive their value from other securities and specify transactions to be completed at a future date as compared with stocks and bonds, which involve immediate transactions. Derivative securities include options and futures contracts. With an option, an investor has an opportunity to buy or sell a stock at a specified price within a given period of time. *Options* are contracts that give the holder the right but not the obligation to buy (*call option*) or sell (*put option*) a specified financial asset at a specified price within a given period of time. Financial assets could be stocks, stock indexes, or currencies.

Futures are contracts between two parties who agree to buy and sell a financial security or commodity at a specified price at a specified future date. In addition to financial securities, such as stock indexes, interest-rate futures, and monetary currencies, futures are traded actively on commodities, such as precious metals, oil, coffee, orange juice, pork bellies, corn, and soybeans. The major difference between investing in a financial security directly versus investing in the same financial security through a futures contract is the use of borrowed funds. With futures contracts, investors put up a small fraction of the total value of the contract, which magnifies the potential returns but also increases potential risk of loss. Chapter 2 discusses the risk-return tradeoff of the different investments.

WEB EXERCISE

Web sites such as www.smartmoney.com and www.troweprice.com have financial calculators to help you determine how much money you would need to save for a college education and retirement. Go to one of these sites and use its financial calculators to determine how much money you would need to save for graduate school, a college education for a child, and retirement.

CHAPTER 2

Investment Risk and Return

KEY CONCEPTS

- Types of investment risk
- The relationship between risk and return
- Calculating a rate of return
- Returns as measured by stock market indices
- Making sense of the measurement of risk and return of stocks
- Asset allocation and the selection of investments

The discussion in Chapter 1 highlighted why we invest our money—namely, to earn a return on our investments that compensates us for inflation, taxes, and uncertainties and results in greater future purchasing power. We therefore look for the types of investments that can earn expected returns to achieve future objectives. Before making the decision of which investments to choose, we subjectively estimate the likelihood of attaining those expected returns. An understanding of this risk and return process can help you to choose the types of investments that will achieve your objectives within your set time frames.

TYPES OF INVESTMENT RISK

Risk is defined as the variability of returns from an investment. Risk is the uncertainty related to the outcome of an investment, and all investments are subject to risk of one type or another. The greater the variability in the price, the greater is the level of risk. Understanding the risks associated with different securities is critical to building a strong portfolio. Risk is probably what deters many investors from investing in stocks and prompts them to keep their money in so-called safe bank accounts, CDs, and bonds. Returns from these passive savings vehicles often have lagged the rate of inflation. Although investors will not lose their capital, they risk losses in earnings owing to inflation and taxes when they merely hold cash and cash equivalents.

Business Risk

Business risk is the uncertainty that pertains to a company's sales and earnings, namely, that a company generates poor sales and earnings for a period of time. By their nature, some companies are riskier than others, and the riskier companies see greater fluctuations in their sales and earnings. If a company's sales and earnings decline significantly, its stocks and bonds experience downward pressure when the company is not able to cover its interest, principal, and dividend payments. Deterioration in sales and earnings at worst could move the company into bankruptcy, which makes its securities (stocks and bonds) worthless. A company with stable sales does not have this problem of not being able to cover its regular expenses.

Investors' expectations of a company's earnings affect the prices of its stocks and bonds. Shareholders who anticipate a decline in earnings will sell their shares, which can cause a decline in the stock's price. Similarly, if investors anticipate an increase in earnings, they are willing to pay higher prices for the stock. If the company's earnings decline significantly, the company's bonds could be downgraded by ratings services such as Moody's and Standard and Poor's, causing the bonds to decline in price.

Common stocks of automobiles, home building, construction, and durable goods companies are referred to as *cyclical stocks*. A cyclical stock is the stock of a company whose earnings and prices move directly up or down with expansion and contraction of the economy. Business risk for a cyclical company increases when changes in the economy result in reduced consumer or business spending for that company's products. This occurred in 2001 and 2002 when the telecommunications equipment sector (companies such as Lucent, Nortel Networks, and Ciena) experienced a downturn due to an economic recession, which caused the telecom companies (AT&T, Sprint, and WorldCom) to reduce their spending on new equipment.

By investing in the common stocks of companies with stable earnings rather than those of cyclical companies, you can reduce business risk. *Stable stock* is the stock of a company whose earnings are not influenced by changes in the activity of the economy. Some examples are electric utility and consumer goods companies.

Financial Risk

Financial risk is the inability of a company to meet its financial obligations, and the extent of a company's financial risk is measured by the amount of debt the company holds in relation to its equity. A company with a high proportion of debt relative to its assets has an increased likelihood that at some point in time it may be unable to meet its principal and interest obligations. The greater the debt-to-equity ratio, the higher is the financial risk because the company will need to earn at least enough to pay back its fixed interest and principal payments. When a company carries a high ratio of debt to equity, the company becomes a *default risk (credit risk)*. In addition to financial risk, business risk also can increase default risk, in that if a company's earnings are impaired, ratings agencies downgrade the company's bonds. Ratings agencies grade securities of companies based on their ability to pay bondholders their interest and principal payments. When bonds are downgraded, creditors then may impose restrictions on the company, such as limitations on further debt and the payment of dividends. These restrictions may not pose problems, but a company may find it harder to comply with them during periods of declining earnings.

Companies that have little or no debt have little or no financial risk. Looking at a company's balance sheet reveals the amount of debt relative to total assets and equity. At worst, financial risk, like business risk, can lead a company to bankruptcy, making its securities worthless. To reduce financial risk, invest in the securities of companies with low debt-to-equity or low debt-to-total asset ratios. See Table 2-1 for the steps to determine the financial risk for a company using the Internet. Figure 2-1 shows the categories of total risk, which can be broken down into unsystematic and systematic risk.

Unsystematic risk is the risk specific to a company or industry. This risk pertains to a company's business, its operations, and its finances. *Operating risk* refers to contingent risks such as the death of a CEO, a labor strike, or litigation. Unsystematic risk is also known as *diversifiable risk*.

TABLE 2-1

How to Determine the Financial Risk of a Company Using the Internet to Obtain the Information

You can determine the financial risk of companies that interest you by reviewing their financial statements using the Internet.

1. Go to www.yahoo.com and click on "Finance."
2. In the Enter symbol(s) box, type the ticker symbols of the company or companies that you want to research. If you want to know the financial risk of General Electric Company, Intel Corporation, and Applied Materials, Inc., type "GE," "INTC," and "AMAT." Make sure to separate each symbol with a comma. If you do not know the symbol for a company, click "Symbol Lookup."
3. Click the Summary view.
4. Click "profile" for information on that company.
5. In the left column, click "Income Statement" in the Financials section. A screen with an income statement appears. Look for "Earnings before interest and taxes" (operating income) and "Interest expense" for the year (or quarter). Determine the company's coverage of its interest expense as follows:

$$\text{Coverage ratio} = \frac{\text{earnings before interest and taxes}}{\text{interest expense}}$$

Low coverage indicates that a sales decrease or an operating expense increase may result in the company being unable to meet its interest payments.

6. Go to the left of the screen and click on "Balance Sheet." Scroll down to "Liabilities," and add the total current and long-term liabilities. Look for the "Total assets," and determine the debt ratio for the year or quarter as follows:

$$\text{Debt ratio} = \frac{\text{total current and long-term liabilities}}{\text{total assets}}$$

A large debt ratio with low coverage indicates high financial risk.

7. Evaluate the financial risk for each of the companies that you researched.

Systematic risk is caused by factors that affect all securities. Systematic risk includes external risks to the company, such as market risk, event risk, interest-rate risk, exchange-rate risk, liquidity risk, and purchasing-power risk. You cannot reduce market risk through diversification.

Alleviating Business and Financial Risks

You can lessen your exposure to business and financial risk in your portfolio of investments through *diversification*, which refers to the purchase of different investment assets whose returns are unrelated.

By building a diversified portfolio, you reduce the variability in returns (risk).

For example, if you invest your savings of $1 million in the common stock of Intel Corporation on August 31, 2003, at $28 per share, a year later your loss would have been 25 percent of your investment. Intel stock fell to $21 per share. Intel's stock performance was dismal when compared with the market for the same period, August 31, 2003 to August 31, 2004. The Dow Jones Industrial Average (DJIA) increased by 7 percent, the Standard and Poor's (S&P) 500 Index increased by 8 percent, and the Nasdaq Composite Index was down by 1 percent for the same one-year period. See Table 2-2 for the loss in the portfolio for an investment in Intel Corporation's stock.

Suppose that instead of investing the entire $1 million in Intel stock for the one-year period, you decided to divide the money equally into 10 stocks, as shown in Table 2-3. At the end of the one-year period, your diversified portfolio would have increased by 6 percent as opposed to the loss of 25 percent from investing the entire

FIGURE 2-1

Breakdown of Total Risk

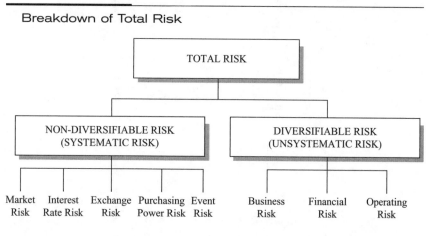

TABLE 2-2

Portfolio of Stocks

Date	Security	Price Share	No. of Shares	Symbol	Cost	Market Price (8/31/04)	Loss
8/31/03	Bought Intel	$28	35,714	INTC	$1,000,000	$749,994	($250,006)

TABLE 2-3

Portfolio of Stocks

8/31/03 Transaction	Stock Price	Symbol	Cost	Stock Price/Market Price 8/31/04	Gain (Loss)
Buy 2702 shares Boeing	$37.01	BA	$100,000	$52/$140,504	$40,504
Buy 2,000 shares Johnson & Johnson	$50	JNJ	$100,000	$58/$116,000	16,000
Buy 2,222 shares Pepsi	$45	PEP	$100,000	$50/$111,100	11,100
Buy 5,025 shares Mattel	$19.90	MAT	$100,000	$16/$80,400	(19,600)
Buy 2,531 shares Washington Mutual	$35	WM	$100,000	$38.80/$98,202	(1,798)
Buy 3,571 shares Intel	$28	INTC	$100,000	$21/$74,991	(25,009)
Buy 2,631 shares ExxonMobil	$38	XOM	$100,000	$46/$121,026	21,026
Buy 1,669 shares Wal-Mart	$59.90	WMT	$100,000	$52.60/$87,789	(12,211)
Buy 5,000 shares Tyco	$20	TYC	$100,000	$31/$155,000	55,000
Buy 4,717 shares Applied Materials	$21.20	AMAT	$100,000	$15.90/$75,000	(25,000)
Totals			**$1,000,000**	**$1,060,012**	**$60,012**

amount in Intel. The gains in the portfolio came from aerospace, pharmaceutical, beverage, oil, and conglomerate stocks (Boeing, Johnson & Johnson, Pepsi Cola, ExxonMobil, and Tyco). The losses were due to Mattel in the recreational sector of the economy, Washington Mutual in the financial sector of the economy, Intel and Applied Materials in the technology sector, and Wal-Mart in the retail sector.

The importance of diversification can be looked at in another way. With a portfolio consisting of one stock, a 50 percent decline in that stock results in a 50 percent decline in the total value. In a portfolio of 10 stocks with equal amounts invested in each stock, a decline of 50 percent in one stock's value results in a 5 percent decline in the total value. Thus too few stocks in a portfolio means that you have too much risk placed on each stock. Too many stocks in a portfolio dilutes the potential upside appreciation in the total value of the portfolio.

By investing in a number of stocks from different sectors of the economy rather than investing in one stock, we have reduced our risk of loss. The returns on stocks from different sectors of the economy are not perfectly correlated, thereby reducing the variability in the returns. For example, the two technology stocks in the portfolio, Intel and Applied Materials, have returns that generally move together, a high correlation. Stocks from different sectors of the economy have returns that are not related, which means a low or negative correlation. By increasing the number of stocks in your portfolio to 30 or 40 that have low or negative correlations you can effectively eliminate all company-related risks. Thus, of the total risk, you can reduce unsystematic risk (operating, business, and financial risks) through diversification.

Market Risk

Market risk refers to the movement of security prices, which tend to move together in reaction to external events, unrelated to a company's fundamentals. Market risk is the risk that market pressures will cause an investment to fluctuate in value. Although you can diversify investments to virtually eliminate business, financial, and operating risks, you cannot do the same with market risk. Diversification does not provide a safety net when an external event causes a landslide in the stock markets. For example, when the stock market goes up, most stocks go up in price, including those with less-than-spectacular sales, growth, and earnings. Similarly, if a sell-off occurs in the stock market, stocks with better than average sales, growth, and earnings will be included in the downslide.

External events that move security prices (stocks, bonds, and other assets such as real estate) are unpredictable. Such an event could be a terrorist incident or news of a war, death of a prominent leader of a foreign nation, changes in inflation rate, labor strikes, or floods in the Midwest. Investors cannot do much to avoid these volatile short-term fluctuations in stock, bond, and real estate prices.

Over long periods of time, however, stock prices tend to appreciate in relation to their intrinsic value (their growth and earnings). In other words, a stock's long-term returns are determined by a company's investment fundamentals. Market risk highlights the dangers for investors who invest short-term money in the stock market. If you need cash when the market has declined, you will need to sell your stocks, which may have produced losses. For stock investments, you should have a long time horizon so that you are not forced to sell in down markets. The same long time horizon applies to investments in real estate.

Reducing Market Risk

Investors cannot do much about the volatility of the markets with a short time horizon because the risk of potential loss is high with stocks and other real investment assets. Stocks are more volatile in price than bonds. Table 2-4 shows the historic returns of different financial securities over a 74-year period from 1926 to 2000. With a holding period of 74 years, annual returns averaged 12.4 percent for small-capitalization (small-cap) stocks, 11 percent for large-cap stocks, 5.5 percent for intermediate-term government bonds, and 3.9 percent for Treasury bills. Stocks clearly outperformed bonds, and Treasury bills. However, large- and small-cap stocks also have the greatest risk, as measured by their standard deviations. For example, the variability of returns for small-cap stocks can range from a gain of 45.8 (12.4 + 33.4) percent to a loss of 21 (12.4 − 33.4) percent. The variability of returns for intermediate-term government bonds is considerably less (a range of 11.3 percent to a loss of 0.3 percent).

With a short time horizon, the potential risk of loss from investing in stocks increases. Table 2-5 shows historic returns for financial

TABLE 2-4

Historic Returns 1926–2000

	Return	Risk (Standard Deviation)*
Small-cap stocks	12.4%	33.4%
Large-cap stocks	11%	20.2%
Intermediate-term government bonds	5.5%	5.8%
Treasury bills	3.9%	3.2%
Inflation	3.3%	4.4%

*Source of risk: Ibbotson Associates.

TABLE 2-5

Historic Returns During the Period
2000 to February 2002

	Returns
Small-cap stocks	−1.3%
Large-cap stocks	−9.4%
Intermediate-term government bonds	9.9%
Treasury bills	4%
Inflation	2.5%

securities during the period 2000 to February 2002. Stocks earned negative returns, but government bonds and Treasury bills produced positive returns. When inflation is factored into returns, the real rates of return for stocks become much more compelling over long periods of time than those earned on bonds and Treasury bills (see Table 2-4).

These statistics show that patient investors with long holding periods can reduce significantly the market risks from investing in stocks. However, stock investors cannot escape from market risk completely because there is always volatility in the stock market. However, with the reinvestment of dividends and capital gains, the range of returns is less variable over longer holding periods.

Using asset allocation to choose a balanced portfolio of different investments also reduces the effects of market risk, as shown in Table 2-6. A mix of half large-cap stocks and government bonds would

TABLE 2-6

Historic Returns from Asset Allocation during Period from 1926 to 2000

	Return	Greatest 5-Year Return	Minimum 5-Year Return
100% large-cap stocks	11%	28.6%	−12.5%
50% bonds, 50% large-cap stocks	8.7%	18.5%	−3.2%

have returned less than stocks alone, but the risk of loss is reduced. The lowest five-year return for this mix over the 74-year period was a negative 3.2 percent return for bonds and stocks versus a negative 12.5 percent for large-cap stocks. Bond markets, stock markets, and real estate markets do not always rise and fall in tandem. During a stock market decline, the bond and real estate markets could be rising, and this provides some form of balance for shorter-term objectives.

Interest-Rate Risk

Interest-rate risk is the rise or fall in interest rates that affects the market value of investments. Interest-rate risk refers to changes in market rates of interest, which affect all investments. Fixed-income securities (bonds and preferred stocks) and real estate are affected most directly. In periods of rising interest rates, market prices of fixed-income securities decline to make them competitive with yields of new issues that come to the market. This decline in price causes a loss of principal for fixed-income security holders. Similarly, in periods of declining interest rates, prices of fixed-income securities increase, resulting in capital appreciation. Rising and declining interest rates have the same effect on real estate prices.

Changes in interest rates have a lesser effect on common stocks than on fixed-income securities. High levels of interest rates tend to depress stock prices, and low levels of interest rates tend to go hand in hand with bull markets. High interest rates prompt many investors to sell their stocks and move into the bond markets to take advantage of the higher coupon rates of bonds. When interest rates decline, investors move from bond and money-market securities to stocks.

Purchasing-Power (Inflation) Risk

Purchasing-power risk is the risk that changes in consumer prices will erode the future purchasing power of returns from investments. If prices in the economy rise (inflation), your future dollars will purchase fewer goods and services than they do today. This is called *purchasing-power risk*, and it has the greatest effect on investments with fixed returns (bonds, savings accounts, CDs) and no returns (non-interest-bearing checking accounts and the hoard under the mattress).

Assets with values that move with general price levels, such as common stocks, real estate, and commodities, perform better during periods of slight to moderate inflation. To protect against purchasing-power risk, choose investments with anticipated returns that are higher than the anticipated rate of inflation.

Of all the financial assets, common stocks have fared the best during periods of low to moderate inflation. During periods of high inflation, all financial assets, including common stocks, do poorly. However, common stocks perform less poorly than bonds and money-market securities under these circumstances.

Event Risk

Event risk is broadly defined as the possibility of the occurrence of an event specific to a company that could affect bond and stock prices. Such a specific company event could be that a company takes on more debt; this action could result in a reduction of the price of its existing bonds. Event risk also could result from a general event, such as a political upheaval, government intervention in the private sector, or a natural disaster. For instance, Taiwan Semiconductor's stock dropped after an earthquake in Taiwan because investors feared that the firm's production facility had been damaged. Because external events are difficult to predict, investors can do little to prevent this type of risk. They can, however, estimate the effects that an event would have.

Exchange-Rate Risk

Exchange-rate risk is the risk that the exchange rate of a currency could cause an investment to lose value. An increase in the value of the dollar against a foreign currency could decimate any returns and result in a loss of capital when the foreign securities are sold. This is called *exchange-rate risk*. For example, a 10 percent rise in the price of the dollar versus the British pound negates a 10 percent increase in the price of British stocks. A declining dollar hurts not only U.S. bond and stock markets but also the U.S. economy because imported goods become more expensive, which is inflationary. To temper potential increases in inflation, the Federal Reserve Bank does not hesitate to raise interest rates. This has a negative effect on both the bond and stock markets. Bond prices decline when interest rates rise, and investors sell their stocks when they can get higher returns by moving into bonds.

Liquidity Risk

Liquidity risk is the risk of not being able to convert an investment into cash quickly without the loss of a significant amount of the invested principal. Certain securities are more liquid than others; the greater the liquidity, the easier it is to buy and sell the investment without suffering a price concession. When investing in a particular security, you should consider the following two factors:

- The length of time you will need to hold the investment before selling it
- The relative certainty of the selling price

If you plan to use the funds in a short period of time, invest in securities that are high in liquidity (savings accounts, Treasury bills, money-market mutual funds). A Treasury bill can be sold quickly with only a slight concession in selling price, whereas a 20-year-to-maturity junk bond not only may take time to sell but also may sell at a significant price concession.

This (price concession) is especially true for bonds that are *thinly traded*, which means that relatively few of these bonds are traded and that the trades occur only with large disparity between the bid and ask prices. Thinly traded bonds are not *marketable*, which means that they cannot be sold quickly.

Common stocks of actively traded companies on the stock exchanges are marketable because they will sell quickly. They also may be liquid if the selling price is close to the original purchase price. However, inactively traded common stocks on the stock exchanges and on the over-the-counter (OTC) markets may be marketable but not liquid because the spreads between the bid and ask prices may be wide, and the sale price may be significantly less than the purchase price. This could be a problem when you need to sell inactively traded common stocks unexpectedly, and there are no buyers for the stocks. You would have to sell the stocks at a lower price to entice a buyer. Anticipate liquidity risks for inactively traded common stocks and medium- and long-term bonds. Other investment assets such as real estate and collectibles may be both illiquid and non-marketable.

THE RELATIONSHIP BETWEEN RISK AND RETURN

By now you should understand that even with the most conservative investments, you face some element of risk. However, not investing your money is also risky. For example, putting your money under the mattress invites the risk of theft and the loss in purchasing power if the prices of goods and services rise in the economy. When you recognize the different levels of risk for each type of investment asset, you can better manage the total risk in your investment portfolio.

A direct correlation exists between risk and return: The greater the risk, the greater is the potential return. However, investing in securities with the greatest return and, therefore, the greatest risk can lead to financial ruin if everything does not go according to plan.

Understanding the risks pertaining to the different investments is of little consequence unless you're aware of your feelings toward risk. How much risk you can tolerate depends on many factors, such as the type of person you are, your investment objectives, the dollar amount of your total assets, the size of your portfolio, and the time horizon for your investments.

How nervous do you think you'll be about your investments? Will you check the prices of your stocks and bonds daily? Will you be able to sleep at night if your stocks decline in price from their acquisition prices? Will you call your broker every time a stock falls by a point or two? If so, you do not tolerate risk well and should weigh your portfolio toward conservative investments that generate income through capital preservation. The percentage of your portfolio allocated to stocks may be low to zero depending on your comfort zone.

Figure 2-2 illustrates the continuum of risk tolerance. If you are the type of investor who is comfortable with accepting greater risk, you might want to invest a greater percentage of your portfolio in stocks and possibly other assets such as real estate.

FIGURE 2-2

Continuum of Risk Tolerance

	50%	
100%	% Allocation to Fixed Income Securities	0%
0%	% Allocation to Stocks	100%

Nervous	Investor with moderate risk	Risk Seeker,
Investor	tolerance	Speculator

A wide range of returns is associated with each type of security. For example, the many types of common stocks, such as blue-chip stocks, growth stocks, income stocks, and speculative stocks, react differently. Income stocks generally are lower risk and offer returns mainly in the form of dividends, whereas growth stocks are riskier and usually offer higher returns in the form of capital gains. Similarly, a broad range of risks and returns can be found for the different types of bonds.

You should be aware of this broad range of risks and returns for the different types of securities so that you can find an acceptable level of risk. Figure 2-3 illustrates the general risk-return tradeoff for different types of securities. The greater the risk, the greater is the expected return. This does not mean, however, that investing in riskier securities always will bring the greatest returns. It means only that the returns are expected to be greater for these securities. For example, the level of certainty with regard to returns from Treasury bills is often referred to as the *risk-free rate*. The risk-free rate is the rate of return on a riskless investment such as a Treasury bill.

Bear in mind that with a broad range of risk and returns for each type of security, you may be exposed to more risk with junk bonds than with blue-chip stocks. For example, the data in Table 2-4 indicate that over the 74-year period 1926–2000, real returns on a portfolio of large-cap common stocks averaged 7.7 percent a year (11 percent − 3.3 percent, the rate of inflation), whereas the average real rate of return for small-cap stocks averaged 8.1 percent (12.4 percent − 3.3 percent). Yearly real returns from intermediate-term government bonds averaged 2.2 percent (5.5 percent − 3.3 percent), and real returns from Treasury bills averaged 0.6 percent (3.9 percent − 3.3 percent) for the same 74-year period. *Real returns* are the nominal average returns minus the average rate of inflation. The risk of loss in any one-year period was greater for common stocks than for bonds during that 74-year period.

FIGURE 2-3

Level of Risk and Rates of Return for Different Types of Investments

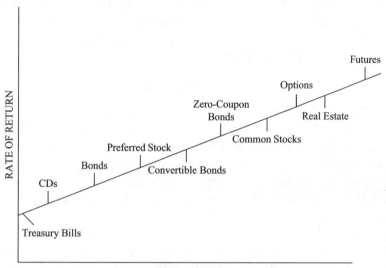

CALCULATING A RATE OF RETURN

A *rate of return* is a measure of the increase (or decrease) in an investment over a period of time. You invest to earn a return in the form of income (interest and dividends) and/or capital appreciation (when the price of the investment sold is higher than the purchase price). Some investments, such as savings accounts and CDs, offer only income with no capital appreciation; others, such as common stock, offer the potential for capital appreciation and may or may not pay dividends. If the price of a stock declines below the purchase price and you sell the stock, you have a capital loss. The simple definition of total return includes income and capital gains and losses.

Calculating a return is important because it measures the growth or decline of your investment, and it provides a yardstick for evaluating the performance of your portfolio against your objectives.

You can calculate the total rate of return as follows:

$$\text{Rate of return for the holding period} = \frac{(\text{ending value} - \text{beginning value}) + \text{income}}{\text{gross purchase price}}$$

You should include spreads and commissions in the calculations. For example, if you bought a stock at the beginning of the year for $1,500 (including the commission), sold it at the end of the year for $1,800 (net proceeds received after deducting the commission), and earned a dividend of $50, the rate of return is 23 percent:

$$\text{Rate of return} = \frac{(1{,}800 - 1{,}500) + 50}{1{,}500}$$

$$= 23 \text{ percent}$$

This rate of return is simple and easy to use, but it is somewhat inaccurate if the investment is held for a long period of time because the time value of money is not taken into account. The *time value of money* is a concept that recognizes that a dollar today is worth more in the future because of its earnings potential. For example, if you invested a dollar at 5 percent for one year, it would be worth $1.05 at the end of one year. Similarly, if you receive a dollar at the end of one year, it would be worth less than a dollar at the beginning of the year.

This simple average rate of return of 23 percent does not take into account the earnings capacity of the interest. In other words, if you were to reinvest the $50 of dividends you received, the rate of return would increase above 23 percent.

Using the time value of money to calculate the rate of return gives you a more accurate-rate-of return figure. However, it is more difficult to calculate because the rate of return on a stock equates the discounted cash flows of future dividends and the stock's expected sale price to the stock's current purchase price. This formula works better for bonds than for common stocks because the coupon rate for bonds is generally fixed, whereas dividend rates on common stocks fluctuate (and you therefore need to make assumptions). When companies experience losses, they might reduce their dividend payments, as Ford Motor Company did to preserve its cash. If a company's earnings increase, the company might increase the amount of its dividend payments. The future sale price of a stock has even less certainty. Bonds are retired at their par price ($1,000 per bond) at maturity; but when a stock eventually is sold, the future sale price is anyone's guess.

How to Calculate a Return for a Portfolio

It is useful to be able to compute a return for a portfolio of investments. The following example illustrates the steps to determine such a return. The portfolio has five stocks with the following returns:

Stocks	Return
A	7.5%
B	6.2%
C and D	2.0%
E	−3.1%

The returns for the stocks are weighted and then summed to give the portfolio weighted-average return.

Stock	Weighting		Rate		Weighted-Average Return
A	⅕	×	0.075	=	1.5%
B	⅕	×	0.062	=	1.24%
C and D	⅖	×	0.02	=	0.8%
E	⅕	×	−0.031	=	−0.62%
					2.92%

Weighted-average portfolio return = 2.92 percent

To be able to compare your portfolio return with the return of the market, you need to be able to determine your return accurately. This process may not be easy if you add funds to purchase securities and withdraw funds during the holding period. You may recall that a few years ago the Beardstown Ladies Investment Club had a problem calculating its returns accurately. The members claimed to have earned average annual returns in the low 20 percent range for an extended period, beating annual market averages, only to find that they had computed their returns incorrectly. In fact, an audit by a prominent accounting firm showed that their average annual returns were in single digits during that same period.

For a portfolio in which you have not added or withdrawn any funds, the simple holding-period return discussed earlier is sufficient:

$$\text{Holding-period return} = \frac{\text{ending balance} - \text{beginning balance}}{\text{beginning balance}}$$

Table 2-7 illustrates how to calculate a return for a portfolio in which funds have been added and withdrawn.

TABLE 2-7

Measuring a Portfolio Return with Additions to and Withdrawals from the Portfolio

For example, if you had $100,000 in your portfolio at the beginning of the year, and at the end of the year your portfolio had increased to $109,000, you had a 9 percent return ($109,000 - $100,000)/$100,000.

For additions and withdrawals during the year, the holding period return for a portfolio is calculated as follows:

$$\text{Holding-period return (HPR)} = \frac{\text{interest} + \text{dividends} + \text{capital gains} + \text{unrealized capital gains}}{\text{beginning investment} + [\text{new funds} \times (\text{number of months in portfolio/12})] - [\text{funds withdrawn} \times (\text{number of months not in portfolio/12})]}$$

For example, suppose that a portfolio began with $110,500 at the beginning of the year, received dividends of $8,600 and capital gains of $12,000, and suffered unrealized losses of $6,000 during the year. New funds of $10,000 were added at the beginning of April, and $4,000 was withdrawn at the end of October. The portfolio had an annual return of 12.44 percent:

$$\text{HPR} = \frac{\$8,600 + 12,000 - 6,000}{110,500 + 10,000\,(9/12) - 4,000(2/12)}$$

$$= 12.44 \text{ percent}$$

This portfolio earned a 12.44 percent return before taxes and can be compared with a comparable benchmark index for the same period of time.

RETURNS AS MEASURED BY STOCK MARKET INDICES

A number of stock market indices give you different measures of the stock market. You can use these indices in the following ways:

1. To determine how the stock markets are doing
2. As comparison benchmarks for the performance of your individual portfolio and mutual funds
3. As forecasting tools for future trends.

These market indices give a glimpse into the movement of individual stock prices. However, you should understand the relationship between the indices and individual stocks before taking any action. For example, a panic attack is not necessary when the Dow Jones Industrial Average drops 150 points in any one day, and neither should you order champagne for the neighborhood when the Nasdaq Index goes up 40 points.

In general, the different stock market indices move up and down together by greater or lesser amounts, although they sometimes diverge. Figure 2-4 presents a comparison of the three major stock market indices. These differences are due to the composition of stocks in each index, the manner in which each index is calculated, and the weights assigned to each stock.

These differences explain the discrepancies between the rates of return of the different indices. Following is a discussion of the most widely used stock indices.

Dow Jones Industrial Averages

The Dow Jones Industrial Average (DJIA) is the oldest and most widely quoted measure of the stock market. The DJIA is comprised of the stock prices of 30 large blue-chip companies. The closing stock prices of each of the 30 stocks are added and then divided by an adjusted divisor. This divisor is a very small number (e.g., 0.13532775 as of May 3, 2005), which makes the DJIA a greater number than the average of the stock prices. When the DJIA was introduced, it was calculated as a simple average using the number of stocks in the calculation. However, because of stock splits and the addition of new stocks to replace stocks that were dropped, an adjusted divisor was used to keep the average from changing for stock splits and

FIGURE 2-4

Comparison of Selected Stock Market Indices, 1988–2003

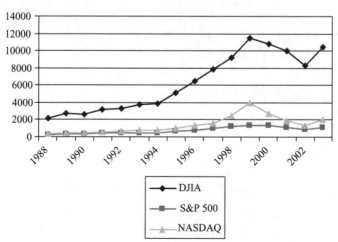

the addition of new stocks. This adjusted divisor explains why the DJIA can be a large number such as 10,000 with the addition of only 30 share prices of the companies in the average.

Owing to the small number of companies in the Dow, care has been taken over the years to make sure that these companies are broadly representative of the market. Thus, in 1997, four companies [Bethlehem Steel, Texaco, Westinghouse (now Viacom), and Woolworths (now Venator Group)] were dropped and were replaced by Hewlett-Packard, Johnson & Johnson, Citigroup, and Wal-Mart. Later changes included the addition of Microsoft Corporation and Intel Corporation.

Much criticism surrounds the DJIA. First, the stocks are not equally weighted; consequently, an increase of a higher-priced stock has a greater impact on the DJIA than an increase of a lower-priced stock. Second, with a sample of only 30 large blue-chip stocks, the DJIA is hardly a representative measure of the market.

Yet the DJIA still can be of use to investors. First, by looking at a chart of the DJIA over a period of time, investors can see the ups and downs of the market, which can help you to decide when to buy and sell stocks. Second, the DJIA can be used as a yardstick for comparing how your blue-chip stocks and blue-chip mutual funds have performed in comparison with the DJIA for the same period of time. However, because the DJIA is composed of only 30 stocks, you also should look at more broad-based measures of the market. Table 2-8 presents a comparison of the DJIA and the Standard and Poor's 500 Index and the Dogs of the Dow for the past 10 years.

The *Dogs of the Dow* is an offshoot of the DJIA. It involves a strategy of investing in the 10 highest dividend-yielding stocks in the DJIA at the beginning of the year and then replacing the stocks with the 10 highest-yielding stocks the next year.

Other Dow Jones averages are the *Dow Jones Transportation Average* (DJTA), which is composed of the stocks of 20 major transportation companies; the *Dow Jones Utility Average* (DJUA,), which consists of 15 major utility stocks; and the *Dow Jones Composite Average*, which combines the three Dow Jones averages and all their stocks.

Standard & Poor's 500 Index

Standard & Poor's 500 Index (S&P 500) consists of 500 stocks listed on the New York Stock Exchange and on the Nasdaq. The 500 companies included in the S&P 500 Index also can be broken down into the following indices:

- S&P Industrial Index, which consists of 400 industrial stocks
- S&P Transportation Index, which consists of 20 companies
- S&P Utilities Index, which consists of 40 companies
- S&P Financial Index, which consists of 40 companies

The most often cited of the S&P indices is the S&P 500 Index. The S&P 500 Index is a market-value-weighted index, which is computed by calculating the total market capitalization (value) of the 500 companies in the index, dividing that by the total market capitalization of the 500 companies in the base year, and then multiplying the number by 10. The percentage increase or decrease in the total market value from one day to the next represents the change in the index.

With 500 stocks, the S&P 500 Index is more representative than the DJIA with only 30 stocks. The S&P 500 Index occasionally adds and drops stocks to maintain a broad representation of the economy.

TABLE 2-8

Performance of the Indices

Year	DJIA	S&P 500	Dogs of the Dow
1989	31.7%	31.5%	26.5%
1990	−0.4%	−3.2%	−7.6%
1991	23.9%	30.0%	34.3%
1992	7.4%	7.6%	7.9%
1993	16.8%	10.1%	27.3%
1994	4.9%	1.3%	4.1%
1995	36.4%	37.6%	36.5%
1996	28.6%	23.0%	27.9%
1997	24.9%	33.4%	21.9%
1998	18.1%	28.6%	10.7%
1999	27.2%	21.1%	4%
2000	−4.7%	−9.2%	6.4%
2001	−5.4%	−11.9%	−4.9%
2002	−14.9%	−22.1%	−8.9%
2003	28.3%	28.7%	28.7%
10-year return	14.4%	13%	12.9%*

*Ten years ended December 31, 2003.

The S&P 500 Index is an important measure of the performance of larger stocks in the market, which is further confirmed by the growing popularity for S&P 500–indexed mutual funds (mutual funds that hold portfolios of stocks designed to match the performance of the S&P 500 Index). These mutual funds outperformed most of the actively managed funds in 1998 primarily because many actively managed mutual funds invested in value stocks and small-cap stocks, which all underperformed the 50 large growth stocks in the S&P 500 Index. From 1995 to 1999, both the DJIA and S&P 500 Index more than doubled, only to decrease by about half in the bear market of 2000–2002. The broader market of small-cap stocks lagged and did not participate in the four-year rally from 1995–1999.

New York Stock Exchange Composite Index

The *New York Stock Exchange Composite Index* is a more broad-based measure than the S&P 500 Index because it includes all the stocks traded on the New York Stock Exchange (NYSE). It is a market-value-weighted index and, like the S&P 500 Index, relates to a base period, December 31, 1965. On that date, the NYSE Composite Index was 50. In addition to the NYSE Composite Index, the NYSE also has indices for industrials, utilities, transportation, and financial stocks.

Nasdaq Composite Index

The *Nasdaq Composite Index* is a measure of all the stocks traded on the Nasdaq (National Association of Securities Dealers Automated Quotations) system. The Nasdaq Index is more volatile than the DJIA and the S&P 500 Index because companies traded on the OTC market are smaller and more speculative than the larger companies that trade on the NYSE. Thus an increase in the Nasdaq Composite Index can be interpreted as investor enthusiasm for small stocks.

Other Indices

The *American Stock Exchange Index* (AMEX) is value-weighted and includes all stocks listed on that exchange.

The *Wilshire 5000 Index* is the broadest index and includes all companies listed on the NYSE and AMEX, as well as many of the larger stocks traded on the OTC market.

The *Value Line Composite Index* differs from the other indices in that it is calculated using a geometric averaging method using 1,700 stocks listed on the NYSE, AMEX, and OTC markets.

The *Russell 3000 Index* is a broad-market index that offers investors access to 98 percent of the U.S. market. The largest 1,000 stocks in the Russell 3000 Index make up the Russell 1000 Index, and the smallest 2000 stocks in the Russell 3000 make up the Russell 2000 Index (a measure for the performance of small-cap stocks).

The *EAFE Index* is the benchmark for foreign stocks and foreign stock mutual funds. The EAFE is the Morgan Stanley Capital International Europe, Australasia, Far East Index, which includes 1,026 stocks from 20 countries.

Determining Which Index to Use

Studies have shown that all the indices are correlated; that is, they all move together in the same direction. However, there are some differences. The Nasdaq and the AMEX indices are not as highly correlated with the S&P 500 and the DJIA. This makes sense because companies in the Nasdaq and AMEX stock indices are younger, smaller, and riskier companies than the companies in the DJIA and S&P 500. The best approach is to choose the index that closely resembles the makeup of your stock portfolio.

Individual measures of the market are convenient indicators or gauges of the stock market and also indicate the direction of the market over a period of time. By using these market indices, you can compare how well individual stocks and mutual funds have performed against comparable market indicators for the same period.

MAKING SENSE OF THE MEASUREMENT OF RISK AND RETURN OF STOCKS

As pointed out earlier, a diversified portfolio of greater than 20 to 40 stocks reduces the unsystematic portion of risk in the portfolio, leaving only the systematic part of risk. Reducing some of the risk should reduce the variability of the returns in the portfolio. However, market risk is not reduced by diversification, but having a long time horizon can lessen a portion of this risk. If the market declines with a short time horizon, you would have to sell your stocks at

lower prices, whereas with a long time horizon, you are able to liquidate your stocks when they have appreciated in value.

ASSET ALLOCATION AND THE SELECTION OF INVESTMENTS

As mentioned earlier, diversification can reduce some of the risks
inherent in investing. For example, when the stock of one company
in your portfolio declines, other stocks might increase and offset your
losses. However, diversification does not reduce market risk. If the
stock market as a whole declines, the stocks of a diversified portfolio
decline also. When the bond and stock markets move together, even
a diversified portfolio during down markets is not immune from
market risk. Another element that can help to combat market risk is
time. When selecting securities with long time horizons, you can wait
for stock prices to recover from down markets to sell.

The securities you select depend on your objectives, your circumstances (marital status, age, family, education, income, net worth,
and the size of the portfolio), level of risk, expected rate of return, and
the economic environment. *Asset allocation* is the assignment of funds
to broad categories of investment assets, such as stocks, bonds,
money-market securities, options, futures, gold, and real estate. The
asset allocation model in Figure 2-5 shows how some of these asset
allocation factors determine the selection of investments.

For example, if you are seeking capital growth and are young,
single, and a professional with an excellent salary, you may be able to
tolerate greater risk in order to pursue higher returns. With a long
time horizon and less need for income generation from investments,
a greater portion of your portfolio can be invested in common
stocks. Such an asset allocation in this case could be as follows:

Stocks	75 percent
Real estate	10 percent
Bonds	5 percent
Money-market equivalents	10 percent

If, however, you do not tolerate risk as well, a more conservative asset allocation model would be as follows:

Stocks	60 percent
Bonds	30 percent
Money-market equivalents	10 percent

FIGURE 2-5

Asset Allocation and the Selection of Investments

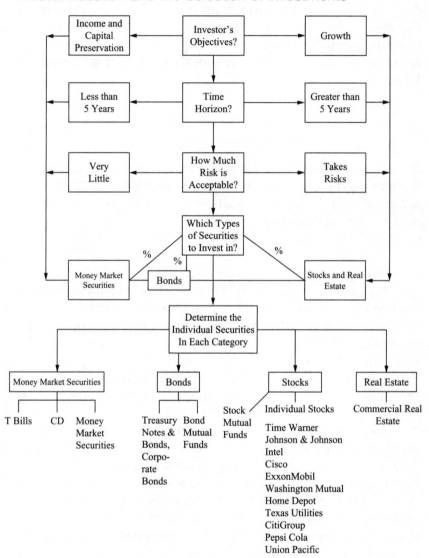

An older, retired couple with limited net worth and whose objectives are income generation and capital preservation would have a different allocation of their assets. They cannot tolerate much risk, and their time horizon is shorter. To generate regular receipts of income, a greater portion of their investment portfolio would go into fixed-income securities with varying maturities. Generally, the longer the maturities, the greater are the returns, even though risk increases with the length of the maturities. Depending on their circumstances, a small percentage of their portfolio might be allocated to common stocks to provide capital appreciation. A suggested asset allocation model might be set up as follows:

Stocks	15%
Bonds	65%
Money-market equivalents	20%

As you can see, the percentage allocated to stocks, bonds, and money-market equivalents varies depending on your circumstances and the size of your portfolio. What works for one investor may not be appropriate for another. For example, the financial characteristics of two investors may be identical, but one investor may need to set aside greater amounts in money-market securities to meet ongoing medical bills or some other expected expenditure.

An asset allocation plan should be flexible enough to accommodate changes to fit personal and economic circumstances. For example, when market rates of interest are declining, a greater percentage of the portfolio may be allocated to stocks. Similarly, when interest rates are rising, you could put more of your funds in money-market equivalents, and when conditions become more favorable, you can move some money back into stocks (see Table 2-9).

After you've determined an asset allocation mix of the broad categories of investments (stocks, bonds, money-market funds, and other asset types), your next step is to make your selection of individual investments and amounts to allocate to each. For stocks, it may be useful to review the different categories of common stocks. For example, allocating equal amounts of money to value stocks, growth stocks, foreign stocks, blue-chip stocks, and small-cap stocks reduces the total risk of your stock portfolio. The same process applies to the division of the total amount allocated to bonds. The portfolio of individual stocks listed in Figure 2-5 can be classified into sectors and types, as illustrated in Table 2-10.

Table 2-10 presents a broad representation of the different industry sectors, and most of the companies listed are leaders in their respective sectors. Noticeably absent from this portfolio are small-cap

TABLE 2-9

Guidelines for Asset Allocation

1. Review your objectives and personal financial circumstances. To generate current income and preserve capital, the asset allocation model should be weighted more toward bonds and money-market securities. If current income is not needed and the investor is investing for capital growth in the future, the weighting would be more toward stocks and real assets.

2. Determine your tolerance for risk. If you have a long time horizon and can accept the risks of the stock and real estate markets, a greater amount can be invested in stocks and real estate. If you cannot tolerate risk, the allocation should be weighted more toward bonds and money-market securities.

3. Consider your time frame. If you are young and have a long time horizon (about 25 years), allocate a larger percentage to stocks. If you have a short time frame, the allocation would be weighted more toward bonds, with a smaller percentage in stocks.

4. You should not be unrealistic in your expectations of your investments. The returns of the past two decades have been quite spectacular. Long-term bonds in the decade of the 1980s returned, on average, around 13 percent annually. Stock returns were abnormally high during the late 1990s owing to the technology boom and the Internet bubble, only to decline to more realistic levels of valuation in the early 2000s. For example the S&P 500 Index earned, on average, around 37 percent in 1995, 22 percent in 1996, and 33 percent in 1997. The past two decades have been abnormally good for both the bond and the stock markets owing to the decline in interest rates from around 17 percent in 1980 to the current low of 3 to 5 percent in the early 2000s. You should lower your expected returns to more realistic levels into the future.

5. Consider the risk-return tradeoff in the asset allocation model. How you allocate your assets can affect both risk and returns. For example, according to Ibbotson and Sinquefield (1994), diversification among different classes of investment assets lowered the levels of risk and improved returns. The three portfolios in the study used data during the 1926–1993 time frame. The first portfolio consisted solely of long-term government bonds and had an average annual return of 5.5 percent with a risk (standard deviation) of 11.3 percent. A second, more diversified portfolio consisted of 63 percent in Treasury bills, 12 percent in long-term government bonds, and 25 percent in common stocks of large companies. This portfolio had the same annual returns as the first portfolio, 5.5 percent, but the risk fell to 6.1 percent. A third portfolio consisted of 52 percent in stocks of large companies, 14 percent in long-term government bonds, and 34 percent in Treasury bills. This portfolio returned 8 percent annually with 11.3 percent risk. This is the same risk as the first portfolio of bonds, but the returns are much greater.

6. After determining your asset allocation model, the next step is to determine your individual investments. In a speech to the American Association of Individual Investors National Meeting, July 10, 1998, John J. Brennan used the example of a portfolio invested in 100 percent international stocks for the five-year period ending 1990. This portfolio, based on the Morgan Stanley EAFE Index, would have outperformed a portfolio of stocks based on the S&P 500 Index. However, in the five-year period from 1992 to 1997 a 100 percent portfolio of stocks based on the S&P 500 Index would have outperformed the portfolio of foreign stocks. To reduce overall risk, you should divide your stock allocation into different sectors of the economy and then choose the individual stocks for each sector. You should do the same for a bond portfolio.

TABLE 2-10

Portfolio of Stocks

Stock	Sector or Industry	Type of Stock
Time Warner	Media	Growth stock
Johnson & Johnson	Pharmaceutical	Defensive stock
Intel	SemiConductor	Technology growth stock
Cisco Systems	Network communications	Technology growth stock
ExxonMobil	Oil	Energy blue-chip stock
Washington Mutual	Savings & Loan	Value stock
Home Depot	Discount retailer	Growth stock
Texas Utilities	Utility	Income stock
CitiGroup	Financial services	Blue-chip stock
Pepsi Cola	Beverage	Defensive stock
Union Pacific	Transportation Stock	Cyclical stock

Note: This is not a recommendation to buy any of these stocks. Some stocks may be trading at high multiples of earnings owing to increases in price, whereas others may be depressed as a result of the bear market

stocks and foreign stocks, which are riskier investments. This portfolio was chosen with the following considerations:

- Large-cap stocks instead of mid- or small-caps
- Greater emphasis on growth stocks instead of value stocks
- U.S. stocks instead of foreign stocks

REFERENCES

Brennan, John J.: "Strategic Asset Allocation in Today's Market." Speech given to the American Association of Individual Investors National Meeting, Washington, DC, July 10, 1998.

Faerber, Esmé: *All About Stocks,* 2nd Ed. New York: McGraw-Hill, 2000.

Higgins, Michelle: "Savings Accounts Earn So Little, They Lose Ground to Inflation,"*Wall Street Journal,* May 8, 2002, p. D2.

Ibbotson, Roger G., and Rex A. Sinquefield: *Stocks, Bonds, Bills and Inflation: Historical Return (1926-1993).* Chicago: Dow Jones–Irwin, 1994.

Malkiel, Burton G.: *A Random Walk Down Wall Street.* New York: W.W. Norton, 1990.

CHAPTER 3

Security Markets and How Stocks Are Traded

KEY CONCEPTS

- The security markets
- How the securities markets work
- Types of orders
- Financial planners and stockbrokers
- Types of accounts at brokerage firms
- How short selling works

Security markets are sensitive to changes in the economy, such as rising and falling interest rates, political events, anticipated events, and those events that you might think would have no bearing on the markets. In addition, securities markets themselves have been in constant flux because they too have changed as a result of external events. Understanding these changes and how the security markets work can help you to lower your transaction costs when buying and selling securities.

THE SECURITY MARKETS

The security markets are cornerstones of the capitalist system where securities (stocks, bonds, options, futures, and commodities) are traded. The stock markets in the United States consist of the two major exchanges and an over-the-counter (OTC) market. The New York Stock Exchange (NYSE), and the American Stock Exchange

(AMEX) are the major exchanges, and they have trading floors where stocks are traded. The Nasdaq market is the OTC market, and it trades primarily new, small-capitalized (small-cap) stocks of companies over telephone lines and computer networks.

The stock and bond markets have changed significantly because of advances in technology. The widespread use of personal computers and, more specifically, the Internet has given investors direct access to information that was previously unavailable. In addition, daily trading hours for investors have been lengthened. Whereas the stock markets were once open for trading only during specific hours, after-hours trading now takes place. The exchanges still close at the end of the official trading day (4:30 P.M., Eastern U.S. time); after-hours trades transpire via electronic computer networks (ECNs) before the market opens at 9:30 A.M. Eastern U.S. time and after 4:30 P.M.

Trades on the NYSE are matched by specialists on the floor through open-outcry auction, but the NYSE is moving toward allowing widespread automatic matching of buy and sell orders like its rival Nasdaq.

One of the many advantages for investors using the Internet is that they can trade securities online without a broker. Another advantage of the Internet is greater stock-pricing transparency. In other words, you can see the price that buyers and sellers are willing to settle on for a particular stock. The bond markets still have a long way to go in making their prices transparent to potential buyers.

Transaction costs have decreased with the switch to decimalization. This switch has had the effect of narrowing the lowest bid-and-ask spread from 1/16 point ($0.06) to the minimum of $.01 per share.

The advent of computers, online trading, extended trading hours, and decimalization has made investing in different securities easier, but you also need to be more informed about the securities that you can buy or sell so easily.

The function of the security markets is to provide continuous and fair pricing. Buying and selling financial securities are auction processes. A buyer submits a *bid* price (the amount he or she is willing to pay), and a seller submits an *ask* price (the amount at which he or she wants to sell). If these prices do not match, the bid and ask prices from other buyers and sellers are sought so that trades can be made.

Efficient markets provide up-to-date prices for certain securities. For stocks, you can get instantaneous prices through real-time pricing on the Internet or by calling your broker. You can easily obtain spreads between the bid and ask quotes for stocks. The *spread* is the difference between the bid and ask prices. Continuous pricing for bonds is not as readily available. Prices of bonds are also available on the Internet, although they are not as transparent as stocks. The reason is that each dealer has his or her own pricing for each of the bonds in inventory, and the markups and transactions costs are buried in this pricing. Consequently, many investors find that comparing the prices on similar bonds to determine the best available prices is difficult.

The security markets in the United States are large, in that they have many buyers and sellers. The larger the number of buyers and sellers in a market, the more investors are assured of receiving fair pricing. Use of the Internet, along with the viewing of stock information on television stations (such as on CNBC and Bloomberg), has provided stock price transparency, where investors can see changing prices from trade to trade, as well as the rapid transmittal of information that affects stock prices. Because stock prices in efficient markets reflect all relevant information, little likelihood exists that investors will trade their stocks at unfair prices.

Because bond pricing is less transparent, you have a greater chance of being cheated on price, particularly for thinly traded or illiquid bonds. The reason is that each dealer marks up the bonds in his or her portfolio without regard for the markups on similar bonds by other dealers. These transaction costs are an indication of the liquidity of the securities in the market. For example, buying a bond at $1,000 and then immediately selling it at $910 indicates not only a wide spread but also illiquidity. A *liquid* security is one in which prices are fairly certain, and only small amounts are lost when trades are made.

Stock Exchanges

Stocks are listed on the national exchanges—New York Stock Exchange (NYSE) and American Stock Exchange (AMEX)—or on regional exchanges (or both). If stocks are not listed on these exchanges, they may be traded on the Nasdaq OTC market.

The *New York Stock Exchange* (NYSE), also referred to as the "Big Board," is the largest and oldest exchange in the United States. It has the most stringent listing requirements. In addition to maintaining the requirements for listing on the exchanges, companies are expected to comply with certain regulations administered by the Securities and Exchange Commission (SEC), such as publishing quarterly reports and annual reports and releasing any information that affects the company's ongoing operations. Companies that do not meet the listing requirements can be delisted. Generally, the largest, best-known, and most financially secure companies that meet the listing requirements are listed on the NYSE.

When a buy or sell order is placed for a company listed on the NYSE, the broker or registered representative transmits the order electronically to the floor of the exchange. The order is then taken to the trading post for that stock, where a specialist executes the order. The ticker tape reports executed transactions. You can watch the trades on the ticker tape, which are shown on television such as CNBC, during the trading session. After you place an order to buy or sell shares, you receive a confirmation of your executed trade from your brokerage firm. The daily number of shares traded on the NYSE has increased consistently over the years and since 2000 has exceeded 1 billion shares each day.

The *American Stock Exchange* (AMEX) has less stringent listing requirements than the NYSE and generally has the listings of younger, smaller companies. The exchange has added the trading of stock options, stock indices, and exchange-traded funds (ETFs). The AMEX, like the NYSE, has a physical trading floor, whereas the Nasdaq is an electronic exchange. The AMEX uses a specialist system like the NYSE. A company can be listed on the NYSE or the AMEX, as well as on a regional exchange.

Five *regional exchanges* (Philadelphia, Boston, Cincinnati, Chicago, and Pacific Exchanges) list the stocks of companies in their geographic areas that are not large enough to qualify for listing on the two larger exchanges. These exchanges also can dual list the same company. For example, General Electric is listed on the NYSE and on several regional exchanges. The advantage of these regional exchanges is that local brokerage firms that do not have memberships on the NYSE have access to these dual-listed shares. The Pacific Exchange has given up its physical trading floor and has become an *electronic communications network* (ECN). An ECN is a privately owned trading network that matches investors' buy and sell orders electronically. The Pacific Exchange accounts for a large percentage of the options traded. The Philadelphia Exchange trades in options, stock, bond, and currency indices. If trades are not transacted on the NYSE or AMEX, they can be routed to the regional exchanges to get better prices.

A number of companies that issue stocks to the public might not be listed on any of the exchanges described in this section for a variety of reasons. Rather, they are traded over the counter. *The over-the-counter (OTC) market* is linked by a network of computers and telephones and can include stocks listed on the NYSE or AMEX. The most actively traded issues are listed on the *Nasdaq* (National Association of Securities Dealers Automated Quotations) national market system. The least actively traded issues that do not meet the listing requirements trade on the *Over-the-Counter Bulletin Board.* These thinly traded stocks tend to consist of companies that may be more speculative with regard to their future survival. A stockbroker can provide the bid and ask prices for these bulletin board stocks by entering a company's code into the Nasdaq computer system. Many large, reputable companies, such as Intel, Microsoft, Cisco, and Dell, have chosen to remain on the OTC market rather than move up to the AMEX or the NYSE. The listing fees are lower on the OTC market, which is another reason why a majority of these companies are small-cap companies.

In the OTC market, orders are executed differently from the way they are executed on the exchange floors. A customer's order to buy is sent to the trading desk of the brokerage firm. From there, a trader at the brokerage firm contacts market makers (in the case of an OTC stock) or dealers (for a stock exchange–listed stock) in that stock to determine the lowest ask price. *Market makers* are the firms that buy stocks for or sell stocks from their own inventories. A markup is added to the ask price; you can determine this amount from the stock listings in the Nasdaq National Market Issues in the newspaper or online. Similarly, whenever a stock is sold, an amount called a *markdown* is subtracted from the bid price. In OTC trades, a brokerage firm cannot charge a commission and also act as the market maker. The brokerage firm has to choose between charging a commission and earning a markup or markdown.

Market makers or dealers buy and sell securities for and from their own accounts. The AMEX and the Nasdaq merged in 1999, which has narrowed some of the differences between a floor exchange and a computerized market. Two benefits cited by those in favor of the merger are lower costs and better trades. Over many years, *spreads* (the difference between bid and ask prices) were much higher for Nasdaq stocks than for those traded on the floor of the exchanges. In 1997, Nasdaq was fined for creating extraordinary high spreads on stock trades.

Nasdaq has made some changes to attract greater trading volumes. It inaugurated the SuperMontage trading system on October 14, 2002, to stem the loss of trades to ECNs. The ECNs took away 49 percent of trading in Nasdaq-listed stocks in 2002 (McNamee, p. 80). The SuperMontage system allows brokers to post several quotes, rather than one, to buy and sell stocks. Additionally, it shows how much stock is available at five pricing levels rather than merely at the best bid and ask prices. Which system prevails does not matter because the greater the competition between Nasdaq and the ECNs, the better is the pricing for investors.

Some structural flaws in the Nasdaq trading system encouraged the growth of ECNs. Not a single clearinghouse for OTC trades existed, so buy and sell orders were not always available to interested parties. This lack of centralization led to the charging of high spreads, which resulted in a $1 billion fine against Nasdaq in 1997. In 1997, the SEC allowed ECNs to display their orders on the Nasdaq electronic trading bulletin board along with the orders of Nasdaq market makers in a system known as *Level 2 quoting.* Level 2 quotes are bid and ask prices provided by all market makers of securities carried on the Nasdaq system.

ECNs provide individual and institutional investors with alternative trading systems. ECNs match trades (buy and sell orders) electronically and have increased their trading volume by lowering spreads. Trading on ECNs is advantageous for large institutional investors who want to trade large blocks of shares. If these institutional investors used the Nasdaq market makers (or exchanges), the general investing public would see their trades, and the stock prices would change. ECNs allow these institutional investors to trade their stocks anonymously. ECNs also allow individual investors to trade stocks before the stock market opens for the day and after the stock market has closed for the day.

The diversion of trades from Nasdaq to ECNs reduces Nasdaq's revenue in that it cannot resell the quotes and trade data to brokers and investors (McNamee, p. 81). Sustained competition between Nasdaq and the ECNs can only produce better prices for investors.

The NYSE's plan to acquire ECN Archipelago in April 2005 could fundamentally change how the stock exchange operates. This combination will allow the NYSE to broaden its position in options and futures markets, as well as being able to compete with the automated transactions market for Nasdaq-listed stocks and ETFs. Following this announcement, to increase its own competitive position and boost offerings, Nasdaq announced that it would acquire Instinet, an ECN. This combination would allow investors to trade NYSE stocks more easily on the Nasdaq system.

Foreign stock exchanges list and trade the stocks of their respective markets. Financial newspapers and financial online Web sites such as Yahoo quote the prices of the most actively traded foreign companies listed on the major European, Asian, Australian, South African, and Canadian exchanges (foreign exchanges).

Bond Exchanges

Corporations, the federal government, agencies of the federal government, municipal governments, and foreign corporations and governments issue bonds. Bonds are listed on the exchanges or are traded on the OTC markets. After a bond is brought to the market, it trades in the secondary markets, which include the exchanges and the OTC markets. The *secondary market* is one in which existing securities are traded among investors through an intermediary (dealer or market maker).

Some corporate bonds are listed on the *New York Bond Exchange* and the *American Bond Exchange*. Price quotes of these bonds can be found in financial newspapers. NYSE-listed bonds trade through the *Automated Bond System* (ABS), a terminal-based system for trading corporate bonds and agency and government bonds. The ABS matches prices of orders executed and then reports quotes and trades on a real-time basis to market data vendors. Many corporate bonds are not listed on exchanges but are traded on the OTC markets through bond traders. U.S. government securities, government agency bonds, and municipal bonds are also traded in the OTC markets through bond traders.

An active secondary market for Treasury securities exists, made up of security dealers. The Federal Reserve Bank also participates in this market; it buys and sells Treasury securities as part of its open-market operations.

A secondary market exists for government agency bonds, for example, Federal National Mortgage Association (FNMA) securities, Government National Mortgage Association (GNMA) securities, municipal bonds (such as state and local government issues and highway authorities), and foreign bonds. FNMA and GNMA bonds are issued by privately owned and government-owned corporations. These bonds are backed by mortgage securities.

The OTC markets consist of thousands of broker-dealers who are not in any single location but rather are spread throughout the country. They use computers and telephones for their transactions. These broker-dealers buy for their own accounts or on behalf of their customers, for whom they are acting as agents. In the latter type of transaction, the agent or broker receives a commission for placing the order. Broker-dealers can act as brokers and receive commissions or as dealers and earn a markup on sales and a markdown on purchases. *Brokers* are individuals or firms that bring together buyers and sellers and do not take a position in the investment being traded. A *markup* is an increase in the price of a security; it is also the difference between the price charged by a dealer and the price offered by a market maker. A *markdown* is a decrease in the price of a security; it is the difference between a price paid by a dealer and the price at which a dealer can sell the securities to a market maker.

Many broker-dealers specialize in certain types of bonds. In other words, they make a market in buying and selling these bonds. How this works with respect to orders from individual investors is shown in the following two steps:

1. An individual investor places an order for a particular bond with a brokerage firm.
2. If the brokerage firm is a market maker for that particular bond, it will sell the bond to the customer. If the brokerage firm is not a market maker for that particular bond, the firm negotiates with a firm that is a market maker for that security.

Most bonds are bought through brokerage firms. The exception is Treasury securities, which are relatively easy to buy directly through the Federal Reserve banks at issue. Because most bonds are traded through broker-dealers, no central display of trade prices exists, which results in a lack of pricing transparency for bonds.

Other Exchanges

Options are traded at the *Chicago Board Options Exchange* by using a combination of market makers and brokers. This options exchange is the largest. The regional *Philadelphia Exchange* also lists options. Both *futures* and options on futures are traded at the *Chicago Mercantile Exchange*. The *New York Mercantile Exchange* also trades futures contracts.

HOW THE SECURITY MARKETS WORK

New issues of common stock, preferred stock, and bonds are sold in the *primary markets*. In other words, the primary market is the market in which new securities are sold to the market. The *secondary markets* are where existing securities are traded among investors through an intermediary. This section includes a discussion of how these securities markets work for the major types of securities. The discussion is limited to stocks, but the same procedures occur for the issuance of new bonds to the public.

Primary Markets and Initial Public Offerings (IPOs) for Common Stocks

New issues of stocks that are sold for the first time are *initial public offerings* (IPOs). If a company that has already issued stock on the market wants to issue more stock, it is referred to as a *new issue*. eBay, Yahoo, and Google were extremely successful IPOs on the market in the late 1990s and early 2000s.

Most IPOs and new issues of stocks and bonds are marketed and sold through underwriters (brokerage firms). Most of the underwriting of common stocks takes one of three forms: negotiated arrangement, competitive bid, or best-efforts arrangement. These different arrangements are due to different terms and conditions agreed to between the issuing company and the brokerage firm and do not have a direct affect on the individual purchaser of the securities.

What you should know about buying new issues or IPOs is that you do not pay a commission to buy the securities from underwriters. These fees are paid by the issuing company.

Companies issuing securities in the primary market are required to provide you with a legal document, called a *prospectus*, so that you can make prudent investment decisions. The prospectus is a formal document related to the offering of new securities that provides information to investors interested in purchasing the securities

Returns from IPOs

IPOs generally give investors a wild ride with regard to returns. In September 1998, eBay, an Internet company, was brought to market at an issue price of $18 per share, and 3½ months later the stock was trading at $246. This 1,267 percent return took place over 3½ months. Not all IPOs are like eBay, though.

Many investors have been burned in the IPO market. One of the largest losers for 1998 was USN Communications, which came to market at a price of $16 in February and ended the year around $0.31 per share, a loss of 98 percent. Investors who placed market orders on the first day of trading for the new Internet issue Globe.Com also were burned. The stock was first offered at $9 per share and then rose to $97 per share before falling back down and closing in the low double digits on the first day of trading. Investors who had their market orders filled at those lofty prices took a tremendous beating because the stock ended up trading at around $5 per share at the end of December 1998. Globe.Com is no longer in business.

Palm, Inc., is another example of an IPO with phenomenal short-term returns and very poor long-range returns. On the day Palm came to the market in the first quarter of 2000, it traded briefly around $165 per share. Two years later it was trading at below $1 per share. A 1-for-500 reverse stock split subsequently took place to raise the price of the stock.

You should not be blinded by the spectacular returns of some IPOs because the long-term average returns of IPOs are not compelling. A study done by Christopher B. Barry and Robert H. Jennings in 1993 shows that the greatest return on an IPO is earned, on average, on the first day the stock comes to the market. Professor Jay Ritter concluded that an IPO's long-term performance is much poorer than that of companies trading on the secondary markets (existing shares traded on the markets). In addition, the Wall Street practice of imposing penalties on brokers who sell their client's shares immediately after issue is disadvantageous for small investors (Zweig et al., pp. 84–90). For example, investors who bought shares in the after-market on the first day of trading of Lazard in May 2005 saw the shares close at below the offering range on the first day of trading. Table 3-1 offers an explanation of how IPO shares are allocated and who gets them.

One reason for a decline in price of IPO shares after a period of time might be that company insiders sell their shares. Executives, managers, and employees of a company can purchase their own stock or are granted options on the stock. Insiders usually must hold the stock for a period, known as a *lock-up period*, which typically ranges from three months to a year. When the lock-up period expires, the insiders can sell their shares, which can cause the share price to fall.

The IPO market has some disadvantages that you should be aware of before investing:

- Institutional investors get very large allocations of shares, leaving a small percentage available for individual investors.

- Institutional investors are privy to better information than individual investors.
- Individuals rely on information primarily from a prospectus; institutional investors can attend road shows and meet company executives. *Cheat sheets,* provided by brokerage firms to their preferred institutional clients, contain management forecasts and income projections that are not part of a prospectus. Companies are reluctant to include cheat sheets in their public documents; if a company misses its published projections, it might be vulnerable to lawsuits.
- Individual investors are penalized for selling their shares immediately after issue, although institutional investors are allowed to quickly "flip" their shares.

If you want to participate directly in the IPO market, you should be aware of these disadvantages. You might consider instead mutual funds that concentrate on IPOs. The next section shows how you as an individual investor can do your research homework to limit your risk of loss.

Protecting Against Losses in Choosing IPOs

Every successful IPO has, unfortunately, more than a corresponding number of failures for investors. If you are an individual investor intent on investing in IPOs, you should take precautions to lower your risk of loss over the long term. Although paying attention to

TABLE 3-1

How IPO Shares Are Allotted and Who Gets Them?

Investors of all types have tried diligently to obtain IPO shares because of the spectacular returns earned by many IPOs over short periods. Therefore, if individual investors have a hard time getting these shares at issue, who does get them?

The issuing company distributes a portion of the IPO to its friends and family members. The underwriter also allocates its shares to privileged investors, such as institutional investors and mutual funds. Smaller allocations go to the brokerage firm's wealthy investors. The average small investor is positioned low on the institutional totem pole.

No rules or regulations govern the allocation process. The National Association of Securities Dealers (NASD) bars investment banks from selling these IPO shares to senior officers who are in a position to direct future business back to their investment banks (underwriters). This rule might have been violated when Salomon Smith Barney allocated hot IPO shares to the executives of WorldCom in return for their future investment banking business (Craig, P. C10).

a prospectus does not ensure success, it certainly is a good defensive measure.

Check the prospectus for the following:

- *The underwriters:* Is the underwriting company well known? Large, well-known underwriting firms are generally busy enough to screen out the more speculative IPOs. Even so, some new issues of immature companies are still underwritten by top underwriters, and the stock prices have fallen into oblivion after being brought to the market. Check the underwriter's record by asking the broker for a list of recent underwritings or by checking on the Internet at *www.iporesources.org*.

- *Check the number of underwriters in the syndicate.* Large syndicate groups generally give an IPO more exposure. Additionally, large syndicates provide more brokerage firms to trade the new stock, supporting its price (Barker, pp. 168–169).

- *Financial Statements:* Look at the financial statements in the back of the prospectus. From the *balance sheet*, determine who has provided the capital for the assets? Is it primarily from the debt holders or shareholders? If total liabilities exceed shareholders' equity, this is a red flag and requires further investigation. If the company has a downturn in revenues, can it still service its debt? If the shareholders' equity is negative, look carefully at the financial details of the company. Companies that have posted losses that exceed the amount of their retained earnings have negative retained earnings. If these negative retained earnings exceed the amounts in the capital accounts, the company has a negative shareholders' equity. Determine whether this company has the ability to turn its losses into profits in the not too distant future to maintain its business? Lazard had sizeable debt and negative book value, explaining its lackluster share price performance.

  Related to the income and losses is the cash flow a company generates. For example, Friendly Ice Cream, the restaurant chain, chalked up losses from operations since 1992, but this company had positive cash flows (Barker, p. 169). You can calculate *cash flow* by starting with net income or loss and adding back the noncash items such as depreciation and amortization.

  From the *income statement*, determine whether sales and earnings are growing. If a company experiences growth in sales but shows a loss in income, examine its prospectus for comments about profits in the foreseeable future. If profits are not anticipated soon, another red flag is raised. A note of irony: If investors had listened to this advice, they would never have bought any of the new Internet IPOs in October and November 1998, whose share prices mostly went up in the same trajectory as a rocket taking off for Mars. Most of these companies did not have anticipated earnings for years to come and were trading at rich multiples of sales. Although the Internet is here to stay, many Internet companies are not future beneficiaries of the technology. Internet IPO fever is not typical even for IPOs, and you should not continue to assume that every stock with an idea and no earnings always will be a tremendous success.

- *Read the section "Discussion and Analysis by Management":* See if there is any cushioning of future trouble signs ahead. Take a step back and ask what could go wrong with this company? What are its risks? Who are its competitors? Who are its customers? Assess the overall risks of the company. If it is too risky, walk away from it.

These precautions can help you limit the risk of loss from investing in IPOs.

New Issues of Securities

New issues of securities occur whenever exchange-listed companies want to raise new capital by issuing more securities. The procedure for issuing new securities to the public is roughly the same as with an IPO. Before securities are sold to the public, they must be registered with and approved by the SEC. The prospectus, called a *shelf registration*, is less detailed than that of an IPO because the company has already filed the necessary reports with the SEC, in addition to quarterly and annual statements and the necessary initial reports. The price of the issue approximates the market price of the company's securities, and less fine-tuning of that point takes place between the investment bankers and the company.

Secondary Markets and How Securities Are Traded

After new stocks and bonds have been sold, investors can trade them on the secondary markets. The company (original issuer of the securities) does not receive any proceeds on these trades. Instead, the trades are made between the owners of the securities and new investors willing to buy the securities. The secondary markets are important for providing not only liquidity and fair pricing for securities but also a baseline for the pricing of new issues and IPOs.

How Bonds Are Traded

Treasury securities are traded in the Treasury market through 35 primary dealers that include some of the largest investment banks and money-center banks. These dealers also can make a market in (buy and sell) government agency bonds. Banks and investment banks are also market makers in the municipal bond market because they underwrite and invest in many municipal-bond issues. Although a small percentage of corporate bonds are listed on the bond exchanges, dealers, who make a market in the bonds, trade the majority of corporate bonds on the OTC market.

Bonds are traded through brokers on the secondary market. Most bonds are traded over the counter rather than on the bond exchanges. Many brokerage firms act as *brokers* or *dealers,* using their own inventories to fill buy and sell orders. The major difference between a broker and a dealer is that a broker acts on behalf of clients to place their orders, whereas a dealer trades securities from his or her own account. A dealer is also known as a *market maker.* Consequently, an individual investor's order to buy or sell bonds can be filled from the brokerage firm's own inventory, in which case the broker is acting as a dealer. If it is not, the order goes to a dealer who makes a market in that particular bond. Transaction costs are much higher for bonds than for stocks because of their wider *spreads.* The spread is the difference between what a dealer pays for a bond and the price at which he or she sells the bond.

Pricing transparency is poor for bonds, and investors are seldom aware of the spreads. Markups are set by the dealer and incorporated into the price of the bond. Some progress is taking place toward making prices available to investors, and some bond prices are listed on the Bond Market Association's Web site www.bondmarkets.com. Other Web sites to obtain bond prices and yields are www.investinginbonds.com and www.munidirect.com.

How Stocks Are Traded

Individual investors place their orders for stocks through their brokers, who buy and sell stocks for their investors. These orders can be filled in two major trading systems: the auction market and the dealer market.

An *auction market* is a centralized location where bid and ask prices are given for stocks. Bid and ask prices are matched by specialists and floor brokers in an open-outcry auction, and shares with the lowest ask prices are bought from investors, and shares with the highest bid prices are sold to investors. This process takes place on the NYSE and AMEX. A *specialist* is a member of an exchange who makes a market in one or more of the securities listed on the exchange.

An example best illustrates the process of order execution on the NYSE. Suppose that you are interested in buying 200 shares of Home Depot, Inc. You call your broker for a quote or go online for this information. The bid is $39.90, and the ask is $39.91 per share. The *bid* means that the specialist is willing to buy Home Depot shares at $39.90 per share, and the *ask* means that the specialist is willing to sell Home Depot shares at $39.91 per share. The *spread* is $0.01 per share. On the NYSE, the Home Depot specialist makes a market in the stock.

You then decide to buy 200 shares of Home Depot at the market price. The transaction should be close to the $39.91 price per share if you place the order immediately after receiving the quote and if the market price of Home Depot does not fluctuate widely. Your broker fills out a buy order (or you fill out an online order), which is transmitted electronically to the floor of the exchange. Figure 3-1 provides an example of an online buy-sell order. There, the *floor broker* (member of an exchange who executes orders on the exchange floor) takes the order to the Home Depot trading post to execute the buy order, from either another floor broker who has a sell order for 200 Home Depot shares or from the specialist. When your order is executed, the brokerage firm mails or e-mails you a confirmation that the order has been executed.

Specialists are allowed to trade the assigned stocks in their own accounts and to profit from those trades. However, specialists are required to maintain a fair and orderly market in the stocks assigned to them. For example, specialists are not allowed to compete with customers' orders. If a customer places a market order to buy, the specialist cannot buy for his or her own account ahead of the unexecuted market order. Similarly, specialists cannot sell from their own accounts ahead of unexecuted market orders to sell. The purpose of allowing specialists to act as traders is to minimize the

FIGURE 3-1

A Typical Online Order Ticket

Symbol/Name _____

Quantity _____ shares

Transaction Type: Select one
                   Buy/Sell/ Sell Short/ Buy to Cover

                   _____

Order Type: Select one
             Market/Limit/Stop

             _____

        Limit Price _____   Stop Price _____

Duration: Select one
          Day/Good-Till Canceled

          _____

Account Type: Select One
               Cash/Margin

               _____

effects of imbalances in the supply and demand of assigned stocks. Specialists are prohibited by law from manipulating stock prices. Even though the SEC monitors the trading activities of specialists and ensures that they follow its numerous rules, maintaining an orderly market, along with the profit motivations of specialists, means stepping into a gray area. The reputation of the NYSE was tarnished by trading abuses of specialists and floor brokers on the exchange floor who traded stocks ahead of investors' orders for their own profits in 2003. The repercussions from the probe into these trading scandals could lead the way for trading on the NYSE to become more like the Nasdaq dealer market, where trades take place electronically.

Dealer Market. Although the NYSE claims that the auction process on the exchange floor results in a better price for customers in more than a third of all trades, the exchange floor has lost some of its trades to the dealer market. In a dealer market, dealers make markets in stocks from their inventories by using an electronic computerized system. Numerous dealers can provide both bid and ask prices for the same stock. This form of trading takes place on the Nasdaq system for OTC trades. The National Association of Securities Dealers (NASD) implemented the National Association of Securities Dealers Automated Quotation (Nasdaq) system, which allows subscribing brokerage firms to obtain price quotations on stocks in the system.

When buying or selling stock, you place an order with a brokerage firm. That order is sent to the brokerage firm's trading department, which then shops among that stock's market makers for the best price. To serve the needs of different brokerage firms, Nasdaq provides three levels of quotes:

- *Level 1.* This basic level provides a single quote for each stock. The price is updated continuously.
- *Level 2.* This level provides instantaneous quotes (bid and ask prices) for Nasdaq stocks from all the different market makers. A brokerage firm takes an investor's order for a particular stock to find the best price (the lowest ask price if the investor is buying and the highest bid price if the investor is selling) from those quotes. See Table 3-2 for an example.
- *Level 3.* This level, for market makers and dealers, provides Level 2 quotes and the capacity to change those quotes.

Many criticisms have been leveled at the potential conflict of interest between market makers and dealers regarding execution of trades on the OTC market. That brokerage firms can act simultaneously as agents for their customers and self-interested dealers might be a conflict of interest. Acting as an agent, a broker should find the best price for his or her customers. This responsibility becomes blurred when the agent's brokerage firm is also looking to profit from the deals it makes. You have no need to look for more competitive prices if your brokerage firm can fill your order as a market maker and thereby fulfill its profit objective. Table 3-3 discusses the importance of spreads.

TABLE 3-2

Examples of Level 2 Quotes and What They Mean

Some online brokerage firms provide Level 2 quotes for OTC stocks for their online clients. The following example illustrates the quotes offered by market makers and ECNs for a particular stock. Many actively traded stocks could have as many as 40 market makers. Microsoft, for example, might have 20 to 40 market makers.

Market Maker/ECN	Bid	Size	Ask	Size
1	19.25	20	19.26	20
2	19.24	5	19.27	5
3	19.25	7	19.27	5
4	19.24	20	19.26	20
5	19.22	5	19.28	5

With Level 2 quotes, a market buy order for a particular stock receives each market maker's or ECN's best bid offer. In this example, the best offer (ask) price is $19.26 per share for this particular company from ECNs 1 and 4. A market order to sell transacts at the best bid price, which is from ECNs 1 and 3 at $19.25 per share.

When a market order is entered, it is executed at the best price and continues to be filled incrementally until the order is completed. For example, a market order to buy 5,000 shares of the stock listed above would be transacted as follows:

2000 shares from Dealer 1 at $19.26 per share

2000 shares from Dealer 4 at $19.26 per share

 500 shares from Dealer 3 at $19.27 per share

 500 shares from Dealer 2 at $19.27 per share

An investor also can place an all-or-none order to make sure that it fills at the same price. The identity of each market maker or ECN is available to the investor. The size indicates the inventory that is available.

TYPES OF ORDERS

When you are buying and selling securities, you can place different types of orders to improve your execution prices. The incremental size of an order is also important. Using a *round lot* usually means that the number of shares traded is 100 or multiples of 100. For very cheap stocks (*penny stocks*), a round lot may be 500 or 1,000 shares; for high-priced shares, a round lot could be considered 10 shares. These 10-share round lots are referred to as *cabinet stocks*. Berkshire Hathaway A stock is a good example of a cabinet stock. It was trading at around $84,400 per share in May 2005. This is the most expensive stock on the NYSE. An *odd lot* for most cabinet stocks consists of a

TABLE 3-3

What Spreads Disclose

Stock spreads are determined by their bid and ask prices. Bid and ask prices are determined in some ways by supply and demand for the stocks but more specifically by the availability of the stock at particular prices. Bid and ask prices change rapidly in real time. Paying attention to the bid and ask sizes (the amount of stock available from each market maker) of each stock can provide more information about the supply and demand for the direction of the stock price. Spreads have narrowed because of the greater pricing transparency gained from access to real-time quotes through technology. The result of having narrower spreads is better execution prices. For example, the reduction in spreads from $0.03 to $0.02 per trade of 1,000 shares results in a $10 savings. If you make 100 trades per year, the total saving is $1,000. These savings can increase the returns on your portfolio meaningfully. You can draw these inferences about spreads:

- A wide spread indicates an illiquid stock.
- A narrow spread indicates a liquid stock.

Use limit orders when buying and selling stocks to specify the exact purchase or sale price. With a market order, the purchase (or sale) price could be higher (or lower) than the ask (or bid) price.

The bid and ask size also indicates the relative strength or depth of the bid and ask prices. When the supply of a stock (the ask size) is larger than the demand for the stock (the bid size), the short-term price indication is that the stock price will fall. Conversely, if the ask size is smaller than the bid size, the short-term price of the stock is pressured upward. The following quote illustrates the price direction using the bid and ask size:

Ticker Symbol	Bid Price	Ask Price	Size (Bid/Ask)
GE	34.71	34.73	1,000 × 200

In this example the bid size is larger than the ask size, indicating greater demand for the stock than the supply. In other words, the short-term price is headed upward. You can use the bid and ask size to assist in determining whether to use a market or limit order.

---

trade of between one and nine shares. On normally priced shares, an odd lot is composed of between one and 99 shares; for very cheap stocks, an odd lot consists of fewer than 500 shares. Investors trading in odd lots generally pay more to trade than investors trading in round lots. The commissions paid in order to execute odd lot trades may be higher.

Orders for stocks in excess of 10,000 shares are called *block trades*. These orders, typically placed by institutional customers, are handled in a variety of ways. Commissions are much lower than for normal trades, and orders are executed instantaneously.

By knowing the types of orders to use and how they are executed, you might be able to lower your transactions costs and avoid any misunderstandings with your brokers.

Market Order

A *market order*, the most frequently placed type of order, is an instruction to buy or sell a stock at the best available price at the time that the order is executed. If you obtain a price quote for Intel stock, for example, and place an order to buy 100 shares without specifying the price, it is a market order. Market orders are given priority in the communications systems of brokerage firms, so the stock is purchased before the price changes much. Market orders generally are executed within a few minutes (or even a few seconds) of being placed. In a few situations, a market order might not be executed, when curbs are in effect on the exchange floor, for example, or when the trading of that particular stock has been halted.

The good news is that market orders are filled soon after they are placed. The downside is that you do not know in advance the price at which the order will be executed. The order generally is executed at or close to the quoted price because of the order's prompt execution. However, if the stock is actively traded at the time the order is placed, some price deviation from the quoted price might take place. For example, a market order placed to buy a newly issued stock that begins trading for the first time on the secondary market might be executed at a much higher price than the offering price. When a fast-moving market occurs for a particular stock or stocks, a market order can be transacted at a significant price discrepancy from the price that is quoted.

These fast markets have a bearing on online trading. Even if investors receive real time quotes, a market order might not keep pace with those real-time quotes. By the time an order is placed online, the market might have moved considerably, making the quote that is received only an approximation of what is happening. Because market orders are executed on a first-serve basis, if numerous orders are already ahead of the one that is placed, the execution price can be significantly different from the quoted price. In this type of market, you should use limit orders to protect against the risk of large price deviations.

Market orders are usually *day orders*, which mean that they expire at the end of the day if they are not executed by then.

Limit Order

A *limit order* is an instruction to buy or sell a stock at a specified price. The specified price can be different from the market price. A limit order specifies a maximum price for buying a stock or a minimum price for selling a stock. For example, if the price of a stock is anticipated to fall from its current price, you can place a limit order to buy that stock at a specified lower price. If you want to buy 100 shares of General Electric, for example, which has fluctuated between $28 and $34 per share, you can place a limit order to buy General Electic at $28 even though the market price is $34 per share at the time the order is placed. The length of time that the order stands before being executed depends on the instructions you give to your broker. Using a good-till-canceled (GTC) order, you can have the order remain active until it is either executed or canceled. If a time limit is not specified, the order is assumed to be a day order; in that case, if the stock price does not fall to the limit price, the order is canceled at the end of the day.

Similarly, a limit order to sell stock can be placed above the current market price. For example, if IBM stock is trading at $87 per share, and you think that the stock will continue on an upward trend, you might decide to place a limit order to sell at $89 per share or higher. This order is then executed if and when IBM's shares reach $89.

A limit order for an NYSE stock is sent from an investor's brokerage firm to the commission broker on the exchange floor who sees whether the order can be filled from the crowd (other commission brokers). A *commission broker* is an employee of a member firm on the exchange who transacts the firm's orders on the exchange floor. If the limit order's price does not fall within the quotes of the current bid and ask prices, the order is given to the specialist (a member of the exchange who makes a market in one or more stocks listed on the exchange). If the specialist does not execute the order, the limit order is entered into the specialist's book for future execution. In this case, the specialist is acting as a broker for the commission broker. If the price of IBM, for example, rises days or months later, the higher priced limit orders in the specialist's book are executed in the order in which they were entered, known as the first-in, first-out (FIFO) basis. The specialist receives part of the customer's commission for executing this limit order.

The advantage of placing a limit order is that investors have an opportunity to buy (or sell) shares at a lower (or higher) price than the market price. The obvious disadvantage is that limit orders might never be executed if the limit prices are never reached. Placing a limit order does not guarantee that your order will be executed; with a market order, however, you are assured of execution, but not the price of execution.

Stop Order

A *stop order* is an instruction to buy or sell a stock whenever the stock trades at or past a specified price, when it then becomes a market order. You can use a stop order to protect existing profits or reduce losses. Although a stop order might appear similar to a limit order, they have some differences.

A stop order differs from a limit order in that after the stock's price reaches the stop-order price, the stop order becomes a market order. Suppose that you buy some stock at $20 per share that is now trading at $30 per share. Selling those shares would result in a $10 per share profit. To protect this profit from a rapid price drop, you can place a stop order to sell at $28 per share. If the stock drops to $28, the stop order then becomes a market order and is executed at the prevailing market price. If the stock is sold at $27.75 a share, you have protected a profit of $7.75 per share. On the other hand, if the stock keeps increasing from $30 per share after the stop order is placed, the stop order lies dormant (if it has no time limit and is a GTC order) until the share price falls to $28.

Similarly, you can protect profits on a short sale by using a stop order to buy. (Short selling is explained in the next section of this chapter).

In addition to protecting profits, stop orders can be used to reduce or prevent losses. Suppose that you buy a stock at $10 in anticipation of a price increase. Soon after your purchase, news from the company suggests that the price may go down rapidly. You can place a stop order to sell at $9, which limits your loss, if the stock price declines below $9 per share.

Limiting losses on a short sale is the other use for stop orders, which is explained in the section on short selling.

Another danger waits when you are setting a stop-order price. If you place the stop-order price too close to the current price, a temporary surge or fall in the price of the stock can trigger the execution of a market order. Then, although the stock price might move back in the direction you anticipate, you no longer have a position in that stock. On the other hand, if the stop-order price is set further away from the current market price, less profit is protected (or you risk a greater loss).

Of course, the use of stop orders does not increase profits if you do not anticipate the direction of the market price correctly.

FINANCIAL PLANNERS AND STOCKBROKERS

Financial advisors provide investors with assistance in their financial planning. A financial advisor evaluates your financial situation and then formulates a financial and investment plan. Stockbrokers provide investment advice about individual securities and place investors' trade orders.

Financial Planners

A *financial planner* is someone who has paid a $150 fee and in some states has registered with the Securities and Exchange Commission (SEC). Virtually anyone who pays a fee of $150 and registers with the SEC can be a financial advisor. (Some states require registration also.) Consequently, you should do your homework before hiring a financial planner or advisor and then evaluate that person's advice carefully. Ask the planner for his or her credentials.

Stockbrokers

To trade securities, you need access to the marketplace, and you attain access through a brokerage firm. The selection of a stockbroker is a personal decision. You can choose from three types of brokers:

- Full service
- Discount
- Online

The amount and level of services among these basic types of brokers differ, as do methods of compensation. The following guidelines are helpful in choosing a brokerage type.

Services Required

Stockbrokers charge commissions for executing trades. These commission costs vary considerably and can affect your profits and losses. Commission charges can be based on three factors: number of shares traded, the share price, and the total amount of the order.

Full-service and national brokerage firms generally charge the highest fees and commissions, followed by *regional* brokerage firms, which tend to be marginally cheaper. Discount brokerage firms offer reduced commissions, and they charge either no fees or reduced fees for miscellaneous services. Commissions are discounted even more at deep discount brokerage firms.

Paying $91 at a full service brokerage firm versus $7 at a deep discounter for the same trade certainly makes a difference to the total return. If the stock price is $30 per share for a 100 share trade, you are paying 3 percent of the stock price (91 divided by 3,000) at a full-service broker versus 0.2 percent at the deep-discount broker. The stock would have to go up 6 percent, therefore, to cover your transactions costs with the full-service commission broker compared with a rise of 0.4 percent for the deep-discount broker. The greater the number of trades, the more significant the commissions become to your profit or loss.

Individual brokers at *full-service brokerage firms* earn commissions on the volume of trades they make. Brokers, if pushed by their clients, sometimes are willing to discount their commissions, particularly for clients with large accounts. Full-service brokers familiarize themselves with the financial circumstances of their clients, provide opinions about specific stocks and bonds, and provide research by client request. Investors pay higher commissions for the investment advice and research available from a full-service brokerage firm. A personal relationship exists between the investor and full-service broker. The full-service brokerage firms offer a diversified range of financial services, in addition to information, research reports, and the execution of trades.

Discount brokerage firms offer reduced commissions and in some (not all) cases reduced services compared with full-service brokerage firms. Brokers at discount brokerage firms execute trades for clients, but they do not necessarily provide the same personal service as full-service brokers. In fact, personal brokers are not necessarily assigned to investors who use discount brokerages. Research might or might not be available for the asking. Some discount brokerage firms provide research for free, and others charge for information.

Traditionally, *deep-discount firms* offer only basic mechanical access to the markets, price quotes, and trade executions. Since the advent of online trading, though, competition among deep discounters has resulted in limited full-service features being introduced. In these cases, some amount of information and research are combined with very low trade commissions.

Electronic trading or *online brokers* allow you to place your own trades using a computer linked to the Internet. The costs of online trading can vary from $5 per trade to $40 per trade. Research is widely available through these online trading services. Some brokerage firms charge nominal amounts for Standard & Poor's (S&P's) reports or Zack's research reports, and others provide them for free. Online investing can mean online research no matter which type of brokerage firm is used. The government's Web site, Edgar Online (www.freeedgar.com), provides data derived from the thousands of SEC documents filed by publicly traded companies. Table 3-4 illustrates what to look for in an online brokerage firm.

If you are comfortable using a computer and do not require information and research from a personal broker, you can benefit from the lower commissions charged by online brokerage firms. You also should ask about the broker's fee structure for custodial services, account management, and transactions before making a final choice.

TYPES OF ACCOUNTS AT BROKERAGE FIRMS

Opening an account at a brokerage firm is as easy as opening a bank account. Many brokerage firms require little more than a deposit. You are asked to supply basic information, such as your occupation and Social Security Number, in addition to more specific information about your financial circumstances. Brokers are required to get to know their customers and to be able to use judgment with regard to sizable transactions and determine whether customers can use credit to finance their trades.

Brokerage firms must ask their customers how securities are to be registered. If you decide to leave your stock certificates, for example, in the custody of your brokerage firm, the securities are registered in street name. *Street name* refers to the registration of investor-owned securities in the name of the brokerage firm. Accrued dividends of street named securities are mailed to the brokerage

TABLE 3-4

What to Look for in an Online Brokerage Firm

You can choose from many online trading firms. They have different commission rates and offer a variety of services. A few features of an online brokerage firm are *fast and reliable executions, immediate confirmations*, and *free real-time quotes*. If orders take a long time to be executed, choose another online broker. When a market order is placed in normal circumstances, it should be transacted almost instantaneously. Your trades also should be executed at *the best prices.* You can determine whether the best price was passed on to you by watching real time price quotes for the stock around the same time that your order was transacted. Some investors also want an online firm that provides them with *research.*

In addition to these features, your choice depends on several factors, such as

- The type of investor
- The frequency of trades
- The level of services required

If you're a long-term investor who requires help with investment decisions, and you want to trade online, look for an online brokerage firm that offers personal service. The trading costs at this type of firm are usually at the higher end of the range.

If you're a long-term investor who does not need any handholding, look for lower-end trading commissions from an online broker that provides research, free real-time quotes, an easy-to-use Web site, and fast executions at the best prices.

Investors who trade stocks actively need low-cost brokers who provide information needed for trading. Active traders and day traders require tick-by-tick trading activity of individual stocks. These traders need to know the highest bid prices, the lowest ask prices, and the best available price for any stock in real time in order to make quick, nimble trades. Active traders and day traders require Level 2 service to stay on top of ever-changing prices from all market makers. Some online brokerage firms provide Nasdaq Level 2 quotes free of charge. By monitoring buy and sell quotes, day traders can get better insights into the possible direction of the movement of stock prices. Armed with this information, day traders can profit by buying the shares of a stock from a lower-quoted market maker and selling to a higher-priced market maker. Taking large positions in a stock and attempting to profit from fractional point moves is not for the faint hearted. Online trading fostered the growth of day traders. Day trading as a fad collapsed with the deflating tech-stock bubble in 2002. Specialized day-trading brokerage firms still operate, but any investor interested in opening an account in one of them should understand the special training required and the dangers incurred by day trading. The risk of loss is much greater than with a buy-and-hold style of investing.

firms, where they are then credited to customers' accounts. The main disadvantage of registering stocks in street name is that the brokerage firms might not forward to you all the mailings of company reports and news. The advantage of holding securities in street name is that when securities are sold, the customer has no need to deliver the signed stock certificates within the three days required before settlement of the transaction.

Securities that are registered in your name can be kept either in your broker's vaults or mailed to you. You should store these security certificates in a bank safe-deposit box because they are negotiable securities. If they are stolen, you might face losses.

Three types of accounts are used for buying and selling securities:

- Cash
- Margin
- Discretionary

Cash Account

A *cash account* with a brokerage firm requires that cash payments be made for the purchases of securities within three days of the transaction. With a cash account, you are required to pay in full for the purchase of securities on or before the settlement date. The *settlement date* is now defined as three business days after an order is executed and the date on which the purchaser of the securities must pay cash to the brokerage firm and the seller of the securities must deliver the securities to the brokerage firm. If you buy stock on a Monday, for example, your payment is due on or before the Wednesday of that week, assuming that no public holidays take place during those three days. That Monday is referred to as the *trade date* (the date on which an order is executed). If you do not pay for the securities by the settlement date, the brokerage firm can liquidate them. In the event of a loss, the brokerage firm can require additional payments from you to make up for the loss and to keep your account in good standing. For online accounts, the money generally needs to be in the account before the trade is made.

When stocks are sold, stock certificates must be delivered or sent to the brokerage firm (if securities are not held in street name) within three days to avoid any charges. After the settlement date, the proceeds of the sale, minus commissions, are either mailed to the investor or deposited into a cash account with the brokerage firm, depending on the arrangements made in advance. Determine whether any fees are charged for the management of cash in the account or for access to a money-market account.

Margin Account

A *margin account* with a brokerage firm allows a brokerage client to purchase securities on credit, and to borrow securities to sell short. In other words, a margin account with a brokerage firm allows you to buy securities without having to pay the full cash price. The balance is borrowed from the brokerage firm. The maximum percentage of the purchase price that a client can borrow is determined by the *margin requirement* set by the Federal Reserve Board. Brokers can set more strict requirements for their clients. For example, with a margin requirement of 50 percent, if you are buying stock worth $12,000, you would have to put up at least $6,000 in cash and borrow the other $6,000 from the brokerage firm. If the margin requirement is 60 percent, you would have to put up at least $7,200 and borrow the balance. The brokerage firm uses the stock as collateral on the loan. These securities are held in street name and also can be loaned to other clients of the brokerage firm who are selling short. Short selling is discussed later in this chapter.

The brokerage firm charges interest on the amount borrowed by the margin investor. Risks are magnified in margin trading because losses represent a greater portion of the money invested. However, if the price of the stock goes up, the rate of return is greater for the margin investor than for the cash investor because the margin investor has invested less money. In both cases, the investor must pay interest on the margin loan, increasing a loss and slightly reducing a profit. This concept is illustrated in Table 3-5.

If stock prices decline in a margin account, the amount owed to the brokerage firm becomes proportionately larger. In order to protect their positions, brokerage firms set *maintenance margins*, which are minimum equity positions investors must have in their margin accounts. When funds fall below the maintenance margin, the broker sends the investor a *margin call*. A margin call is a notice requesting that the investor pay additional money to maintain the minimum margin requirement. If the investor does not deposit additional funds, the brokerage firm can liquidate the securities. The investor is then liable for any losses incurred by the brokerage firm. Table 3-6 shows how margin maintenance works.

Two types of transactions can be performed with only a margin account: selling stocks short (described in the next section) and writing uncovered stock options (discussed in the chapter on options).

TABLE 3-5

Rate of Return Using a Cash Account Versus a Margin Account

An investor buys 100 shares of Johnson & Johnson (JNJ) at $45 per share and sells at $54 per share. The margin requirement is 50 percent. Commissions per trade are $50. Interest on the margin account is $45.

	Cash Account		Margin Account
Proceeds from sale of 100 shares of JNJ at $54	$5,400		$5,400
Less commissions	(50)		(50)
Net proceeds	5,350		5,350
Cost of 100 shares plus commission	(4,550)		(4,550)
Gross profit	800		800
Less interest expense			45
Net profit	800		755
Rate of return = profit/invested funds 800/4,550	17.58%	755/2,275*	33.18%

*Invested funds = $2,275 (4,550 × 50%)

The proceeds and the gross profit are the same for both the cash and margin accounts. The differences are that the investor deposits the entire cost of the shares for the cash account ($4,550), whereas the investor in the margin account only puts up 50 percent ($2,275). The rate of return is greater for the margin investor because the amount invested is much less than that of the cash investor despite the lower net profit caused by the interest expense for the margin investor.

Determine the rate of return if the preceding data are the same except for JNJ stock being sold at $41 per share.

	Cash Account		Margin Account
Proceeds from sale of 100 shares of JNJ at $41	$4,100		$4,100
Less commissions	(50)		(50)
Net proceeds	4,050		4,050
Cost of 100 shares plus commission	(4,550)		(4,550)
Gross loss	(500)		(500)
Interest expense			45
Net loss	(500)		(545)
Investment	4,550		2,275*
Rate of loss −500/4,550	−10.98%	−545/2,275	−23.95%

*Margin requirement $2,275 (4,550 × 50%)

The rate of loss is magnified with a margin account because the net loss is greater and the amount invested is less than the figures in the cash account.

TABLE 3-6

Margin Maintenance

Determine whether a margin call takes place in the following situation:

The margin requirement set by the Federal Reserve is 50 percent, and the brokerage firm's maintenance margin requirement is 40 percent. The investor buys 100 shares of Cisco at $15 per share. The share price drops to $13 per share. Ignore commissions.

Purchase price 100 shares of Cisco at $15 per share		$1,500
Investor's equity: 50% × 1,500		750
Borrowing in margin account		750
Value of Cisco at $13 per share		$1,300
Less borrowed amount		(750)
Investor's equity		550
Investor's equity percentage	550/1,300	42.3%

Because this percentage exceeds the maintenance margin requirement of 40 percent, no margin call is placed.

Discretionary Account

A *discretionary account* is a brokerage account in which the broker is permitted to buy and sell securities on behalf of the investor. If you have this type of account, you agree to allow your brokerage firm to decide which securities to buy and sell, as well as the amount and price to be paid and received. (For an unethical broker, a discretionary account is the answer to all prayers!)

You should monitor the activity in your discretionary account monthly to determine whether your broker has engaged in any excessive trading for the sole purpose of earning more commissions. In this process, called *churning*, stocks are turned over frequently, even though they have only moved up or down a few points. Unless you know the broker and trust him or her implicitly, be careful with a discretionary account.

HOW SHORT SELLING WORKS

Most investors invest in common stocks by buying them and then selling them later. Outright ownership of shares is referred to as a *long position*. The opposite is a *short position*, which is based on the expectation that the price of the security will decline. A short position indicates that a security is borrowed and then sold but not yet replaced. When stock prices are expected to increase, you can benefit from buying stocks. On the flip side, you can benefit by selling short stocks before their prices decrease.

In a short sale, you borrow stocks to sell and hope that the price then declines. If it does, you can buy the stocks back later at a lower price and then return them to the lender. An example illustrates this process.

Ms. X thinks that the stock of Schering Plough, ticker symbol SGP (the pharmaceutical company), is overvalued and that its price will drop. She places an order with her broker to sell short 100 shares of SGP, which is transacted at $43 per share (the total proceeds are $4,300 without commissions). The brokerage firm has three business days to deliver 100 shares of SGP to the buyer and has several sources from which to borrow these securities. It might borrow the 100 shares of SGP from its own inventory of SGP stock, if it has any, or from another brokerage firm. The most likely source is from its own inventory of securities held in street name from its margin accounts. In this example, the brokerage firm locates 100 shares of SGP in a margin account belonging to Mr. Y. The brokerage firm sends these shares to the buyer who bought the shares sold short by Ms. X, and SGP is notified of the new ownership.

All parties in this transaction are satisfied. The buyer has acquired the shares. The short seller, Ms X, has $4,300, minus commissions, in her margin account, and the brokerage firm has received the commissions on the trade. The $4,300 (minus commissions) is held in the margin account (and cannot be withdrawn by Ms X) as protection in case Ms X defaults on the short sale.

Mr. Y, who more than likely signed a loan consent form when he opened his margin account, is indifferent to the process. He still has all his rights to the ownership of the 100 shares of SGP. This process is illustrated in Figure 3-2.

When the stock in question is a dividend-paying stock, who receives the dividend? Before the short sale, the brokerage firm would have received the dividend on the 100 shares of SGP held in street name in Mr. Y's margin account, and this amount then would be paid into his account. However, those shares have been used in the short sale and have been forwarded to the new buyer, who receives

FIGURE 3-2

A Short Sale

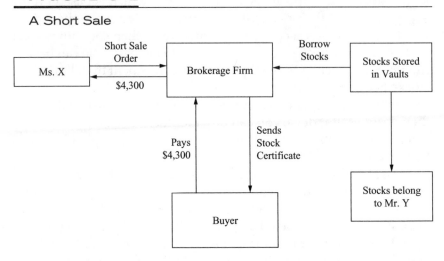

the dividend from Schering Plough. Mr. Y is still entitled to his dividend. The short seller, Ms X, who borrowed his securities, must pay to Mr. Y an equal dividend amount via the brokerage firm.

When SGP declines to $18 per share, Ms X puts in a buy order to cover her short position. The securities are returned to the brokerage firm, and Ms X has made a profit of $25 per share, not counting the commissions on the trades and the dividend.

As mentioned earlier, short sales are transacted in margin accounts. The possibility always exists that Ms X could skip town, and then the brokerage firm would be short the 100 shares of SGP. By using a margin account, the short seller (Ms X) has to leave the proceeds from the short sale in the account and is also required to pay in an additional amount of cash—this is the margin requirement discussed earlier. Assuming a margin requirement of 50 percent, the example shown in Table 3-7 illustrates Ms X's margin account.

Margin accounts provide greater leverage than cash accounts, as shown in Table 3-7. Ms X paid $2,125 and received a 111 percent return (2,358/2,125). Cash transactions require the entire investment in the stock to be put up in cash, which reduces the rate of return. *Leverage* is the creation of profit or loss proportionately greater than an underlying investment by using other people's money. The use of leverage has the effect of a double-edged sword. In the event of losses, the percentage loss is greater on margin trading than on cash trades.

TABLE 3·7

Margin Account Illustrating a Short Sale

Proceeds from short sale of 100 shares of SGP at $43	$4,300
Less commissions and fees	(50)
Net proceeds	4,250
Plus total margin requirement (50%)	2,125
Balance	6,375
Minus interest expense on borrowed funds	(42)
Net proceeds	6,333
Cost to purchase 100 shares of SGP at $18	$1,800
Plus commission	50
Total cost	1,850
Balance	4,433
Less margin deposit	2,125
Profit	$2,358

What Are the Risks of Short Selling?

Short selling allows you to sell a security without owning it (which, for virtually everything other than stocks, can land a person in prison!). If a stock's price falls below its short-sale price, you make a profit.

If the stock price increases, however, you can lose money. The potential loss is limitless because if the stock keeps going up, the amount of the loss increases. Suppose that you thought that certain Internet stocks were overvalued during their period of "irrational exuberance" and decided to sell some of them short. Tremendous losses would have resulted during the wild inflation of prices. AOL stock (now part of Time Warner) went from $100 to about $400 per share on a pre split basis in a short period. If you had sold short at $100 and had not covered your position (bought back the stock), you would have faced the prospect of buying back the stock at an enormously high price, resulting in a large loss per share. With a long position, the most that you can lose is the amount of your investment (buy a stock at $12 per share and it falls to $0), whereas short selling imposes no limits. The higher the price, the greater is the loss.

You have to be aware of other risks. Stocks can be sold short only if the price of the stock on its preceding trade was traded on an uptick or a zero-tick. An *uptick* means that the price of the existing trade must exceed the price of the preceding trade. A *zero-tick* means that the price of the most recent trade is the same as that of the preceding trade. Thus, if the price of a stock declines precipitously, your short sale might not be executed.

The short seller is also required to pay any dividends that are declared by the company to the owner of the borrowed securities. In addition, the proceeds of the short sale are held as collateral for the securities borrowed by the brokerage firm. The short seller is also required to provide additional funds (the margin requirement of 50 percent set by the Federal Reserve). If the stock remains in a flat trading range, the short seller's funds and the margin requirement are tied up in the account.

Using Stop Orders to Protect Profits on a Short Sale

Stop orders can be used to protect profits on a short sale. If you sell short a stock at $40 and the stock declines to $32, you might be reluctant to buy back the short position, hoping that the stock will decline even further. To protect profits against an unanticipated price increase, you place a stop order at $34 to preserve the $6 profit per share.

Similarly, the use of a stop order can reduce the losses in an unfavorable short sale. If you sell short a stock at $15, you might place a stop order to cover a short position at $16. This strategy limits the losses should there be a rise in the price of the stock. Without a stop order, the investor potentially could face a large loss if the stock keeps going up in price.

With a long position in stocks, the most that an investor could lose is the entire investment (if the company goes bankrupt and the stock falls to zero with nothing left for the shareholders). However, with short selling, if the price of a stock keeps rising, the losses theoretically could be unlimited.

Selling short may be risky for investors who do not have the stomach to watch the price of the stock turn in an unanticipated direction.

There are rules governing short sales on the NYSE and the AMEX, as well as for stocks on the Nasdaq. Short sales may not be made when stocks are falling in price because this will exacerbate the price declines. On the exchanges, short sales may be made for a higher price than that of the previous trade, on an *uptick,* or for a price that is equal to the previous trade but more than the trade prior to that, on a *zero-plus tick.*

What Is Short Interest?

Short interest is the number of shares of a company's stock that has been sold short and has not been bought back. In other words, the shares borrowed have not been bought back and returned to the lenders. Both the NYSE and the AMEX, as well as the Nasdaq, publish monthly figures of the short sales of listed companies. These are published in the financial newspapers monthly.

R E F E R E N C E S

Barker, Robert: "Just How Juicy Is that IPO?" *Business Week,* October 6, 1997, pp. 168–169.

Craig, Susanne: "IPO Allotments: A Guide to the Game," *Wall Street Journal,* August 29, 2002, pp. C1, C10.

Faerber, Esmé: *All About Stocks, 2d ed.* New York: McGraw-Hill, 2000.

Hennessey, Raymond: "St. Paul Unit IPO Gets a Boost," *Wall Street Journal,* September 24, 2002, p. C5.

McNamee, Mike: "A Magic Bullet for NASDAQ?" *Business Week,* September 30, 2002, pp. 80–81.

New York Stock Exchange: "NYSE to Retain Automated Bond System Operations," press release, April 11, 2001; available at http://www.nyse.com/marketinfo/nysebonds.html (September 19,2002).

Schroeder, Michael, and Anita Raghavan: "SEC to Fine Firms, Ending Nasdaq Probe," *Wall Street Journal,* January 6, 1999, p. C1.

Zweig, Philip L., Leah Nathans Spiro, and Michael Schroeder: "Beware the IPO Market," *Business Week,* April 4, 1994, pp. 84–90.

CHAPTER 4

Investment Companies (Mutual Funds)

KEY CONCEPTS

- Funds and how they work
- Distinguish between the different types of funds
- Understand the different types of closed-end funds, unit investment trusts, real estate investment trusts, and exchange-traded funds
- Types of mutual funds
- An analysis of the prospectus can assist in the choice of a fund
- The risks of mutual funds.
- Should an investor invest in individual securities or use funds?

Investment companies have come close to providing the ideal type of investment for millions of investors who do not want to manage their own investments. The managers of these investment companies invest the funds of these investors in diversified portfolios of stocks, bonds, and money-market instruments. Investors receive shares in these investment companies' funds related to the size of their investments. Thus, even with a modest investment, an investor owns a share of a diversified portfolio of stocks or bonds. An advantage of this type of investment is that investors who do not have the time to manage their financial investments or knowledge of the individual financial securities can invest their money in diversified stock, bond, and money-market portfolios of mutual funds.

Yet mutual funds have come under increased scrutiny from regulators (Securities and Exchange Commission and the New York Attorney General, for example) over excessively high fees charged and the practice of market timing shares in some mutual funds. These scandalous practices by some mutual funds have left many investors in a quandary over whether to invest their money in mutual funds. Many investors have turned to exchange-traded funds as a popular investment alternative.

The growth in the amount of money managed by investment companies in mutual funds has made them important players in the securities markets. According to the Investment Company Institute (www.ici.org), the mutual fund industry managed over $16.06 trillion of investors' assets worldwide at the end of 2004. With so many mutual funds to choose from, investors should be as careful in their selection of mutual funds as they are in investing in individual securities. Three steps can facilitate the choice of which fund to invest in:

1. Understand how these funds work.
2. Determine what the objectives of the funds are and the types of investments they make.
3. Evaluate the performance of funds from their prospectuses and other sources.

FUNDS AND HOW THEY WORK

All mutual funds work in similar ways. The investment company that sponsors a mutual fund sells shares to investors and then invests the funds that are received in a portfolio of securities. By pooling the investors' funds, a fund manager can diversify the acquisition of different securities, such as stocks for stock funds and bonds for bond funds. The objectives of the fund determine the types of investments chosen. For example, if a stock fund's objective is to provide capital appreciation, the fund invests in growth stocks. Similarly, a bond fund with an objective of providing tax-free interest at the federal level invests in municipal bonds. The fund buys different municipal bond issues to achieve a diversified portfolio, which also reduces the risk of loss due to default.

Interest earned on invested securities is paid to the fund's shareholders as dividends. An investor who invests $1,000 gets the same rate of return as another investor who invests $100,000 in the same fund, except the latter shareholder receives a dividend that is 100 times greater (proportionate to the share ownership in the fund).

When prices of securities in the portfolio fluctuate, the total value of the fund is affected. Many different factors—such as the intrinsic risk of the types of securities in the portfolio, in addition to economic, market, and political factors—cause these price fluctuations. The fund's objectives are important because they indicate the type and quality of the investments chosen by the fund. From these objectives, investors can better assess the overall risk the fund is willing to take to improve income (return) and capital gains.

Investment companies offer four different types of funds:

- Open-end mutual funds
- Closed-end funds
- Unit investment trusts (UITs)
- Exchange-traded funds (ETFs) (Exchange-traded funds are mostly sponsored by brokerage firms and banks.)

Table 4-1 outlines the differences between closed-end funds, UITs, and open-end mutual funds.

The Different Types of Funds

Two basic types of funds are open-end or closed-end. *Open-end funds* issue unlimited numbers of shares. Investors can purchase more

TABLE 4-1

Closed-End Funds and Unit Investment Trusts Versus Open-End Funds

Closed-End Funds and Unit Investment Trusts	Open-End Funds
1. Issue a fixed number of shares.	1. Issue an unlimited number of shares.
2. Shares (after issue) are traded on the stock exchanges.	2. Shares (including new shares) may be bought (and sold) from (to) the fund.
3. Shares can trade at, above, or below net asset values.	3. Shares trade at net asset values.
4. Share prices depend not only on fundamentals but also on the supply and demand for the shares.	4. Shares prices depend on the fundamentals of the assets in the fund.
5. Closed-end funds do not mature. Unit investment trusts do.	5. Open-end funds do not mature except for zero-coupon funds.
6. Unit trusts invest in bond securities, which are held to maturity.	

shares from the mutual fund company and sell them back to the fund company, which means that the number of shares increases or decreases, respectively. A *closed-end fund* issues a fixed number of shares, and when all the shares are sold, no more are issued. In other words, closed-end funds have fixed capital structures. Investors who want to invest in closed-end funds after all the shares are sold (for the first time) have to buy the shares from shareholders who are willing to sell them in the market. Shares of closed-end funds are listed on stock exchanges and over-the-counter markets, whereas shares of open-end mutual funds are bought from and sold to the investment company sponsoring the fund. As a result, share prices of closed-end funds are a function of not only their net-asset values but also of the supply of and demand for the stock in the market.

Another type of closed-end fund is the unit investment trust. A *unit investment trust* (UIT) issues a fixed number of shares, which are sold originally by the sponsor of the trust. The proceeds from the sale are used to buy stocks or bonds for the trust, which are held to maturity. Unlike an open-end or closed-end fund, no active trading of the securities in the portfolio takes place. Consequently, no active management of the trust takes place, which should mean lower management fees, although this is not always the case. A trust has a maturity date, and the proceeds are then returned to the shareholders of the trust.

All UITs charge sales commissions, whereas investors in open-end funds have a choice between the purchase of a fund that does or does not charge a sales commission.

Open-End Mutual Funds

You invest your money in a mutual fund by buying shares at the *net asset value* (NAV). Net asset value is the market value of the fund's assets at the end of each trading day minus any liabilities divided by the number of outstanding shares.

Open-end funds determine the market value of their assets at the end of each trading day. For example, a balanced fund, which invests in both common stocks and bonds, uses the closing prices of the stock and bond holdings for the day to determine market value. The total number of shares of each of the stocks and bonds that the fund owns is multiplied by the closing prices. The resulting total of each investment is added together, and any liabilities associated with the fund (such as accrued expenses) are subtracted. The resulting

TABLE 4-2

How the Net Asset Value of a Fund Is Determined

Market value of stocks and bonds in the fund		$100,000,000
Minus total liabilities		− 130,000
Net worth		$ 99,870,000
Number of shares outstanding		7,500,000
Net asset value	$ 13.316	(99,870,000/7,500,000)

total net assets are divided by the number of shares outstanding in the fund to equal the net asset value price per share. Table 4-2 shows how the net asset value (NAV) is determined.

The NAV changes daily because of market fluctuations of the stock and bond prices in the fund. NAVs are important because

1. The NAV is used to determine the value of your holdings in the mutual fund (the number of shares held multiplied by the NAV price per share).
2. The NAV is the price at which new shares are purchased or redeemed.

NAVs of the different funds are quoted in daily newspapers or on the funds' Web sites.

Mutual funds pay no taxes on income derived from their investments. Under the Internal Revenue Service Tax Code, mutual funds serve as conduits through which income from investments is passed to shareholders in the form of interest or dividends and capital gains or losses. Individual investors pay taxes on income and capital gains distributions from mutual funds.

Shareholders receive monthly and annual statements showing purchases and sales of shares, interest income, dividends, capital gains and losses, and other relevant data that they should retain for tax purposes. In addition, when investing in mutual funds, investors also should keep track of the NAV prices of shares purchased and sold. This information is used in the computation of gains and losses when shares are redeemed.

The value of a mutual fund increases when

- Interest and dividends earned on the fund's investments are passed through to shareholders.

- The fund's management sells investment securities at a profit. The capital gains from such a sale are passed through to shareholders. If these securities are sold at a loss, the capital loss is offset against the gains of the fund, and the net gain or loss is passed through to shareholders;
- The NAV per share increases.

Closed-End Funds

As discussed earlier in this chapter, closed-end funds issue a fixed number of shares that are traded on the stock exchanges or in the over-the-counter (OTC) market. When the shares are sold, the fund does not issue more shares. At the end of 2004, there were 620 closed-end funds consisting of 463 bond funds and 157 stock funds. These funds have professional managers who assemble and manage the investment portfolios according to the goals and objectives of the funds. Unlike open-end funds, closed-end funds do not trade at their NAVs. Instead, their share prices are based on the supply of and demand for their funds and other fundamental factors. Consequently, closed-end funds can trade at premiums or discounts to their NAVs, as shown in Table 4-3. Closed-end fund prices can be obtained from financial newspapers or from Web sites on the Internet.

TABLE 4-3

Closed-End Fund Premiums and Discounts

Company	Net Asset Value (NAV)	Market Price*	Premium/Discount
Gabelli Equity Trust	8.33	8.60	3.2%
Asia Tigers	11.43	10.58	−7.4%
Corporate High Yield	9.03	9.19	1.8%
How to Calculate the Discount or Premium			

$$\text{Premium/discount} = \frac{\text{market price} - \text{net asset value}}{\text{net asset value}}$$

$$\text{Gabelli Trust} = \frac{8.60 - 8.33}{8.33}$$

$$\text{Premium} = 3.24 \text{ percent}$$

*Prices as of November 8, 2004.

Shares of closed-end funds are bought and sold through brokers. You should be aware of the following facts about the purchase of closed-end funds:

- Brokerage firms underwrite and sell newly issued shares of closed-end funds.
- The brokerage fees on these newly issued shares can be quite high, which then erodes the price of the shares when they trade on the market. For example, if a closed-end fund sells 1 million shares at $10 per share and there is a brokerage commission of 7 percent, the fund receives $9.3 million to invest ($700,000 is deducted from the $10 million proceeds). The share price drops in value from the $10 originally paid and trades at a discount to the offer price.
- Another reason not to buy newly issued shares in a closed-end fund is that the portfolio of investments has not yet been constituted, so investors do not know what the investment assets are and, in the case of bond funds, the yields on those investments.

Unit Investment Trusts

Unit investment trusts UITs are registered investment companies that sell units (shares) of a relatively fixed investment portfolio consisting of bonds or stocks. UITs have a stated termination date when the investments either mature or are liquidated. The proceeds are then returned to the unit-holders (shareholders). Consequently, these trusts are well suited to bonds, with their streams of income and maturity of principal. With stock UITs, the stocks are sold at the termination date, and the proceeds are returned to the unit-holders. The majority of UITs sold consist of tax-exempt municipal bonds, followed by taxable-bond trusts and then equity (stock) trusts.

UITs are bought through brokers who sponsor their own trusts and through brokerage firms that represent the trusts. If you do not want to hold your trust through maturity, you can sell it back to the sponsor of the trust. The trust sponsors are required by law to buy the shares back at their NAVs, which can be more or less than the amount the investor paid initially. Under certain conditions, shares of these trusts can be quite illiquid, particularly for bond trusts when interest rates are rising.

The same caveats apply for buying initial public offerings (IPOs) of UITs as for closed-end funds:

- Investors do not know the composition of the portfolio's investments.
- Investors pay sales charges, or *loads*, which may be as much as 4 to 5 percent higher than the net asset values.

In a UIT, the portfolio of investments generally does not change after purchase. In other words, no new securities are bought or sold. Theoretically, therefore, management fees should be lower on UITs than on closed-end funds because the portfolio remains unmanaged. The only time securities are sold in a UIT is generally when a severe decline in the quality of the issues occurs. Consequently, no management fees should be incurred on a UIT. In most instances, this is not the case, and fees can be high.

Real Estate Investment Trusts (REITs)

A *real estate investment trust* (REIT) is a fund that buys and manages real estate and real estate mortgages. REITs offer individual investors the opportunity to invest in real estate without having to own and manage individual properties. REITs were popular during the middle of 1996 when inflation was expected to surge. In 2001–2002, when the stock market declined, investors again turned to REITs as safe-haven investments.

A REIT is a form of closed-end mutual fund, in that it invests in real estate the proceeds received from the initial sale of shares to shareholders. REITs buy, develop, and manage real estate properties and pass on to shareholders the income from the rents and mortgages in the form of dividends.

REITs do not pay corporate income taxes, but in return, they must, by law, distribute 95 percent of their net income to shareholders. Consequently, not much income remains to finance future real estate acquisitions.

Following are three basic types of REITs:

- *Equity REITs* buy, operate, and sell real estate such as hotels, office buildings, apartments, and shopping centers.
- *Mortgage REITs* make construction and mortgage loans available to developers.

- *Hybrid REITs*, a combination of equity and mortgage REITs, buy, develop, and manage real estate and provide financing through mortgage loans. Most hybrid REITs have stronger positions in either equity or debt. Few well-balanced hybrid REITs exist.

The risks are not the same for each type of REIT, so you should evaluate each type carefully before investing. Equity REITs generally tend to be less speculative than mortgage REITs, although the risk level depends on the makeup of the assets in the trust. Mortgage REITs lend money to developers, which involve a greater risk. Consequently, shares of mortgage REITs tend to be more volatile than shares of equity REITs, particularly during a recession.

Equity REITs have been the most popular type of REIT recently. Their cumulative performance of 55 percent total returns since year end 1999 through August 2002 have outpaced the Standard and Poor's (S&P) 500 Index, which declined by 35 percent for the same period (Clements, p.D1). Equity REITs derive their income from rents received from the properties in their portfolios and from increasing property values.

Mortgage REITs are more sensitive than equity REITs to changes in interest rates in the economy. The reason is that mortgage REITs hold mortgages whose prices move in the opposite direction of interest rates. Although equity REITs might be less sensitive to changes in interest rates, they too suffer the consequences of rising interest rates. Mortgage REITs generally do well when interest rates fall. Because of the different property holdings in mortgage REITs, they tend to be more income-oriented in that their emphasis is on current yields, whereas equity REITs offer the potential for capital gains in addition to current income. For example, Annaly Mortgage Management, Inc. (a mortgage REIT), paid a dividend yield of 9 percent in the first quarter of 2005, which was a premium dividend rate to stock and bond yields.

REITs can have either finite or perpetual lives. Finite-life REITs, also known as FREITs, are self-liquidating. In the case of equity REITs, the properties are sold at the end of a specified period. In mortgage REITs, profits are paid to shareholders when the mortgages are paid up.

Little correlation exists in the performance of REITs and the stock market. Consequently, investors should hold a small percentage (no more than 5 percent) of their investment assets in REITs. Table 4-4 lists some of the guidelines for buying REITs.

TABLE 4-4

Guidelines for Selecting REITs

- Investigate a REIT before buying into it. Get the REIT's annual report from a broker, or call the REIT directly. You also can get additional information from the National Association of Real Estate Investment Trusts, 1101 17th Street N.W., Washington DC 20036.
- Look to see how long the specific REIT has been in business. How long have its managers been in the real estate business, and how well do they manage the REIT's assets? How much of a personal stake do its managers have in the REIT? According to Byrne (1994, p. 32), insiders should own at least 10 percent of the stock.
- Look at the REIT's debt level. The greater the level of debt, the greater is the risk because more of the revenue is needed to service the debt. If a downturn in revenue occurs, interest payments become harder to service. Look for REITs with debt-to-equity ratios of less than 50 percent (Byrne, p. 32).
- Don't choose a REIT because it has the highest yield. The higher the yield, the greater is the risk. In some cases, underwriters raise the yields to hide poor fundamentals (Zuckerman, 1994 p. 35).
- Select REITs that have low price-to-book values (1-to-1 or less).
- Check the REIT's dividend record. Be wary of REITs that have cut their dividends recently. Check the source of cash for the payment of dividends. Cash for dividends should come from operations, not from the sale of properties.
- Location is everything in real estate. Look at the locations of the properties in the trust. Avoid REITs that have invested in overbuilt or depressed locations.

Caveats

- Avoid REITs that are blind pools. These might be set up by well-known management firms that raise funds to invest in unidentified properties. Before investing in any project, it is important to see what the real estate assets and liabilities are.
- Investors should not invest more than 5 percent of their total investment portfolio in REITs.

Exchange-Traded Funds (ETFs)

Exchange-traded funds (ETFs)are baskets of stocks or bonds that track a broad-based index, sector of an index, or stocks in countries. ETFs are similar to closed-end funds in that investors buy these listed shares on the stock exchanges. The predominant listings are on the American Stock Exchange (AMEX). These shares represent ownership in a portfolio of stocks or bonds that track a broad index or sector indices. Investors buy or sell these shares through brokers just like they do with individual stocks. ETFs are priced based on the types of securities that they hold in addition to the supply of and demand for the shares. These shares can be sold short or bought in margin accounts, and they can be traded using market, limit, or stop orders.

The greatest competition to mutual funds has come from ETFs. ETFs have become popular investment alternatives to mutual funds for many investors who want diversification and low-cost investment options. The typical costs charged to investors in equity ETFs are 0.4 percent of assets annually compared with 1.4 percent of assets for the average equity mutual funds, according to Standard and Poor's (Young, p. 124).

There are over 150 ETFs to choose from; this number has grown significantly since the first ETF, the S&P Depository Receipts (SPDRs, known as "Spiders") was introduced in 1993. Table 4-5 lists a few of the many ETFs traded on the market. Some of the more popular ETFs are the SPDRs, which track the S&P 500 Index; Diamonds, ticker symbol DIA, which track the 30 stocks in the Dow Jones Industrial Average; and the Qubes, ticker symbol QQQQ, which track ownership in the 100 largest stocks on the Nasdaq. There are numerous ETFs that are specialized in sectors of the broad indices (financial, technology, and industrials, for example), as well as in foreign stock market indices [iShares, which track the Morgan Stanley Capital

TABLE 4-5

List of Some Exchange-Traded Funds

Name	Ticker Symbol	Category/Index
SPDRs	SPY	S&P 500 Index (large cap)
Diamonds	DIA	Dow Jones Industrial Average (large cap)
Nasdaq 100 Trust	QQQQ	100 largest stocks on the Nasdaq
iShares MSCI EAFE Index	EFA	International Index (large cap)
Semiconductor HOLDRs	SMH	Semiconductor stocks
BLDRS Asia 50 ADR	ADRA	Pacific/Asia stocks
BLDRS Europe 100 ADR	ADRU	European stocks
iShares Lehman TIPS Bond	TLT	Inflation government bonds
Pharmaceutical HOLDRs	PPH	Pharmaceutical stocks
Financial Select Sector	XLF	Financial stocks in the S&P 500 Index
iShares Russell 2000	IWN	Small cap stocks in the Russell 2000 Index
iShares MSCI Spain	EWP	Spanish stocks

Note: For a complete list of ETFs, visit the following Web sites: www.amex.com, www.ishares.com, and www.yahoo.com click on *"Finance"*, and then click on *"ETFs."*

International indices (MSCI) for 20 countries and many regional sectors around the world]. Visit the AMEX Web site at www.amex.com for information on the various ETFs listed. See Table 4-6 for a description of Spiders, Diamonds, and the Nasdaq 100 tracking stock.

The description of the net asset value (NAV) implies that the share price of an ETF can trade above or below its NAV. This discrepancy generally will not occur because of the issuance by the ETF of shares in kind. Whenever a discrepancy in price occurs and an institutional investor wants to exploit this price differential with large

TABLE 4-6

More About Spiders, Diamonds, and Nasdaq 100 ETFs

There is a family of ETFs that is based on the S&P 500 Index and its component sectors, such as technology, energy, and financials, for example. The SPDR Trust holds shares of all companies in the S&P 500 Index. The purchase of a single share in this trust gives its owner a share of the 500 companies in the S&P 500 Index. Several select, specialized SPDRs allow investors to track, for example, the financials in the S&P 500 Index or the 79 tech stocks in the S&P 500 Index. Investors also can track the utilities, industrials, and five other sectors in the S&P 500 Index. These sector ETFs are traded just like the main SPDR (SPY).

The ETF that tracks the 30 stocks of the Dow Jones Industrial Average is called a Diamond (DIA). The purchase of a single share in this fund gives its owner a share of the 30 Dow Jones Industrial Average stocks.

The ETF that mirrors the 100 largest stocks in the Nasdaq is called a Qube (QQQQ). The purchase of a single share in this ETF gives its owner a share of these Nasdaq 100 stocks.

The following is a list of some of the features of these ETFs:

Trading. These ETFs are traded on the AMEX.

Approximate share price ratio. The value of one share of a Spider, a Diamond, and a Qube ETF in relation to the respective indices tracked are 1/10th the value of the S&P 500 Index for one SPY share, 1/100th the value of the DJIA for one DIA share, and 1/20th the value of the Nasdaq 100 Index for 1 QQQQ share.

Dividends. Dividends are paid quarterly (in January, April, July, October).

Risks. Same risk exists for these ETFs, as experienced by individual stocks, namely, price fluctuations. There is also the additional risk that the fund may not replicate the exact performance of the underlying index because of expenses incurred by the fund.

Net asset value. The net asset value per ETF is calculated at the close of each business day. The value represents the market value of the stocks in the underlying index plus any accrued dividends and minus any expenses on a per share basis.

Short Selling. Investors can sell these ETFs short and on a downtick.

Source: American Stock Exchange, www.amex.com.

blocks of shares (a minimum of 50,000), the ETF trust redeems the shares with the underlying stocks in the index rather than paying cash. The institutional investor then sells the shares of the underlying stocks in the index and not the shares of the ETF to realize the price discrepancy. This concept emphasizes the similarities between open-end mutual funds and ETFs. An ETF buys and sells shares and issues new shares when necessary. However, ETF investors can buy or sell shares at anytime during the day on the stock exchanges, whereas transactions involving open-end mutual funds take place only at the end of the day at the closing NAV price. The major difference between an open-end mutual fund and an ETF is that when shareholders in mutual funds sell their shares, the mutual fund might have to sell securities to raise enough cash to pay shareholders, resulting in capital gain or loss transactions. With ETFs, traders buy the shares sold by investors, and this leaves the portfolio intact.

Because of the passive management of ETFs, fees are low, and the turnover of securities is low, which (similar to index mutual funds) results in low capital gains taxes. Table 4-7 lists the advantages and disadvantages of investing in ETFs.

TABLE 4-7

The Advantages and Disadvantages of Investing in Exchange-Traded Funds

Exchange-traded funds (ETF) bear similarities to open-end mutual funds, index funds, and closed-end funds. Knowing the advantages and disadvantages of ETFs will help you to determine which type of investment is more suitable to your needs.

- ETFs offer diversification (similar to mutual funds), but they trade as stocks. Even though the stock prices of ETFs that track the different indices fluctuate when markets are volatile, the effect of the fluctuations on each of the indices might be more muted than in a portfolio of individual stocks.
- ETFs charge low fees and generally are tax efficient in the management of these securities, making them similar to index funds.
- ETFs are bought and sold through brokers, just like any other stocks on the market, at real-time price quotes during the day. Mutual funds can only be traded once a day at their closing prices.
- Investors do not need large amounts of money to be able to buy ETFs, which gives them broad exposure to a market index, a sector of the market, or a foreign country.
- The disadvantage of ETFs is that investors incur commissions to buy and sell shares, whereas no-load mutual funds charge no transaction fees to buy or sell shares. These transaction costs to buy ETFs make it uneconomical for investors who typically invest small amounts of money on a frequent basis.

TYPES OF MUTUAL FUNDS

Investors can invest in stock funds, bond funds, money-market funds, hybrid funds, and commodity funds. Table 4-8 shows the different types of fund classifications based on investment objectives.

A *money-market fund* is a mutual fund that sells shares of ownership in the fund and uses the proceeds to invest in money-market securities. Money-market funds are the only funds that maintain constant share prices. The prices of these funds are mostly $1 per share, and the investment company maintains the NAV at $1 per share. Any expenses or short-term losses from the sale of securities are deducted from revenues generated from investments to keep the share price constant. This goal is accomplished more easily for funds that invest in money-market securities, which are short term, meaning not much volatility in the prices of the investment assets.

Money-market funds provide current income and safety of principal for investors. Most of these funds allow investors to write checks against their accounts, thereby providing liquidity as investors withdraw their money at the constant NAV of $1 per share. Yields on money-market funds tend to exceed those of interest-bearing accounts from banks and savings and loans. The major difference between bank accounts and money market funds is that bank accounts carry Federal Deposit Insurance Corporation (FDIC) insurance. However, within the past few years, a few money-market mutual funds have incurred some losses because of investments in derivative securities, which were aimed at increasing the yields of the funds. When interest rates changed direction unexpectedly, many of these funds incurred large losses. Rather than allow the NAVs to fall below $1 per share, the funds' families quietly propped up the losses of these money-market funds to save their reputations.

The safest money-market funds invest in only U.S. Treasury securities, which are backed by the full faith and credit of the U.S. government. Generally, all money-market funds are relatively safe because

- The securities held are issued by governments and their agencies and by large corporations.
- The securities have short-term maturities, which lowers credit risk and the risk of default.

Large institutions are unlikely to default on securities issued for a short period of time, and the prices of short-term securities

TABLE 4-8

Types of Mutual Funds

Fund Type	Objectives
Money market	Invest in money-market securities with maturities of less than one year.
Equity	
Aggressive growth	Seek maximum capital gains; invest in stocks of companies in new industries and out-of-favor companies.
Growth	Seek an increase in value through capital gains; invest in stocks of growth companies and industries that are more mainstream than those chosen by aggressive growth funds.
Growth and income	Seek an increase in value through capital gains and dividend income; invest in stocks of companies with a more consistent track record than companies selected for growth and aggressive growth funds.
Income equity	Invest in stocks of companies that pay dividends.
Index	Invest in securities that replicate the market, for example, S&P 500 Index, Dow Jones Industrial Average.
International equity	Invest in stocks of companies outside the United States.
Global equity	Invest in stocks of companies both inside and outside the United States.
Emerging market	Invest in stocks of companies in developing countries.
Sector	Invest in stocks in the sector of the economy stated in the fund's objectives, for example, energy, health care sector, technology, and precious metals.
Balanced	Seek to provide value through income and principal conservation; invest in common stocks, preferred stocks, and bonds.
Asset allocation	Invest in securities (stocks, bonds, and money market) according to either a fixed or variable formula.
Hedge	Invest in securities (stocks and bonds) and derivative securities to hedge against downturns in the market, interest-rate changes, and currency values.
Bond	
Corporate bond	Seek high levels of income; invest in corporate bonds, Treasury bonds, and agency bonds.
High-yield bond	Seek higher yields by investing in less-than-investment-grade bonds (junk bonds).
Municipal bond, long term	Seek income that is exempt from federal income taxes; invest in bonds issued by state and local governments with long-term maturities.
Municipal bond, intermediate term	Seek income that is exempt from federal income taxes; invest in bonds issued by state and local governments with intermediate-term maturities.

TABLE 4-8 (Continued)

Fund Type	Objectives
Municipal bond, short-term	Invest in municipal securities with relatively short maturities.
U.S. Government income	Invest in different types of government securities, such as Treasury securities, agency securities, and government mortgage-backed securities.
GNMA	Invest in Government National Mortgage Association securities and other mortgage-backed securities.
Global income	Invest in the bonds of companies and countries worldwide, including those in the United States.

generally do not fluctuate widely. This statement does not mean that no high-risk short-term securities exist. Higher-yielding, high-risk short-term securities do exist, and some aggressive money-market funds invest in them to raise yields. Read the fund's prospectus, which outlines the fund's investment restrictions.

A *stock fund* is a mutual fund that specializes in stock investments. Stock funds vary with regard to the types of stocks the funds choose for their portfolios and are guided by the fund's investment objectives. The Securities and Exchange Commission (SEC) requires that funds disclose their objectives. For example, a fund might have the objective to seek growth through maximum capital gains. This type of fund would appeal to more aggressive investors who can withstand the risk of loss because of the speculative nature of the stocks of the unseasoned, small companies in which the fund invests.

A conservative equity fund's objectives are geared more toward providing current income and capital growth. This type of fund invests in dividend-paying stocks, which also would provide for capital appreciation, even though that might not be a primary objective. Growth and income funds seek a balance between providing capital gains and providing current income. Table 4-8 lists some of the types of stock funds.

Equity funds also can be classified according to *investment style*, namely, growth stocks, value stocks, or a blend of the two. Value stocks have financial characteristics different from growth stocks. Value stocks generally pay dividends and have low price-to-earnings (P/E) ratios, whereas growth stocks have high P/E ratios, and the companies tend to have high sales growth rates for a specified period.

Investing in equity funds does not immunize you from the volatility in the markets. In a market downturn, the more speculative stocks in the funds' portfolios generally decline more than the more established blue-chip stocks. The share prices of aggressive funds therefore are much more volatile than the share prices of the more conservative stock funds.

An index fund is a mutual fund that includes a portfolio of securities designed to match the performance of the market as a whole. An index fund tracks an underlying market index and seeks to match the returns of that particular market index. For example, the S&P 500 Index Fund invests in the stocks of the S&P 500 Index. This strategy does not require active management of the assets in the fund because turnover is very low. The stocks are held in the fund until they drop out of the index. Only then are changes made to the fund. The enthusiasm for index funds has spurred growth into other areas, such as mid cap and small-cap stocks, emerging markets, Europe, Asia, and the Pacific Rim.

A combined stock and bond fund is called a balanced fund. Balanced funds invest in a mixture of stocks and bonds. The equity portion of a fund aims to provide capital growth, and the fixed-income investments provide income for shareholders. The range of percentages allocated to stocks and bonds is stated in the prospectus of the fund.

A *bond fund* invests in a portfolio of fixed-income securities. Bond funds vary considerably because so many different types of bonds exist, such as corporate bonds, Treasury bonds, agency bonds, junk bonds, municipal bonds, zero-coupon bonds, and foreign bonds.

Many people think that by investing in bond funds their principal investments are safe because bonds are more conservative investments than stocks. This is not always the case. You can lose money in bond funds in the same way that you can lose money in stock funds. When market interest rates rise, existing bond prices fall to make their yields competitive with the new issues, and fund prices decline. The types of securities in which funds invest determine the risks of the fund: the reaction to changes in market rates of interest, credit quality, and the risk of default, in addition to the length of time to maturity and the yield of the fund.

Share prices of bond funds fluctuate depending on the value of the fund's assets (investments). Certain types of securities fluctuate more in price than other securities. For example, GNMA (Ginnie Mae) securities are more volatile to changes in interest rates than Treasury notes and bonds with comparable maturities. To gauge the extent of the volatility in a mutual fund's price, you should understand how different bond securities react to changes in interest rates.

Municipal bond funds provide shareholders with interest payments that are tax exempt at the federal level, although the income may be subject to state and local taxes.

Conservative investors should be aware that a bond fund composed of junk bonds (a high-yield bond fund) can fluctuate as much as 50 percent in NAV price.

Generally, the riskier the securities held in the fund, the greater is the potential return and the greater is the potential loss. This statement is true for all types of funds, including stock funds.

Much has been written about hedge funds since the disaster at Long Term Capital Management, a Connecticut hedge fund that had to be bailed out by 14 financial institutions. Long Term Capital Management suffered heavy losses in its positions on Russian bonds because of adverse swings in the prices in the currency markets. Yet, in 2001, the Dow Jones Total Market Index of U.S. stocks declined by 12 percent, whereas hedge funds gained 4.4 percent, as measured by the CSFB/Tremont Index (Clements, p. C1). Table 4-9 defines hedge funds and some of their characteristics.

AN ANALYSIS OF THE PROSPECTUS CAN ASSIST IN THE CHOICE OF A FUND

The best place to learn more about a particular fund is from its prospectus. The SEC requires that investors receive a prospectus before investing or soon afterward. A *prospectus* is a formal written document listing relevant information about the fund, the goals of the fund, the strategies for achieving the goals, securities held by the fund, risk, historical returns, fees charged, and financial data.

A prospectus contains the following information:

- Objectives
- Strategies for achieving the objectives
- Overall risk
- Performance
- Fees

TABLE 4-9

What Is a Hedge Fund?

Before you read a definition of a hedge fund, you should know what it is *not*. A hedge fund is not a mutual fund. Hedge funds with fewer than 99 investors are *not* required to register with the SEC. Hedge funds cater to wealthy investors who have a significant net worth ($1.5 million) and are willing to invest $1 million or more. With the negative stock market returns in 2001 and 2002, hedge funds attracted large amounts of new capital and a broader-based clientele. Although returns for hedge funds were low (1 to 2 percent) or flat for 2001, they were nevertheless much better than the double-digit losses posted by most mutual funds for the same period. The reason is that hedge funds can take both long and short positions in stocks, whereas mutual fund managers can only take long positions. In addition, hedge fund managers can use borrowed money, which can increase their returns. These positive returns resulted in the introduction of *mini-hedge funds* in 2002, a new investment product offered by Wall Street. This type of fund requires a relatively low investment of $250,000, even though investors still must have significant assets to withstand any potential risk of loss (Clements, p. C1).

A hedge fund is a specialized open-end fund that allows its manager to take a variety of investment positions in the market to seek higher-than-average potential gains with exposure to greater-than-average risk. U.S. hedge funds, which have been in existence for almost 50 years, typically take the form of limited partnerships. Hedge funds have numerous investment styles, such as market-neutral strategies, in addition to the high and low-risk strategies. Hedge funds, because they are not as heavily regulated as mutual funds, do not have the same limits on the types of investments they can make and have less stringent disclosure requirements. Investors are limited in how they can withdraw funds. Many hedge funds allow investors to withdraw money only at the end of the year. Others may only allow investors to withdraw money at the end of the year or at the end of each quarter (Scholl and Bary, p. 19).

Objectives

A fund's objectives can be broadly phrased; the most common are

1. To seek long-term capital appreciation through the growth of the fund's value over a period of time.
2. To seek current income through investments that generate dividends and interest income and to preserve investors' principal.

Strategies

A fund's strategy reveals the steps its fund manager might take in achieving the fund's objectives. For example, the manager of a stock fund might buy growth stocks or value stocks of companies with a particular size capitalization (small-cap, medium-cap, or large-cap stocks). Bond-fund strategies reveal the types of bonds the fund buys (Treasury, agency, corporate, municipal, foreign, and zero-coupon bonds, for example), the maturities of the bonds, and the credit ratings of the bonds (the quality of the bonds).

Overall Risk

A fund's objectives describe the types of securities in which the fund invests in addition to the risk factors associated with the securities. For example, if a prospectus states that its fund invests in growth securities, you should not be surprised to find that most of the stocks will have high P/E ratios and can include riskier small-cap stocks. Consequently, a decline in the growth stock prices would cause investors in this fund to lose money. A fund's investment policies outline the latitude the fund manager has to invest in other types of securities, including trading futures contracts, writing options to hedge bets (on the direction of interest rates or the market), and investing in derivative securities to boost the yield of the fund. Many conservative funds, which supposedly only hold blue-chip stocks, occasionally have resorted to small-company and offshore stocks to boost returns. The greater the latitude fund managers have in investing in these other types of securities, the greater is the risk. The types of securities in which the fund invests outline the overall risk of the fund.

Another measure of risk is how diversified the fund is. If the fund cannot invest more than 5 percent of its assets in the securities of one company, it is a *diversified* fund. However, if a fund has no limits, the fund manager can choose to invest in a few securities, which greatly increases the risk of loss if one of these investments declines significantly.

Performance

The overall performance of a fund pertains to these three concepts:

- Yield
- Total return
- Expenses

Funds are required by the SEC to provide annualized returns. These returns can be presented in a table or graphically, showing results for one year, five years, and 10 years. New funds provide their returns from the date of inception. These returns are presented on a before-tax basis and an after-tax basis, which shows how tax efficient the fund is. Funds also must compare their returns to an appropriate market index. Table 4-10 shows the average annual total returns for the Vanguard 500 Index Fund for the period ending December 31, 2004. These returns can be compared with the benchmark indices often presented in the fund's prospectus.

Many funds can boast that they have attained the number one position in some area of performance at some point during their existence. Note, however, that good past performance might not be indicative of good future performance. Some funds that did well in the past no longer even exist.

Several business magazines track the overall performance records of many mutual funds during up and down markets. These performance results are a better yardstick to use than the advertising messages of the mutual funds themselves. From these publications, you can see how well funds have performed in up markets and how the funds protected their capital during periods of declining prices. New funds do not have track records, which means that their performance during a period of declining prices might not be available. This statement is especially true for funds that come into existence during a bull market.

Organizations such as Morningstar (www.morningstar.com) rate a mutual fund's performance relative to other funds with the same investment objectives. However, this rating can be misleading

TABLE 4-10

Vanguard 500 Index Fund: Average Annual Total Returns, December 31, 2004

	One Year	Five Years	Ten Years
500 Index Fund Investor Shares			
Returns before taxes	10.74%	−2.38%	12.00%
Returns after taxes on distributions	10.44	−2.77	11.34
Returns after taxes on distributions and sale of fund shares	7.35	−2.20	10.36

when you are trying to choose a fund. First, the funds might not be comparable, even though they have similar objectives. For example, one fund might have riskier assets than another. Second, past performance might not be a reliable indicator of future performance.

In choosing a fund, you should look at what the fund invests in (as well as can be determined) and then try to determine the volatility in terms of up and down markets.

Yield is the percentage return on an investment and is one aspect of performance. Yield is defined as the interest or dividends paid to shareholders as a percentage of the NAV price. Money-market funds quote yields over a seven-day period, which also can be annualized. In the low-interest-rate climate of 2004, many money-market mutual funds cut their expenses to keep their funds' NAVs at $1. The average taxable money-market funds in 2004 yielded less than 1 percent after expenses were deducted from the fund portfolio's earnings. Some money-market funds with higher expense ratios had difficulty maintaining a constant $1 NAV without having to resort to trimming their fees (Damato, p. C1). Long-term bond funds also quote an annualized average yield, but yields are often quoted on a 30-day period.

Total Return

Yield is a measure of a fund's dividend distribution over a 30-day period. It is only one aspect of the fund's *total return,* however. Mutual funds pass on to shareholders any gains or losses, which can increase or decrease the fund's total return.

Another factor that affects total return is the fluctuation in NAV. When the share price increases by 6 percent, it effectively increases the total return by an additional 6 percent. Similarly, a decline in the NAV price of a fund decreases the total return. This concept explains why funds with positive yields can have negative total returns. That is what happened when Asian currencies went into turmoil in 1998 and affected share prices of Pacific Rim mutual funds. These funds had been doing well, but their returns were diminished by steep declines in their NAV prices.

Interest on reinvested dividends is another factor that also might be included in the total return. When dividends paid out by a fund are reinvested to buy more shares, the yield earned on these reinvested shares boosts the overall return on the invested capital.

The total return of a mutual fund includes the following three components:

- Dividends and capital gains or losses
- Changes in NAV
- Dividends (interest) on reinvested dividends

Expenses are a key factor in differentiating the performances of different funds. By painstakingly looking for funds with the highest yields, you are looking at only half the picture. A fund with a high yield also might be the one that charges higher expenses, which could put that fund behind some lower-cost funds with lower yields. Fees reduce total returns earned by funds. You cannot count on future performance projections unless the fees and expenses charged by mutual funds are fairly consistent. A mutual fund prospectus has a separate table with a breakdown of expenses. This table typically shows the different charges paid for either directly by shareholders or out of shareholders' earnings in the fund: load charges, redemption fees, shareholder accounting costs, 12(b)-1 fees, distribution costs, and other expenses.

The mutual fund industry has been criticized for its proliferation of fees and charges. Granted, these are all disclosed by the mutual funds, but you need to know where to look to find the less obvious fees.

Load Funds versus No-Load Funds

A *no-load fund* is a fund whose shares are sold without a sales charge. In other words, you do not pay any fees to buy or sell shares in the fund. With an investment of $10,000 in a no-load fund, every cent of the $10,000 is used to buy shares in the fund. No-load funds sell directly to investors at the NAV per share.

A *load fund* is a fund whose shares are sold to investors at a price that includes a sales commission. The selling price or offer price exceeds the NAV. These fees can be quite substantial, ranging to as much as 8.5 percent of the purchase price of the shares. The amount of the sales (load) charge per share can be determined by deducting the NAV price from the *offer price*. Table 4-11 illustrates how to determine the effective load charge of a fund. Some funds give quantity discounts on their loads to investors who buy shares in large blocks. For example, a sales load might be 5 percent for amounts less than $100,000, 4.25 percent for investments between $100,000 to $200,000,

TABLE 4-11

How to Determine the Effective Load Charge

A mutual fund quotes its load charge as a percentage of its offer price, which under-states the real charge paid by investors in load funds. For example, for a mutual fund with a load charge of 5 percent and a NAV quoted in the newspapers of $25 per share, the offer price is determined as follows:

$$\text{Offer price} = \frac{\text{net asset value (NAV)}}{(1 - \text{load percent})}$$

$$= \frac{25}{(1 - 0.05)}$$

$$= \$26.32$$

The investor pays a load fee of $1.32 per share ($26.32 − $25.00), which is a 5 percent charge of the offer price. However, this load charge as a percentage of the NAV is higher than 5 percent.

$$\text{Effective load charge} = \frac{\text{load charge}}{\text{net asset value}}$$

$$= \frac{\$1.32}{25.00}$$

$$= 5.28 \text{ percent}$$

and 3.5 percent for amounts in excess of $200,000. Investors buying load funds need to determine whether a load also is charged on rein-vested dividends.

Funds also can charge a *back load* or *exit fee*, which affects investors selling shares in the fund. A back load is a fee charged when shareholders sell their shares. The back-end load can be a straight percentage, or the percentage can decline the longer the shares are held in the fund. For example, if you sell $10,000 in a mutual fund with a 3 percent redemption fee, you only receive $9,700 [10,000 − (0.03 × 10,000)].

The ultimate effect of a load charge is to reduce the total return. The effect of a load charge is felt more keenly if the fund is held for a short time. For example, if a fund has a return of 6 percent and charges a 4 percent load to buy into the fund, your total return for the year is sharply reduced. If you must pay a back-end load to exit a fund, this charge could be even more expensive than a front-end load when the share price has increased. This is so because the load percentage is calculated on a larger amount.

You should not be fooled by funds that tout themselves as no-load funds and assess fees by other names that come right out of investors' pockets like loads. These fees are not called loads, but they work exactly like loads. Their uses are to defray some of the costs of opening accounts or buying stocks for the fund's portfolio. The fees vary from 1 to 3 percent among the different fund groups. From an investor's point of view, the lofty purpose of these fees should not matter. They reduce the amount of the investment.

Why, then, do so many people invest in load funds when these commissions eat away so much of their returns? Some possible answers are

- Investors do not want to make decisions about which funds to invest in, so they leave those decisions to their brokers and financial planners.
- Brokers and financial planners earn their living from selling investments from which they are paid commissions. These investments include only load funds and funds that pay commissions out of 12(b)-1 fees. These funds are promoted as the best ones to buy.
- No-load funds and funds that do not pay commissions to brokers and financial planners are not promoted or sold by brokers and financial planners.

No evidence exists to support the opinion expressed by many brokers and financial planners that load funds outperform no-load funds. According to a study on the long-term performance of mutual funds, there was no statistical difference between the performance of no-load funds and load funds over a 10-year period (Kuhle and Pope). However, after adjusting for sales commissions, investors would have been better off with no-load funds.

A *12(b) -1 fee* is a charge a mutual fund can take from investment assets to cover marketing expenses. A 12(b)-1 fee is less obvious than a load. This type of fee is charged by many funds to recover expenses for marketing and distribution. This type of fee, assessed annually, can be steep when added to a load fee. Many no-load funds boast the absence of sales commissions and then tack on 12(b)-1 fees, which resemble hidden loads. A 1 percent 12(b)-1 fee might not sound like much, but it results in $100 per year less in your pocket on a $10,000 mutual-fund investment.

In addition to the above-mentioned charges, funds have *management fees*, which are paid to the managers who administer the fund's portfolios of investments. These fees can range from a 0.5 to 2 percent of assets. High management fees also take a toll on an investor's total return.

All fees bear watching because they reduce yields and total returns. Critics of the mutual-fund industry have cultivated a sense of awareness regarding the proliferation of these charges. Indeed, do not be deceived by funds that claim to be what they are not. Lowering or eliminating front-end loads does not mean that a fund cannot add fees somewhere else. Many new funds waive some of their fees. Check to see whether and when these waivers are set to expire or whether they can be revoked.

A fund has to disclose its fees. You can find management fees, 12(b)-1 fees, redemption fees (back-end loads), and any other fees charged somewhere in the fund's prospectus. Table 4-12 shows a list of fees for the Vanguard GNMA Fund, compiled from the fund's prospectus on Vanguard's Web site (www.vanguard.com). The Vanguard GNMA Fund has one of the lowest expense ratios among the GNMA category of funds.

Selected Per-Share Data and Ratios

Table 4-13 summarizes a typical fund's performance over the periods shown, and this information can be found in the fund's prospectus or annual report. Although the selected per-share data vary in detail from fund to fund, the format is essentially the same.

TABLE 4-12

Fees and Expenses of the Vanguard GNMA Fund, January 31, 2005

	Investor Shares
Shareholder fees (fees paid directly from your investment)	
Sales charge (load) imposed on purchases	None
Sales charge (load) imposed on reinvested dividends	None
Redemption fee	None
Exchange fee	None
Annual fund operating expenses (expenses deducted from the Fund's assets)	
Total annual fund operating expenses:	**0.20%**

The "Investment Activities" section in Table 4-13 shows the amount of investment income earned on the securities held by the fund; this income is passed on to the fund's shareholders. For instance, in 2005, all the net investment income of $0.37 was distributed to the shareholders (line 4), but in 2004, only $0.30 of the $0.31 of net income was paid out to shareholders. In 2004, the $0.01, which was not distributed to shareholders, increased the NAV (line 7) in the "Capital Changes" section. (The capital loss and distribution of gains were reduced by this $0.01 because it was not distributed.)

Capital gains and losses also affect the NAV. Funds distribute their realized capital gains (line 6), but the unrealized capital gains or losses also increase or decrease the NAV.

Changes in the NAV from year to year give some idea of the volatility in share price. For instance, for the year 2004 the NAV

TABLE 4-13

Selected Per-Share Data and Ratios

	2005	2004	2003
Net asset value (NAV) beginning of the year	$10.02	$11.01	$10.73
Investment activities			
Line 1 Income	0.40	0.35	0.55
Line 2 Expenses	(0.03)	(0.04)	(0.05)
Line 3 Net investment income	0.37	0.31	0.50
Line 4 Distribution of dividends	(0.37)	(0.30)	(0.47)
Capital changes			
Line 5 Net realized and unrealized gains (losses) on investments	$1.00	(0.75)	1.50
Line 6 Distributions of realized gains	(0.70)	(0.25)	(1.25)
Line 7 Net increase (decrease) to NAV	0.30	(0.99)	0.28
NAV beginning of year	10.02	11.01	10.73
NAV at end of year	10.32	10.02	11.01
Ratio of operating expenses to average net assets	0.53%	0.56%	0.58%
Ratio of net investment income to average net assets	0.45%	0.46%	0.84%
Portfolio turnover rate	121%	135%	150%
Shares outstanding (000)	10,600	8,451	6,339

decreased by $1.01, which is a 9.17 percent decrease. If you invest $10,000 knowing it could decline to $9,082.65 (a 9.17% decline), how comfortable would you feel with this investment in the short term?

The portfolio turnover rate gives prospective investors an idea of how actively the investment assets in a fund are traded. A turnover rate of 100 percent indicates that the investment assets are sold an average of once during the year. For example, if a fund holds stocks with a value of $100 million, this means that $100 million of stocks are traded once a year with a 100 percent turnover rate. According to Morningstar Mutual Funds as reported by the Vanguard Group (March 11,1999), the average stock mutual fund turnover was 86 percent. High portfolio turnover (more than 200 percent) might not necessarily be bad for shareholders in that the fund might be generating high capital gains.

High turnover is an indication, however, for shareholders to expect capital gains distributions by the end of the year. In accounting terms, the amount of the distribution per share is deducted from the NAV of the shares in the fund.

Index funds have extremely low turnover, around 5 percent (Vanguard Group, March 11, 1999). The advantages of lower turnover are decreased costs and greater tax efficiency. A fund also might have low turnover because it has been holding low-performing stocks for a long time in the hopes of a turnaround. This situation has occurred with many value funds where value stocks did not participate in the stock market rally of the three years from 1996 to 1999.

The ratio of operating expenses to average net assets is fairly low in the example in Table 4-13 (close to 1/2 of 1 percent).

You can determine an average total return by considering the three types of returns on a mutual fund—dividends distributed, capital gains distributed, and changes in share price—by using the following formula:

$$\text{Average total return} = \frac{(\text{dividend} + \text{capital gains distributions}) + (\text{ending NAV} - \text{beginning NAV})/\text{year}}{(\text{ending NAV} + \text{beginning NAV})/2}$$

$$\text{Average total return for 2005} = \frac{(0.37 + 0.70) + (10.32 - 10.02)/1}{(10.32) + (10.02)/2}$$

$$= 13.50 \text{ percent}$$

This simple 13.5 percent yield indicates that an investor in this fund received double-digit returns mainly because of gains realized and increases in the NAV share price. The more volatile the NAV of the fund is, the greater is the likelihood of unstable returns.

Tables 4-14 and 4-15 show fund profiles for the Vanguard U.S. Mid-Cap Index Fund and the Vanguard Long-Term Investment-Grade Fund, respectively. These fund profiles are listed in the semi-annual or annual reports sent to existing and new shareholders, if requested. Fund profiles provide information about a fund's characteristics, investment focus, volatility measures, sector diversification (for stocks), percentage investment in the different types of bonds, credit quality, maturity of issues, and 10 largest stock holdings of the fund.

The Vanguard U.S. Mid-Cap Index Fund is a blend fund (value and growth stocks) with a total of 453 stocks in the fund. The average P/E ratio is 22.1, which is what you would expect from a mixture of value stocks (which generally have low P/E ratios) and growth stocks (which have high P/E ratios). A fund's risk is measured by the r^2 and beta coefficients. The r^2 coefficient is a measure of the returns of the fund as compared with the returns of the benchmark index, in this case the S&P Mid-Cap 400 Index. A measure of 1 indicates that the returns are the same as the index. A measure of 0 indicates no relationship between the returns of the index and the fund. A beta coefficient of 1 indicates that the share price of the fund fluctuates in relation to the index.

The mutual fund *style box* in the Investment Focus of Tables 4-14 and 4.15 shows the focus of these two funds' investments. For stocks, the investment styles are value, growth, or a blend. Each style can be used with small-cap, medium-cap or large-cap companies. Small-cap companies tend to be riskier than mid-cap or large-cap companies. However, over long periods, historically small-cap stocks have surpassed large-cap stocks in terms of returns.

The style box for bonds (Table 4-15) uses the two dimensions as the criteria for the investment focus, maturity (time horizon), and credit quality (risk tolerance). For low risk tolerance, you would move toward the upper left of the box. Those with a higher risk tolerance and a long time horizon would move to the lower right of the grid.

The fund profile of the Vanguard Long-Term Investment-Grade Fund shows that the fund has 222 bond issues with a yield of 5.1 percent for investor shares. The average coupon yield is 6.7 percent, and

TABLE 4-14

Fund Profile for the Vanguard U.S. Mid-Cap Index Fund as of December 31, 2004

MID-CAP INDEX FUND

Portfolio Characteristics

	Fund	Target Index*	Broad Index**
Number of Stocks	453	452	4,978
Median Market Cap	$5.5B	$5.5B	$27.3B
Price/Earnings Ratio	22.1x	22.1x	22.4x
Price/Book Ratio	2.7x	2.7x	2.9x
Yield	1.2%	1.5%	
Investor Shares	1.1%		
Admiral Shares	1.1%		
Institutional Shares	1.2%		
VIPER Shares	1.1%		
Return on Equity	14.4%	14.4%	15.7%
Earnings Growth Rate	12.5%	12.5%	7.5%
Foreign Holdings	0.6%	0.6%	1.0%
Turnover Rate	16%†	–	–
Expense Ratio		–	–
Investor Shares	0.22%		
Admiral Shares	0.13%		
Institutional Shares	0.08%		
VIPER Shares	0.18%††		
Short-Term Reserves	0%	–	–

Volatility Measures

	Fund	Spliced Index‡	Fund	Broad Index**
R-Squared	1.00	1.00	0.88	1.00
Beta	1.01	1.00	0.97	1.00

Sector Diversification (% of portfolio)

	Fund	Target Index*	Broad Index**
Auto & Transportation	2%	2%	3%
Consumer Discretionary	18	19	17
Consumer Staples	3	3	6
Financial Services	22	22	23
Health Care	8	8	12
Integrated Oils	1	1	4
Other Energy	8	8	3
Materials & Processing	9	8	4
Producer Durables	6	6	5
Technology	13	13	13
Utilities	8	8	6
Other	2	2	4

Ten Largest Holdings (% of total net assets)

Monsanto Co. (chemicals)	0.7%
Starwood Hotels & Resorts Worldwide, Inc. (leisure)	0.6
J.C. Penney Co., Inc. (Holding Co.) (retail)	0.6
Valero Energy Corp. (energy and utilities)	0.6
CIGNA Corp. (insurance)	0.6
Medco Health Solutions, Inc. (health care)	0.6
Network Appliance, Inc. (computer hardware)	0.6
Computer Sciences Corp. (conglomerate)	0.5
Coach, Inc. (retail)	0.5
Eaton Corp. (manufacturing)	0.5
Top Ten	5.8%

"Ten Largest Holdings" excludes any temporary cash investments and equity index products.

Investment Focus

*MSCI US Mid Cap 450 Index.
**Dow Jones Wilshire 5000 Index.
†Excludes the value of portfolio securities received or delivered as a result of in-kind purchases or redemptions of the fund's capital shares, including VIPER Creation Units.
††Annualized.
‡S&P MidCap 400 Index through May 16, 2003; MSCI US Mid Cap 450 Index thereafter.

TABLE 4-15

Fund Profile for the Vanguard Long-Term Investment Grade Fund as of January 31, 2005

LONG-TERM BOND INDEX FUND

Financial Attributes

	Fund	Target Index*	Broad Index**
Number of Issues	489	860	5,836
Yield	5.1%	–	–
Yield to Maturity	5.2%†	5.3%	4.4%
Average Coupon	7.3%	7.3%	5.4%
Average Effective Maturity	19.9 years	20.4 years	7.1 years
Average Quality††	Aa2	Aa2	Aa1
Average Duration	11.0 years	11.0 years	4.3 years
Expense Ratio	0.18%	–	–
Short-Term Reserves	0%	–	–

Volatility Measures

	Fund	Target Index*	Fund	Broad Index**
R-Squared	1.00	1.00	0.94	1.00
Beta	1.00	1.00	2.23	1.00

Sector Diversification‡ (% of portfolio)

Asset-Backed/Commercial Mortgage-Backed	0%
Finance	9
Foreign	7
Government Mortgage-Backed	0
Industrial	24
Treasury/Agency	57
Utilities	3
Total	100%

Distribution by Credit Quality†† (% of portfolio)

Aaa	58%
Aa	4
A	16
Baa	22
Total	100%

Distribution by Maturity (% of portfolio)

5–10 Years	2%
10–20 Years	47
20–30 Years	50
Over 30 Years	1
Total	100%

Investment Focus

*Lehman Long Government/Credit Index.
**Lehman Aggregate Bond Index.
†Before expenses.
††Moody's Investors Service.
‡The agency and mortgage-backed securities may include issues from government-sponsored enterprises; such issues are not backed by the full faith and credit of the U.S. government.

**Visit our website at Vanguard.com
for regularly updated fund information.**

the yield to maturity is 5.3 percent, which indicates that the average bond price in the portfolio is trading at a premium (greater than $1,000 per bond). The expense ratio is 0.25 percent, which is $0.25 for each $100 invested in the fund. The investment focus shows that the bonds in the fund are above investment grade and have long-term maturities (greater than 10 years). The distribution by credit quality shows that 93 percent of the bonds in the fund are rated above investment grade (Baa or less), and 88 percent of the fund's bonds have maturities of greater than 10 years. The greatest concentration of bonds is in the industrial sector.

THE RISKS OF MUTUAL FUNDS

The major risk of investing in a mutual fund is the *risk of loss of principal* owing to a decline in NAV. Many types of risk exist: interest-rate risk, market risk, and quality of the securities, to name a few. Rising market interest rates tend to depress both the stock and the bond markets, resulting in a decline in the NAVs of stock and bond funds. A decline in market rates of interest results in an appreciation of stock and bond prices (and the NAVs of stock and bond funds).

The *quality of securities* determines the volatility of the fund's price swings. Stock funds that invest in small-company stocks and emerging growth stocks see greater upward swings in price during bull markets and greater downward swings during bear markets than conservative income equity funds, which invest in the stocks of larger, more established companies. Some small-company funds have invested in small stocks of dubious value, which has caused some losses to their funds.

Standard & Poor's Ratings Services, known for their ratings of individual bonds, have introducing a rating service for mutual funds. The funds are either rated with a select rating or are not rated.

With bank failures in the past and the shaky financial status of some savings and loan associations in the United States, investors are naturally concerned about the *risk of insolvency* of mutual funds. A mutual fund always can "go under," but the chance of it happening is small. The key distinction between banks and mutual funds is the way in which mutual funds are set up, which reduces the risk of failure and loss owing to fraud.

Mutual funds typically are corporations owned by shareholders. A separate management company is contracted by shareholders to run the fund's daily operations. Although a management company oversees the fund's investments, the company does not have possession of these assets (investments). A custodian, such as a bank, holds the investments. Therefore, if a management company gets into financial trouble, it does not have access to the fund's investments. Yet, even with these checks and balances, the possibility of fraud always exists. The SEC cleared two mutual funds whose prices were quoted in the financial newspapers along with all the other mutual funds, but they turned out to be bogus funds.

A transfer agent maintains shareholders' accounts and keeps track of shareholders' purchases and redemptions. In addition, management companies carry fidelity bonds, a form of insurance to protect the investments of the fund against malfeasance or fraud perpetrated by its employees.

Along with these safeguards, two other factors differentiate mutual funds from corporations such as banks and savings and loan associations:

- Mutual funds must be able to redeem shares on demand, which means that a portion of its investment assets must be liquid.
- Mutual funds must be able to price their investments at the end of each day, which is known as *marking to market*. This adjustment of market values of investments at the end of the trading day reflects gains and losses.

For these reasons, mutual funds cannot hide their financial difficulties as easily as banks and savings and loans can.

The SEC regulates mutual funds, but as noted earlier in this chapter, fraudulent operators always can find a way into any industry. Although the risk of fraud is always present, it is no greater in the mutual-fund industry than in any other industry. Above all, you should be aware that you can lose money through purchasing a fund whose investments perform poorly on the markets.

SHOULD AN INVESTOR INVEST IN INDIVIDUAL SECURITIES OR USE FUNDS?

Stock and bond mutual funds have been popular among investors, and record amounts have been invested in them over the years. The advantages of mutual funds, as stated earlier in this chapter, are the use of professional management, diversification, the freedom to invest small amounts of money, and the ease of buying and selling. For many investors, these advantages far outweigh the disadvantages of mutual funds.

Mutual funds might be the most practical way for investors to buy many types of securities, including bonds that sell in high denominations (minimum investments of $50,000), such as certain mortgage-backed bonds, agency bonds, and some municipal issues. An advantage of bond mutual funds is that investors avoid having to understand the complexity of certain types of individual bonds, such as mortgage-backed bonds, zero-coupon bonds, convertible issues, and derivative securities. Mutual funds specializing in these types of bonds allow investors to own many different, complex types of bonds. Similarly, the decision of which individual stocks to invest in can be avoided by choosing equity mutual funds.

The diversification achieved by mutual funds minimizes the effect of any unexpected losses from individual stocks and bonds in the portfolio. Also, the professional managers of these funds have quicker access to information about the different issues. The managers therefore react sooner in buying or selling the securities in question.

However, in certain cases, a strong argument exists for buying individual securities over mutual funds. The rates of return on individual stocks and bonds often are greater than those earned from mutual funds. This statement is true even for no-load funds because in addition to sales commissions, other fees, such as 12(b)-1 and operating fees, reduce the returns of mutual funds. By investing in individual securities, you avoid these fees. A study by Malkiel (pp. 549–572) during the period 1971 through 1991 on the performance of equity mutual funds indicates that on a yearly basis throughout this period the top-performing funds in one year easily could become underperforming funds in the next year. This phenomenon occurred more in the 1980s than in the 1970s.

A powerful argument for investing in individual bonds is that if they are bought and held to maturity, interest-rate risk is avoided. Changes in market rates of interest affect the prices of both individual bonds and bond mutual funds. However, if you have a set time during which you will not need the money, you can invest in individual bonds with corresponding maturities (to your needs) and not worry about what might happen to market rates of interest.

This concept does not apply to bond mutual funds. If market rates of interest go up, a decline in the NAV of share prices of bond funds occurs.

Some bonds, such as Treasury securities, are easy to buy directly from the Federal Reserve banks and branches. By owning them, you can eliminate many of the fees that mutual funds charge, thereby increasing your return. Moreover, when these bonds are bought directly from the Federal Reserve banks or branches, you do not pay commissions. Buying and holding Treasury securities makes more sense than investing in Treasury bond funds. However, if you do not plan to hold the bonds through maturity, funds might be a better alternative.

If you have a small amount of money to invest, mutual funds are a better alternative. A $2,000 investment in a stock fund buys a fraction of a diversified portfolio of stocks, whereas for individual securities this amount might allow for buying only the shares of one equity company. Investing in mutual funds is good strategy if you do not have enough money to diversify your investments and do not have the time, expertise, or inclination to select and manage individual securities. In addition, a wide range of funds offers you the opportunity to invest in the types of securities that would be difficult to buy individually.

Table 4-16 compares some characteristics of investing in individual securities versus mutual funds, closed-end funds, and exchange-traded funds.

REFERENCES

Byrne, Thomas C.: "Beyond Yield," *Individual Investor*, July 1994, p. 32.

Clements, Jonathan: "Its Not Too Late: Despite Recent Gains, REITs Can Still Generate Tidy Returns," *Wall Street Journal*, September 4, 2002, p. D1.

_____: "Wall Street's Latest: Mini-Hedge Funds," *Wall Street Journal*, March 26, 2002, p. C1.

Damato, Karen: "Money Funds Slash Their Fees to Stay at $1 Net Asset Value," *Wall Street Journal*, October 25, 2002, pp. C1, C15.

Faerber, Esmé: *All About Stocks*, 2d ed. New York: McGraw-Hill, 2000.

Kuhle, James L., and Ralph A Pope: "A Comprehensive Long-Term Performance Analysis of Load vs. No-Load Mutual Funds," *Journal of Financial and Strategic Decisions* 13(2): 1–11, 2000.

Lauricella, Tom: "Is It an Offer Investors Can't Refuse?" *Wall Street Journal*, July 19, 2002, pp. C1, C15.

Malkiel, Burton G.: *A Random Walk Down Wall Street*. New York: W.W. Norton, 1996.

T A B L E   4 - 1 6

Characteristics of Individual Securities Versus Mutual Funds, Closed-End Funds, and ETFs

	Individual Securities	Mutual Funds	Closed-End Funds	ETFs
Diversification	Achieved only if a large number of securities is purchased	Achieved with a small investment	Achieved with a small investment	Achieved with a small investment
Ease of buying and selling	Easy to buy and sell stocks at real-time prices during the trading day; more difficult to buy bonds	Easy to buy and sell shares; trades occur only at the closing price at the end of the day	Easy to buy and sell liquid closed-end funds	Easy to buy and sell ETFs at real-time prices during the day
Professional management	No	Yes	Yes	Replicates a market index
Expenses and costs to buy and sell	Brokerage fees to buy and sell	Low to high expenses depending on fund	Low to high expenses depending on fund	Brokerage fees to buy and sell and low fees
Tax Planning	Easier to predict income and plan capital gains and losses	Can upset careful tax planning owing to unpredictable distributions of income and capital gains	Can upset careful tax planning owing to unpredictable distributions of income and capital gains	More tax efficient than mutual funds

Malkiel, Burton G. "Returns from Investing in Equity Mutual Funds 1971–1991,"
    Journal of Finance 50: 549–572, 1995.
Scholl, Jaye, and Andrew Bary: "A Lousy New Year," *Barron's*, October 12, 1998,
    p. 19.
Vanguard Group: "FUNDamentals: Turnover, " www.Vanguard.com, March 11, 1999.
Young, Lauren: "ETFs: What the Buzz Is About," *Business Week*, March 1, 2004, pp.
    124–126.
Zuckerman, Lawrence: "A Look Under the Hood at Realty Stocks," *New York Times*,
    July 16, 1994, p. 35.

CHAPTER 5

Money-Market Securities

KEY CONCEPTS

- Money-market mutual funds
- Treasury bills
- Certificates of deposit
- Commercial paper
- Bankers' acceptances
- Repurchase agreements

Money-market securities are liquid, marketable, safe investments that have maturities of one year or less. They are used typically for the investment of emergency funds and short-term cash. Examples of these types of investments are certificates of deposit (CDs), money-market mutual funds, Treasury bills, commercial paper, bankers' acceptances, and repurchase agreements. These investments also are used as temporary short-term cash substitutes.

The money-market is a subsector of the bond market and includes debt securities with maturities of one year or less. The money-market is not located in one place but consists of banks and dealers throughout the United States that are connected by telephones and computers. The advantage of investing in money-market securities is that idle cash earns a return until more permanent uses for this cash are found. The characteristics of these short-term investments are low risk of default, high liquidity, and marketability. However, many money-market securities trade in large denominations, precluding

TABLE 5-1

Features of Money-Market Securities

Investment Objectives	Characteristics	Advantages	Disadvantages
Payment of income	Liquid	Provides a return for idle cash and emergency funds	Low yields that might not cover inflation
Preservation of principal	Marketable	Temporary parking place for funds between investments	Many individual money-market securities require large investment amounts
Access to funds	Low risk		

their investment by many individual investors. Table 5-1 summarizes some of the features of money-market securities.

Money-market mutual funds are convenient ways for individual investors to invest their short-term funds in money-market securities. Even though money-market funds offer you a convenient way to invest your funds, you should understand the characteristics of the different individual short-term investments, such as Treasury bills, commercial paper, bankers' acceptances, and repurchase agreements for two reasons:

1. Money-market mutual funds invest their pooled funds in these individual short-term fixed-income securities. Understanding how these securities work will enable you to assess the risks and returns of the different money-market mutual funds.
2. There are times when these individual securities offer greater advantages and returns than using a money-market mutual fund.

MONEY-MARKET MUTUAL FUNDS

Money-market funds compete directly with bank deposit accounts, and over the years, money-market funds have grown considerably at the expense of bank accounts. Banks, brokerage firms, and investment companies offer money-market funds. However, many of the mutual funds from the brokerage houses have higher fees and sales commissions (loads). Brokers and financial advisors are motivated to move your funds away from the investment companies' money-market mutual funds to their own products, where they are compensated through sales commissions, also called *loads*. For example, persuading you to invest in a short-term bond fund yielding 2 percent annually rather than in a money-market fund with a yield of 1 percent annually might look like a better alternative at face value. However, a short-term bond fund is not the same as a money-market fund because the net asset value (NAV) of the bond fund fluctuates, whereas the NAV of a money-market mutual fund has a fixed value of $1 per share. Table 5-2 shows the effects of a short-term bond fund with a load versus a no-load money-market mutual fund. In addition, operating expenses for these brokerage funds might be higher. It will take several years for the bond fund to recoup the load fee just to equal the amount of the funds invested in the no-load money-market fund.

Investment companies offer the majority of money-market mutual funds, which provide an alternative parking place for cash and short-term funds than higher-risk stock and bond investments. Investment companies managing money-market funds pool investors' money and issue shares to investors. Then the fund managers invest the money in short-term securities such as Treasury bills, commercial paper, bankers' acceptances, CDs, eurodollars, repurchase agreements, and government agency obligations.

There are three types of money-market funds:

- *General-purpose funds,* which invest in a wide range of money-market securities such as Treasury bills, commercial paper, bankers' acceptances, CDs, repurchase agreements, and short-term off-shore securities
- *U.S. government funds,* which invest in short-term Treasury securities and U.S. agency obligations

TABLE 5-2

Load Versus a No-Load Fund

Load Fund of 3%		No-Load Fund	
Amount invested	$10,000	Amount invested	$10,000
3% load charge	($ 300)	No load	0
Funds available	$ 9,700	Funds available	$10,000

- *Tax-exempt money-market funds,* which invest in short-term municipal securities (The income from these securities is exempt from federal income taxes.)

How Safe Are Money-Market Funds?

Money-market mutual funds do not carry the Federal Deposit Insurance Corporation (FDIC, an independent agency of the U.S. government) insurance carried by bank money-market deposit accounts, but they are relatively safe because

1. The investments are in securities issued by governments and their agencies and large corporations.
2. The maturities of these securities are short term, lowering the risk.

The safest money-market funds invest only in U.S. Treasury securities because of the full faith and credit backing of the U.S. government. All money-market funds are relatively safe because large institutional issuers of short-term securities are unlikely to default on their obligations, and prices of short-term securities do not fluctuate widely, which accounts for the constant share price of $1 per share.

Before investing in a money-market fund, read the prospectus, which lists the types of securities that the money-market mutual fund invests in. Historically, the risk of default has been low for Treasury bills, CDs, bankers' acceptances, and commercial paper. A few companies have defaulted on their commercial paper, which affected money-market funds holding those issues. However, the investment companies running those funds absorbed the losses instead of shareholders of the fund.

Higher-yielding high-risk short-term securities do exist, and some aggressive money-market funds invest in these to raise their yields. The prospectus of a fund outlines the investment restrictions for that fund.

Another concern for shareholders is fraud. What if someone in the fund steals or embezzles shareholders' savings from their accounts? This, of course, could happen with all investments, but there are certain safeguards with money-market funds:

- The investment company does not physically handle the funds. A custodial bank is appointed to record the deposits into and transfers from shareholders' accounts.

- The custodial bank has insurance as well as being bonded in the event of theft or loss owing to embezzlement or fraud.

Thus money-market funds have the same safeguards against fraud as other short-term investments, such as in savings accounts, and investors' fears should be allayed.

How to Invest in Money-Market Funds

The constant share price of money-market mutual funds offers investors the advantage of being able to add and withdraw funds from these accounts without incurring any tax consequences. By comparison, short-term bond mutual funds do not have constant share prices, with the result that when shares are sold, there are capital gains/losses when the purchase and sale share prices differ. For this reason, you do not want to invest your short-term funds in a short-term bond fund rather than a money-market mutual fund.

To invest in a money-market fund, call the fund company (most have toll-free telephone numbers), or download the prospectus and application form from the fund's Web site. The Internet provides a comprehensive list of all the mutual fund families. One of these Web sites is www.moneymarketmutualfunds.com. Mutual fund companies are required by the Securities and Exchange Commission (SEC) to send the prospectus either by mail or through the Internet to new investors. The prospectus includes information about the fund, such as

- The minimum dollar investment necessary to open an account
- How the investor can withdraw funds from the account
- The investment objectives and policies, as well as the investment restrictions
- Who manages the fund, the fees charged by the management company, and an outline of the operating expenses and other fees
- The fund's financial statements

Read the prospectus before filling out the application form. The completed form can be sent back with a check to open the account or using the Internet with the money transferred electronically. You will receive monthly statements showing the number of shares in your account and your deposits, withdrawals, and dividend income. Most funds have a minimum amount (usually $100) for additional investments.

You can withdraw money on demand from your money-market funds in various ways:

- Through check writing
- Through wire transfers from the fund to your bank account
- Through a check written by the fund and mailed to your account in response to a written withdrawal request
- Through transfer to other funds within the same investment company's family of funds
- By using a systematic withdrawal plan (SWP), where the fund sends a periodic check to you, your bank account, or a third party.

Caveats

- Choose a money-market fund from an investment company that has a wide range of different funds, allowing you greater flexibility in your transfers to other types of investment funds.
- Avoid funds that have sales charges, redemption fees, and high management and expense ratios.
- Avoid keeping too much money in money-market funds because over the long term, real rates of return from money-market funds are unlikely to exceed the rate of inflation.
- Avoid choosing short-term bond funds over money-market mutual funds as a parking place for your cash for short periods of time. You could experience losses in principal if the share price falls below the purchase price with short-term bond funds.

TREASURY BILLS

Treasury bills are short-term debt securities issued by the U.S. government that are sold at a discount from their face value. Although Treasury bills are slightly more difficult to purchase directly than money-market funds, many people prefer to invest directly in Treasury bills rather than indirectly through money-market funds. Treasury bills are the most popular of the short-tem individual investments after money-market mutual funds.

Treasury bills (T-bills) are short-term safe-haven investments issued by the U.S. Treasury and fully backed by the U.S. government.

TABLE 5-3

Auction Details of Treasury Bills

Term	Minimum	Multiples	Auction	Day of Auction
4 weeks	$1,000	$1,000	Weekly	Tuesday
13 weeks	$1,000	$1,000	Weekly	Monday
26 weeks	$1,000	$1,000	Weekly	Monday

Their risk of default is extremely low. In fact, if the U.S. government would default on any of its obligations, all investments in the United States would be suspect. Treasury bills are considered to be the safest of all fixed-income investments.

Treasury bills are negotiable non-interest-bearing securities with maturities of 4, 13, and 26 weeks. They are available in minimum denominations of $1,000 and multiples of $1,000. Table 5-3 describes Treasury bill issues.

A Treasury bill is issued at a discount from its face value. The amount of the discount depends on the prices that are bid in Treasury bill auctions. At maturity, the bills are redeemed at full face value. The difference in the amount between the discount value and the face value is treated as interest income. For example, if you buy a 26-week $1,000 Treasury bill at $985 and hold it until maturity, the interest you earn is $15. Tables 5-4 and 5-5 discuss the determination of Treasury bill yields and prices, describe how to buy and sell Treasury bills, and outline the differences between competitive and noncompetitive bids.

Buying and Selling Treasury Bills

You can buy new issues of Treasury bills directly from any of the Federal Reserve banks in the primary market with no commissions or fees charged. You also can buy new issues of Treasury bills indirectly through banks and brokerage firms, which charge commissions for their services. You also can buy and sell existing T-bills on the secondary markets through banks and brokerage firms.

Direct Purchase

Buying directly from the Treasury involves opening an account and then submitting a tender form. Figures 5-1 shows a new account request form, and Fig. 5-2 shows a tender form for a Treasury bill.

TABLE 5-4

Determining the Yield and Price of Treasury Bills

Because Treasury bills have no stated rate of interest, you can determine the yield on Treasury bills using the following equation:

$$\text{Yield} = \frac{(\text{face value} - \text{price paid})}{\text{price paid}} \times \frac{365}{\text{days to maturity}}$$

A six-month Treasury bill purchased for $990 and redeemed at face value has a 2.02 percent annual yield:

$$\text{Yield} = \frac{\$1{,}000 - 990}{990} \times \frac{365}{182.5}$$

$$= 2.02 \text{ percent}$$

To make matters more complex, however, bids submitted to a Federal Reserve bank are not quoted on an annual basis, as shown in the preceding example, but rather on a bank discount basis.

Yield on a Bank Discount Basis

$$\text{Yield} = \frac{\text{face value} - \text{price paid}}{100^*} \times \frac{360^\dagger}{\text{days to maturity}}$$

*The yield is quoted for each $100 of face value.
†Note the use of 360 rather than 365 days.

Using the same example, the discount is $1 for the T-bill selling at $99 per $100 face value with a six-month maturity. The bank discount yield is shown in this example:

$$\text{Yield} = \frac{100 - 99}{100} \times \frac{360}{180}$$

$$= 2 \text{ percent}$$

The bank discount yield is always less than the annual yield.

The first step is to fill out the new account request form (Fig. 5-1) to establish an account with the Department of the Treasury. The nine-digit routing number on the form is the identifying number of your financial institution. You can find the routing number in front of your account number on the bottom line of a check or deposit slip.

Submit this form to the Federal Reserve bank or branch (you can submit it online at www.publicdebt.treas.gov). You then receive confirmation that the account has been established along with your account number. Your purchases of Treasury securities are recorded in this account, which is free up to the amount of $100,000 of secu-

TABLE 5-5

Determining the Price of Treasury Bills

Treasury bills are sold at a discount that is less than the $1,000 par or face amount and then are redeemed at par at maturity. This difference is attributed to interest. The price for a Treasury bill with a 1.33 percent bid discount (the price that dealers are willing to pay for this bill on that day) and a 1.31 percent ask discount (the price that dealers are willing to sell this security for on that day) with a maturity of 180 days is determined as follows:

The *dealer's selling price,* which is the price at which an investor would buy, can be calculated as follows:

$$\text{Price} = \text{par value} - \text{par value (ask discount)} \times \frac{\text{days to maturity}}{360}$$

$$= \$100 - 100(0.0131) \times \frac{180}{360}$$

$$= \$99.345 \quad \text{or } \$993.45 \text{ per T-bill}$$

The *dealer's purchase price* (the price at which an investor would sell) can be calculated as follows:

$$\text{Price} = \text{par value} - \text{par value (bid discount)} \times \frac{\text{days to maturity}}{360}$$

$$= \$100 - 100(0.0133) \times \frac{180}{360}$$

$$= \$99.335 \quad \text{or } \$993.35 \text{ per T-bill}$$

rities. When you invest more than this amount, the Federal Reserve charges $25 to maintain the account.

Fill in the tender form (Fig. 5-2) to buy Treasury bills directly from a Federal Reserve bank. The Federal Reserve auctions new issues of Treasury bills weekly, and you can submit bids on either a competitive or a noncompetitive basis.

Treasury bills purchased directly through Federal Reserve banks are held in the Treasury direct book-entry system, designed primarily for investors who intend to hold their securities to maturity. If you decide to sell your T-bills before maturity, you have to fill out a transfer request form (PD 5179), which transfers the account to the commercial book-entry system. Then you can sell the T-bills through a broker before maturity. The commercial book-entry system records T-bills bought through financial institutions and government securities dealers. You can find information on Treasury bills on the U.S. government's Web site (www.publicdebt.treas.gov).

FIGURE 5-1

New Account Request Form to Open an Account

PD F 5182 E
Department of the Treasury
Bureau of the Public Debt
(Revised August 2004)

www.treasurydirect.gov
1-800-722-2678

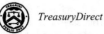 *TreasuryDirect*

OMB NO. 1535-0069

NEW ACCOUNT REQUEST

SEE INSTRUCTIONS - TYPE OR PRINT IN INK ONLY - NO ALTERATIONS OR CORRECTIONS

1. *TreasuryDirect* ACCOUNT INFORMATION	FOR DEPARTMENT USE

ACCOUNT NAME

DOCUMENT AUTHORITY

APPROVED BY

DATE APPROVED

ADDRESS

EXT REG ☐

FOREIGN ☐

BACKUP ☐

City   State   ZIP Code

REVIEW ☐

2. TAXPAYER IDENTIFICATION NUMBER

CLASS ☐

1st Named
Owner   Social Security Number   OR   Employer Identification Number

3. TELEPHONE NUMBERS

Work   Home

4. PAYMENT INFORMATION

ROUTING NUMBER

FINANCIAL INSTITUTION
(Limited to 30 characters/spaces)

NAME ON ACCOUNT
(Limited to 22 characters/spaces)

ACCOUNT NUMBER

☐ Checking   ☐ Savings
(Check One)

5. AUTHORIZATION   I submit this request pursuant of the provisions of Department of the Treasury Circulars, Public Debt Series Nos.
2-86 (31 CFR Part 357), and 1-93 (31 CFR Part 356).

Under penalties of perjury, I certify that:
1. The number shown on this form is my correct taxpayer identification number (or I am waiting for a number to be issued to me), and
2. I am not subject to backup withholding because: (a) I am exempt from backup withholding, or (b) I have not been notified by the Internal Revenue Service (IRS) that I am subject to backup withholdind as a result of a failure to report all interest or dividends, or (c) the IRS has notified me that I am no longer subject to backup withholding, and
3. I am a U.S. person (including a U.S. resident alien).

Instructions. You must cross out item 2 above if you have been notified by the IRS that you are currently subject to backup withholding because you have failed to report all interest and dividends on your tax return.

I further certify that all other information provided on this form is true, correct and complete.

Signature   Date

SEE INSTRUCTIONS FOR PRIVACY ACT AND PAPERWORK REDUCTION ACT NOTICE.   **(OVER)**

FIGURE 5-2

Treasury Bill and Note Tender Form

PD F 5181 E
Department of the Treasury
Bureau of the Public Debt   OMB NO. 1535-0069
(Revised August 2004)   *TreasuryDirect*   (**TREASURY MARKETABLE SECURITIES TENDER**)
www.treasurydirect.gov
1-800-722-2678   For Tender Instructions, See PD F 5382

TYPE OR PRINT IN INK ONLY – TENDERS WILL NOT BE ACCEPTED WITH ALTERATIONS OR CORRECTIONS

1. BID INFORMATION (*Must Be Completed*)	(Bids for bills must end In 0 or 5, see instructions.)	**DEPARTMENT USE**
Par Amount: **Bid Type:** (*Fill in One*) ○ Noncompetitive		TENDER NO.
$ _____ ○ Competitive at _____ % ◄		
(*Sold in units of $1,000*) To place a negative bid for TIPS, see instructions.		RECEIVED BY/DATE

2. *TreasuryDirect* ACCOUNT NUMBER
(*If NOT furnished, a new account will be opened.*)

3. TAXPAYER ID NUMBER (*Must Be Completed*)

_____ OR _____
Social Security Number (First-Named Owner)   Employer ID Number

ENTERED BY

APPROVED BY

4. TERM SELECTION (*Fill in One*)
(*Must Be Completed*)

Bill
    Circle the Number of Reinvestments
○ 13-Week..........0

○ 26-Week..........0

Note
○ 2-Year Note
○ 3-Year Note
○ 5-Year Note
○ 10-Year Note

TIPS
○ 5-Year
○ 10-Year
○ 20-Year

5. ACCOUNT NAME (*Must Be Completed*)

ISSUE DATE

CUSIP 912795-

CUSIP 912828-

6. ADDRESS (*For new account or changes to existing accounts.*)   ☐ **New Address?**

_____
City   State   ZIP Code

FOREIGN ☐

BACKUP ☐

REVIEW ☐

7. TELEPHONE NUMBERS (*For new account or changes to existing accounts.*)
☐ New Phone Number?
Home _____ Alternate _____

8. PAYMENT INFORMATION (*For new account only.*)   Changes? Submit PD F 5178.
Routing Number _____
Financial Institution Name _____
Account Number _____
Name on Account _____
Account Type: (*Fill in One*)   ○ Checking   ○ Savings

9. PURCHASE METHOD
(*Must Be Completed*)
○ *Pay Direct* ® *
(Existing *TreasuryDirect* Account Only)
○ Checks: $_____
   Make checks payable to *TreasuryDirect*. $_____
   Personal checks are acceptable ONLY for notes and TIPS. $_____
○ Other $_____
Total Payment Attached: $ **0.00**
CHECKS ARE DEPOSITED IMMEDIATELY

CHECK #

10. AUTHORIZATION (*Must Be Completed–Original Signature Required*) **Tender Submission:** I submit this tender pursuant to the provisions of Department of the Treasury Circulars, Public Debt Series Nos. 2–86 (31 CFR Part 357) and 1–93 (31 CFR Part 356), and the applicable offering announcement. As the first-named owner and under penalties of perjury, I certify that: 1) The number shown on this form is my correct taxpayer identification number (or I am waiting for a number to be issued to me), and 2) I am not subject to backup withholding because: (a) I am exempt from backup withholding, or (b) I have not been notified by the Internal Revenue Service (IRS) that I am subject to backup withholding as a result of a failure to report all interest or dividends, or (c) the IRS has notified me that I am no longer subject to backup withholding, and 3) I am a U.S. person (including a U.S. resident alien). I further certify that all other information provided on this form is true, correct, and complete.

Certification instructions: You must cross out item 2 above if you have been notified by the IRS that you are currently subject to backup withholding because you have failed to report all interest and dividends on your tax return.

Pay Direct: *(If using this purchase method.) I authorize a debit to my account at the financial institution I designated in *TreasuryDirect* to pay for this security. I understand that the purchase price will be charged to my account on or after the settlement date. I also understand that if this transaction cannot be successfully completed, my tender can be rejected, the transaction canceled, and a **1% penalty assessed**. If there is a dispute, a copy of this authorization may be provided to my financial institution.

_____   _____
Signature (s)   Date

Competitive Bids

A *competitive bid* is a bid to the U.S. Treasury to buy Treasury securities at a particular yield. A competitive bid is submitted with a yield (to two decimal places) on a bank discount basis. For example, if you want to buy $100,000 of six-month Treasury bills and pay $99,000, the competitive bid you submit to the Federal Reserve bank is 2.00 percent. Until 1998, the Federal Reserve accepted the bids that had the lowest discount rates (the highest prices) from all bids received. The accepted bids had a range of yields from the lowest to the highest. The highest yield (the lowest price) accepted for new Treasury securities issued in a Treasury auction is known as the *stop-out yield*. Investors who had their bids accepted at the stop-out yield or close to it received greater returns than those received for bids at the lowest accepted yields. This concept is referred to as the *winner's curse*. However, all Treasury auctions now use the *single-price* or *Dutch auction*, in which all the winning bids that are lower than the stop-out yield are accepted, thereby eliminating the winner's curse. For example, if the range of accepted yields is 1.12 to 1.22 percent, all bidders receive 1.22 percent.

The yields bid depend on money-market yields being offered by competing short-term instruments, as well as expectations of what short-term rates for T-bills would be. By studying these rates, an investor has a better chance of submitting a bid that will be accepted. With competitive bidding, investors face the risk of not having their bids accepted if their bids are above the stop-out yields. The advantage of placing a competitive bid is that an investor can bid for larger dollar amounts in an auction than a noncompetitive bidder.

Noncompetitive Bids

A *noncompetitive bid* is a method of purchasing U.S. Treasury securities without having to submit a price or yield. Noncompetitive bids allow you to buy T-bills at the average accepted competitive bid in the auction. Generally, all noncompetitive bids of up to $1 million per investor per auction for Treasury bills and $5 million for Treasury notes are accepted, which means that investors are assured of their purchases.

There are two disadvantages to submitting a competitive bid. Less experienced investors may not want to calculate their yields, and they might not want to accept the risk of their competitive bids not being accepted.

You can send tender forms to submit bids through the mail or in person to the Federal Reserve banks and branches before the close of the auction. Competitive bids must be received by the time designated in the offering circular. Noncompetitive bids that are mailed must be postmarked no later than midnight the day before the auction and received on or before the issue date of the securities. Payment must accompany the tender form.

After your bid is accepted, you receive a confirmation receipt from the Federal Reserve and a payment, which is the difference between the tender amount submitted and the discounted price of the T-bills. You can stipulate on the tender form whether you want the Federal Reserve to reinvest the T-bills when they mature. If you do not choose the reinvestment option, the Federal Reserve credits your account for the face value of the Treasury bills at maturity. The advantage of buying T-bills directly and holding them to maturity is that you avoid paying commissions or fees.

When you submit a competitive bid, you always run the risk that your bid will not be accepted because of unanticipated fluctuations of money-market interest rates on the day of the auction.

CERTIFICATES OF DEPOSIT

A *certificate of deposit (CD)* is a receipt for a deposit of funds in a financial institution that pays the holder interest on the deposit for a specified time period. CDs offer investors with limited resources a convenient way of investing their short-term funds. CDs can be bought through banks and thrift institutions for small amounts for specified periods. For example, you might decide to invest $500 in a six-month CD that pays interest of 2 percent per annum. The $500 is deposited in the bank, and in six months time, the bank promises to pay you $505 (principal plus interest) at maturity. CDs are not marketable, in that if you need the funds before maturity, there is no market of buyers for your security. You would have to go to the issuing financial institution and pay the early redemption penalty (such as forfeiting the interest for a quarter) to cash in your CD before maturity.

Negotiable CDs are marketable in that they are traded in a secondary market. A negotiable CD is a large-denomination (over $100,000) CD with a specific maturity date and rate of interest that can be bought and sold in the open market before maturity. A *round lot* for a trade in the market is $1 million or greater. Rates and maturities are negotiated individually between lenders and financial institutions. Rates on negotiable CDs generally are comparable with those of other money-market securities such as Treasury bills and commercial paper.

Banks that are members of the FDIC provide insurance of $100,000 per ownership of accounts in a bank. Many investors use CDs as their investment vehicles for their short-term funds.

COMMERCIAL PAPER

Commercial paper is difficult for individual investors to buy, but it is a widely held indirect investment by money-market funds. Understanding what commercial paper is enables you to be able to assess the risks of your money-market funds. *Commercial paper* is an unsecured short-term promissory note (IOU) issued by the largest and most creditworthy financial and nonfinancial corporations as a source of credit. Commercial paper is sold at a discount from its face value, with maturities typically ranging from a few to 270 days. Denominations for commercial paper are large, ranging from $5,000 to $5 million.

Commercial paper is sold either through dealers or directly by the issuers to investors. Dealers buy commercial paper and then immediately resell the paper in large amounts to institutional investors, charging relatively small margins ($\frac{1}{8}$ of 1 percent per annum) (Stigum and Fabozzi, p. 53). Even if individual investors have large amounts ($150,000) to invest, dealers will not sell commercial paper to individual investors because the SEC states that commercial paper should be sold only to sophisticated investors, and dealers consider all individual investors to be unsophisticated. Consequently, individual investors buy dealer paper through brokers who offer the paper in smaller amounts ($25,000 and over) and charge commissions, which can be significant on small purchases (Stigum and Fabozzi, p. 58).

Individual investors might buy commercial paper directly from issuers in relatively small amounts ($25,000). By telephoning or writing to well-known finance companies such as General Motors Acceptance Corp. (GMAC), Chrysler Financial Corp., Sears, etc., you can find out their terms, rates, and maturities.

Commercial paper also may be bought through a bank, for which the bank charges a fee for its efforts.

BANKERS' ACCEPTANCES

Bankers' acceptances are the least understood of all the short-term money-market investments, yet they are good investments for individual investors. *Bankers' acceptances* are negotiable time drafts commonly issued for import-export transactions. For example, if importers want to pay for goods when they are received, not when they are shipped, they arrange a time draft with a local bank to pay for the goods when they arrive three or six months later. If the exporter does not want to wait for payment, the draft can be taken to the firm's bank for payment. The firm's bank can sell the draft to investors, who buy this bankers' acceptance at a discount from its face value and then receive the face value at maturity (when the importer pays the bank). Given the large amounts of money involved in bankers' acceptances, the predominant investors are central banks, not individual investors. Yields on bankers' acceptances generally are slightly lower than those of commercial paper and CDs.

Individual investors can approach large commercial banks and dealers who deal in bankers' acceptances to see what bankers' acceptances are available for investment. The amounts that can be invested typically range from $25,000 to $1 million. Bankers group bankers' acceptances into packages at these higher denominations. Individual investors mostly hold bankers' acceptances indirectly through their investments in money-market mutual funds.

REPURCHASE AGREEMENTS

A *repurchase agreement (repo)* is a contract whereby one party sells securities to another party and simultaneously executes an agreement to buy them back at a contracted price in the future. U.S. government securities are the major types of securities used. The length of the holding period is tailored to the needs of the parties in the transaction, but most repurchase agreements are transacted for only a few days.

The interest is the difference between the selling and the repurchase prices of the repo. Interest is taxed at the federal, state, and local levels of government. There are no regular published repo rates because they are determined through direct negotiations between the buyers and sellers. However, the rates of repurchase agreements are closely related to Treasury bill and federal funds rates. Repo rates may be lower than the federal funds rate because of the security provided by the securities in the repurchase agreement. This does not mean that repurchase agreements are devoid of risk. In 1982, Drysdale Securities, a brokerage company, defaulted on close to $4 billion in repurchase agreements. Since a repo is a loan with security, investors still need to pay attention to

- The ability of the borrower to repay the loan
- Not paying more than the securities are worth, because if the seller defaults, they will lose money

Why, then, would an investor or institution want to buy a repurchase agreement instead of buying the securities?

- The first advantage is that the maturity of a repo can be tailored to the length of time that the short-term money is needed.
- A repo removes the risk of loss owing to market fluctuations of the underlying securities in the transaction. Sellers could, of course, sell their securities when they need the cash, but there is a drawback to this action. If the price of the securities falls below the original purchase price, there is a capital loss. The buyer of the repo avoids this risk and is protected from market fluctuations of the securities.

The major participants in repurchase agreements are securities dealers, corporations, and financial institutions. Unfortunately, owing to the large size of the transactions ($1 million or more), many individual investors do not invest directly in this type of money-market security.

The money-market securities just discussed offer investors the opportunity to have their short-term liquid funds earn a return rather than allowing their money to sit in a non-interest bearing or lower-interest-bearing bank account. The caveat with short-term money-market securities is that over the long term, they do not provide a sufficient hedge against inflation.

Money Market Mutual Funds
or Individual Securities?

Should you invest in money-market mutual funds or in individual money-market securities such as Treasury bills, CDs, bankers' accep-

TABLE 5-6

Money-Market Mutual Funds or Individual Securities?

	Mutual Funds	Individual Securities
Ease of opening an account	Yes	No, except for CDs and Treasury bills
Liquidity and Marketability	Yes	Treasury bills
Loss of principal with early redemption	No	Yes
Higher rate of return	No	Yes

tances, and commercial paper? Table 5-6 shows the advantages of the mutual funds versus the individual money-market securities.

Money-market mutual funds have fixed share prices, which accounts for many of their advantages over individual securities, in that they can be bought and sold without any tax consequences. Income from money-market funds, however, is taxable. Buying and selling individual securities is not as simple as with money-market mutual funds. Treasury bills are both liquid and marketable, but it would take at least three days to receive the proceeds from the sale of Treasury bills in the secondary markets.

The other major advantage of money-market mutual funds over individual securities is that if money is needed earlier than planned, there is no loss in principal. With Treasury bills, which are the most liquid and marketable of the individual investments, there might be a loss or gain in principal owing to fluctuations in market rates of interest. Other than Treasury bills, individual investments may be more difficult to liquidate. With CDs, there are early-withdrawal penalties.

The only disadvantage of money-market mutual funds is that at times individual money-market investments earn higher rates of return. Bear in mind, however, that the purpose of these money-market securities is to provide a parking place for emergency funds and short-term cash, not to be the cornerstone of the bulk of your investments.

Table 5-7 summarizes the advantages and disadvantages of individual money-market securities.

TABLE 5-7

Individual Money-Market Securities

Security Type	Advantages	Disadvantages
Money market funds	Easy to invest and withdraw Access to funds within three days or less Higher rates of return than savings accounts Overnight transfer of funds	Interest income is taxed at federal, state and local levels Earn lower rates of return than individual money-market securities
Treasury bills	No credit or default risk Flexible range of maturities Commission free if bought directly Interest income is exempt from state (and local) taxes Active secondary market	Yields might be less than those on CDs and other short-term individual securities
Certificates of deposit	Rates of return slightly higher than money-market mutual funds Bank CDs carry FDIC insurance	Penalties for early withdrawal of funds Secondary market only for negotiable CDs
Commercial paper	Higher yields than T-bills with similar maturities	Difficult for individual investors to buy Issued in large denominations Interest is taxed at all levels No secondary market
Bankers' acceptances	Higher yields than T-bills with similar maturities Secondary market	Difficult for individual investors to buy Issued in large denominations ($25,000 to $1 million)
Repurchase agreements	Flexible terms and maturities for investors	Large denominations ($1 million or more) preclude individual investors

REFERENCES

Faerber, Esmé: *All About Bonds and Bond Mutual Funds.* New York; McGraw-Hill, 2000.

Schultze, Ellen E.: "Parking Places for Cash can be Costly," *Wall Street Journal,* July 10, 1998, p. C1.

Stigum, Marcia, and Frank Fabozzi: *Dow Jones Guide to Bond and Money Market Investments*: Homewood, IL: Dow Jones–Irwin, 1987.

CHAPTER 6

Common Stock and Preferred Stock

KEY CONCEPTS

- What common stocks are and what they can do for you
- Characteristics of common stock
- Dividends
- Types of common stock
- Preferred stock

WHAT COMMON STOCKS ARE AND WHAT THEY CAN DO FOR YOU

Historically, the stock market has seen many boom and bust cycles. The most recent bear market (an extended period of market declines) began in March 2000 and lasted through 2002. To put this situation into perspective, the last three-year bear market occurred 60 years ago. The Nasdaq Composite Index was hit hardest because of its large composition of technology and Internet-related stocks. The Nasdaq was down 31.5 percent for 2002 and 73.6 percent since March 2000. The total value of U.S. stocks in March 2000 was approximately $17 trillion, which fell to $10 trillion at the end of 2002 (Browning, p. R1). More mainstream stocks also suffered losses during this period, but they were not hit as severely. The Dow Jones Industrial Average was down 15.01 percent for 2002 and 28.8 percent for the three-year period.

Part of the blame for this bear market can be attributed to the excessive overvaluation of many stocks. Many Internet and technology-related companies came into existence based merely on good ideas. Many of these companies generated sales but, unfortunately could not eke out any profits. Consequently, new measures for valuing these companies were developed. The traditional measures using earnings showed the companies to be overvalued, but the new measures using sales as a base provided a sense of euphoria that fueled the speculative bubble. People who had never invested in stocks rushed into the market, investing regardless of the type of business the company was in.

You can learn a great deal from this bear market. First, you must recognize what the different types of stocks are and what they can do for you. Second, you must understand that the valuation of a company is important. Finding undervalued companies is not easy, but investing in overvalued companies is a sure way to lose money.

CHARACTERISTICS OF COMMON STOCK

There are two kinds of stock, *common* and *preferred*. Both common and preferred stock represent ownership in a corporation. Preferred stockholders receive preference over common stockholders regarding payment of dividends and assets in liquidation. Preferred stock is discussed in detail later in this chapter. Common stockholders, however, are the residual owners of the corporation because they have voting rights and bear the ultimate risk associated with ownership. During bankruptcy, common stockholders are last in line (after bondholders and preferred stockholders) for claims on assets. Stockholders' liability is limited to the amount of their investments. With regard to earnings, common stockholders are entitled to receipt of dividends only after all the corporation's obligations have been met.

You can benefit in three ways from investing in stocks:

- They allow you to acquire a store of value.
- They provide capital growth.
- They supply a stream of income (only for dividend-paying stocks).

When a new company is formed, common stock is sold to shareholders to raise money for the company. Similarly, when companies need additional funds to expand, they often sell more common stock.

Bonds are also sold to raise funds. Investors invest in the common stock of companies to earn a return on their money.

Ownership of common stock is evidenced by stock certificates. The front of a certificate shows the name of the issuing company, the name of the owner of the shares, the number of shares of ownership, the identifying serial number, the name of the register, and the par value of the stock. The back of the stock certificate normally includes an assignment statement, which must be signed by the holder of the stock when the holder transfers ownership of the shares.

DIVIDENDS

When the board of directors of a corporation decides to pay out its earnings or part of its earnings in dividends, all its common shareholders have a right to receive them. If the board of directors decides not to declare a dividend, the shareholders receive nothing. Companies are not legally required to pay dividends even if they are profitable and have paid them in the past. In contrast, companies are legally required to pay interest to their bondholders on their debt. This is an important distinction for people who rely on regular income from their investments.

Declaration of Dividends

If the receipt of dividends is important to you, you need to be aware of these four dates:

- *Date of declaration* is the date on which the board of directors declares the dividends.
- *Date of record* is the date that determines which shareholders are entitled to receive the dividends. Only those shareholders owning shares of the company on the date of record are entitled to receive dividends. If shares are purchased after the record date, the owners are not entitled to receive the dividends.
- *Ex-dividend date* is two business days before the date of record. Stock traded on the ex-dividend date does not include the dividend. When common stock is bought, the settlement takes three business days to be completed. Thus, if the record date for a company's dividend is Friday, the ex-dividend date is the preceding Wednesday. Investors who buy these shares on Tuesday (the day before the ex-dividend date) receive the

dividend because the transaction is recorded in the ownership books for that company in three working days.

- *Payment date* is the date on which the company pays the
  dividends.

Companies generally make their dividend policies known to the
public. Because investors use dividend payments, rightly or wrongly,
as a yardstick or mirror of a company's expected earnings, changes in
dividend payments can have a greater effect on the stock price than
a change in earnings does. This phenomenon explains the reluctance
by management to cut dividends when earnings decline. Similarly,
a lag in increasing dividends might occur when earnings increase
because members of management want to be sure that they can
maintain any increases in dividends.

Shareholders who rely on income from their investments generally purchase the stocks of companies that have a history of paying
regular dividends from their earnings. These companies tend to be
older and well established; their stocks are referred to as *income stocks*
or *blue-chip stocks.*

Young companies that are expanding generally retain their
earnings; their stocks are referred to as *growth stocks.* Growth stocks
appeal to investors who are more interested in capital appreciation.

Types of Dividends

Following are the various forms of dividends:

- Cash dividends
- Stock dividends and stock splits
- Property dividends
- Special distributions, extra dividends, spin-offs, and split-offs

Cash Dividends

A *cash dividend* is a dividend paid in cash. To be able to pay cash
dividends, companies need to have not only sufficient earnings but
also sufficient cash. Even if a company shows a large amount of
retained earnings on its balance sheet, this is not enough to ensure
cash dividends. The amount of cash that a company has is independent of retained earnings. Cash-poor companies still can be profitable.

Most American companies pay regular cash dividends quarterly; others pay dividends semiannually or annually. Johnson &
Johnson, the pharmaceutical company, pays quarterly dividends,

and McDonald's pays an annual dividend. A company might declare *extra dividends* in addition to regular dividends. An extra dividend is an additional, nonrecurring dividend paid over and above the regular dividends by the company. Microsoft Corporation paid an extra dividend of $2 per share over and above its regular dividend to shareholders of record holding the stock on November 15, 2004. Rather than battle to maintain a higher amount of regular dividends, companies with fluctuating earnings pay out additional dividends when their earnings warrant it. Whenever times were good for the automobile industry, for example, General Motors declared extra dividends.

Stock Dividends and Stock Splits

Some companies choose to conserve their cash by paying stock dividends, a dividend paid in stock. The companies then recapitalize their earnings and issue new shares, which do not affect its assets and liabilities. Table 6-1 presents an example of a company's balance sheet before and after a 10 percent stock dividend.

TABLE 6-1

Effects of a Stock Dividend on a Company's Balance Sheet

XYZ Company Balance Sheet before a Stock Dividend				
Current assets	$150,000	Current liabilities		$100,000
Fixed assets	200,000	Long-term liabilities		50,000
		Equity: Common stock	100,000	
		$1 par 100,000 shares outstanding		
		Additional paid-in capital	30,000	
		Retained earnings	70,000	
		Total equity		200,000
Total assets	$ 350,000	Total liabilities & equity		$350,000
After 10 Percent Stock Dividend (Market Price $5 per Share)				
Current assets	$150,000	Current liabilities		$100,000
Fixed assets	200,000	Long-term liabilities		50,000
		Equity: Common stock		110,000
		$1 par 110,000 shares outstanding		
		Additional paid-in capital	70,000	
		Retained earnings	20,000	
		Total equity		200,000
Total assets	$ 350,000	Total liabilities & equity		$350,000

In Table 6-1, the "Total equity" section of the balance sheet is the same before and after the split ($200,000). The amounts that are transferred to the different accounts in the equity section depend on the market value of the common stock and the number of new shares issued through the stock dividend. Amounts from retained earnings are transferred to the common stock and additional paid in capital accounts. In this example, 10,000 additional shares have a market price of $5 per share. The "Retained earnings" account is debited for $50,000 ($5 × 10,000 shares), and $10,000 (10,000 shares × $1 par value) is added to the "Common stock" account. The other $40,000 ($4 premium over par value × 10,000 shares) is added to the "Additional paid-in capital" account.

You should realize immediately that receiving a stock dividend does not increase shareholders' wealth. Shareholders who receive a stock dividend receive more shares of that company's stock, but because the company's assets and liabilities remain the same, the price of the stock must decline to account for the dilution. For shareholders, this situation resembles a slice of cake. You can divide the slice into two, three, or four pieces, and no matter how many ways you slice it, its overall size remains the same. After a stock dividend, shareholders receive more shares, but their proportionate ownership interest in the company remains the same, and the market price declines proportionately.

Stock dividends usually are expressed as a percentage of the number of shares outstanding. For example, if a company announces a 10 percent stock dividend and has 100,000 shares outstanding, the total shares outstanding are increased to 110,000 shares after the stock dividend is issued.

Stock Split

A *stock split* is a proportionate increase in the number of outstanding shares that does not affect the issuing company's assets or earnings. A stock split resembles a stock dividend in that an increase occurs in the number of shares issued on a proportionate basis, whereas the assets, liabilities, equity, and earnings remain the same. The only difference between a stock split and a stock dividend is technical.

From an accounting point of view, a stock dividend of greater than 25 percent is recorded as a stock split. A 100 percent stock dividend is the same as a two-for-one stock split. A company might split its stock because the price is too high, and with a lower price, the company's stock becomes more marketable.

The following example illustrates what happens when a company declares a two-for-one stock split. If at the time of the split the company has 1 million shares outstanding and the price of the stock is $50, after the split, the company will have 2 million shares outstanding, and the stock will trade at $25 per share. Someone who owns 100 shares before the split (with a value of $50 per share) would own 200 shares after the split with a value of approximately $25 per share (50 divided by 2). On January 16, 2003, Microsoft Corporation announced a two-for-one stock split that took effect on February 18, 2003. Before the split, Microsoft closed at $48.30 per share. On the morning of the split, it opened at $24.15 per share. An investor with 100 shares before the split would have 200 shares after the split.

Occasionally, companies announce *reverse splits*, which reduce the number of shares and increase the share price. A reverse split is a proportionate reduction in the number of shares outstanding without affecting the company's assets or earnings. When a company's stock has fallen in price, a reverse split raises the price of the stock to a respectable level. Another reason for raising the share price is to meet the minimum listing requirements of the exchanges and the Nasdaq market. For example, a stock trading in the $1 range would trade at $10 with a 1-for-10 reverse split. The number of shares outstanding would be reduced by 10 times after the split. On November 19, 2002, AT&T had a reverse stock split of one-for-five shares. See Table 6-2 for a discussion of whether there are any advantages to stock dividends and stock splits.

Property Dividends

A *property dividend* is a dividend paid in a form other than cash or the company's own stock. A property dividend generally is taxable at its fair market value. For example, when a corporation spins off a subsidiary, shareholders might receive assets or shares of that subsidiary. Distributing the stocks or assets of the subsidiary (rather than cash) allows shareholders to benefit directly from the market value of the dividends received.

Special Distributions

Companies sometimes make special distributions in various forms, such as extra dividends, spin-offs, and split-offs.

TABLE 6-2

Are There Advantages to Stock Dividends and Stock Splits?

If shareholder wealth is not increased by stock dividends and stock splits, why do companies go to the trouble and expense of issuing them?

The first advantage to the issuing company is a conservation of cash. By substituting stock dividends for cash dividends, a company can conserve its cash or use it for other investment opportunities. If the company successfully invests its retained earnings in business ventures, the stock price is bid up, benefiting shareholders. Consequently, shareholders are better off receiving stock dividends, but there are costs associated with the issue of stock dividends. Shareholders pay the cost of issuing new shares, the transfer fees, and the costs of revising its record of shareholders.

Advocates of stock dividends and stock splits believe that a stock price never falls in exact proportion to the increase in shares. For example, in a two-for-one stock split, the stock price might fall less than 50 percent, which means that shareholders are left with a higher total value. This conclusion has not been verified by most academic studies. When the price of the stock is reduced because of the split, the stock might become more attractive to potential investors because of its lower price. The increased marketability of the stock might push up the price if the company continues to do well financially; stockholders benefit in the long run by owning more shares of a company whose stock price continues to increase.

Stock dividends and stock splits do not increase stockholder wealth from the point of view of the balance sheet. Cash dividends, however, increase a shareholder's monetary wealth directly and reduce the company's cash and reinvestment dollars.

Extra Dividends Companies might want to distribute an extra dividend to their shareholders on a one-time or infrequent basis. A company might have had a particularly good quarter financially, or other reasons for this distribution might exist. The company might use a special distribution rather than increase its regular dividends because the distribution is a one-time occurrence. Companies would not want to increase their dividend rates if they could not continue paying those increased rates.

Spin-Offs A *spin-off* is the distribution of shares of a subsidiary company to shareholders. Some companies allocate proportionately to their shareholders some or all of their shares of a subsidiary company as a spin-off. For example, when the Pepsi Cola Company (stock ticker symbol PEP) wanted to focus its attention on its soft drink and snack food businesses, it spun off its restaurant businesses (Pizza

Hut, Kentucky Fried Chicken, and Taco Bell chains). These food businesses now trade under the name Tricon Global with the stock ticker symbol YUM. Pepsi shareholders received 1 share of YUM for every 10 shares of Pepsi owned as of the record date. The market value of the Pepsi stock fell by roughly the value of the YUM shares distributed on the day of the spin-off. Shareholders have the option of keeping or selling the additional shares they receive. In many cases the shares of spin-off companies outperform their parent companies because the new stand-alone companies can expand in directions where they are no longer hindered by their parent companies.

Split-Offs   A *split-off* is the exchange of a parent company's stock for a pro rata share of the stock of a subsidiary company. Split-offs, which differs from spin-offs, do not occur frequently. In a split-off, shareholders are offered the choice of keeping the shares they own in the existing company or exchanging them for shares in the split-off company. For example, on August 10, 2001, AT&T completed a split-off of Liberty Media Corporation. AT&T redeemed each outstanding share of its class A and class B Liberty Media tracking stock for one share of series A and series B common stock, respectively, from Liberty Media Corporation. In a split-off, an exchange of shares takes place, whereas in a spin-off, shareholders receive additional shares in another company.

Although shareholders obviously benefit from receiving cash and property dividends, they also benefit when earnings are not paid out but are instead reinvested in the company. This technique increases the value of the company and hence the value of its stock.

Table 6-3 discusses dividend reinvestment plans for investors wishing to reinvest their dividends directly in the stock of the companies that they already own.

Classes of Common Stock   Some corporations issue different classes of common stock that can have different characteristics. For example, Agere Company has class A and class B common stock. Class A common stock was offered at the initial public offering (IPO), and each share carries one vote on all matters on which shareholders are entitled to vote. Class B common stock entitles shareholders to four votes per share for the election and removal of directors and one vote per share for all other matters. Some companies with more than one class of common stock have different dividend rates.

TABLE 6-3

What Are DRIPS?

A *dividend reinvestment plan* (DRIP) allows shareholders to reinvest their dividends in additional stock rather than receiving them in cash. These plans are offered directly by companies or through agents acting on behalf of the corporation. In the former case, a company issues new shares in lieu of a cash dividend. You also have the option of purchasing additional shares from the company. The advantage is that you pay no brokerage fees, although some companies charge fees for this service.

The other type of plan is offered by agents, such as banks, that collect the dividends and offer additional shares to shareholders who sign up for the plan. The bank pools the cash from dividends and purchases the stock in the secondary market. Investors are assessed fees that cover the brokerage commissions and the fee charged by the bank.

The advantage of DRIPs to shareholders is that they act as a forced savings plan; dividends are reinvested automatically to accumulate more shares. This method is particularly good for investors who are not disciplined savers.

A disadvantage of dividend re-investment plans is that shareholders need to keep, for tax purposes, accurate records of the additional shares purchased. When additional shares are sold, the purchase price is used to determine whether there is a capital gain or loss. These dividends are considered taxable income whether they are received in cash or reinvested automatically in additional shares. Another disadvantage of DRIPs is that the fees charged to participate in the program can be high.

TYPES OF COMMON STOCK

Although all common stock represents ownership interests in companies, many types of common stocks exist. As mentioned earlier, *blue-chip stocks* pay dividends, and *growth stocks* generally do not pay dividends. Stocks can be classified into various categories, which is useful for investors because different types of stocks vary with regard to their returns, quality, stability of earnings and dividends, and relationship to the various risks affecting the companies and the market.

Blue-Chip Stocks

Blue-chip stocks refer to companies with a long history of sustained earnings and dividend payments. These established companies have developed leadership positions in their respective industries and, because of their importance and large sizes, have stable earnings and dividend records. Most, if not all, the companies in the Dow Jones Industrial Average are considered to be blue-chip companies.

However, some financially troubled former Dow stocks such as AT&T, for example, have cut their dividends and have been removed from the Dow Jones Industrial Average and replaced with other, more solid companies.

Not all blue-chip companies are the same. For example, Wal-Mart, the largest retailer in the world, pays an annual dividend of $0.60 per share, whereas Merck, the pharmaceutical company, pays an annual dividend of $1.52 per share, and the ExxonMobil annual dividend is $1.16 per share (as of May, 2005). Wal-Mart sales and earnings have grown rapidly over its early years, during which time it retained its earnings to fuel its growth. In later years it began paying a small dividend. Wal-Mart does not fit into the typical definition of a blue-chip company because it does not pay much of a dividend and has not had a long history of paying out dividends. Merck and ExxonMobil historically also have had growing sales and earnings, but they have elected to pay out a higher percentage of their earnings in dividends and have longer histories of paying dividends.

Blue-chip companies appeal to investors who seek quality companies with histories of growing profits and regular dividend payouts. These types of companies tend to be less risky in periods of economic uncertainty because of their dependable earnings. In bear markets, the stock prices of blue-chip stock companies tend to decline less than those of the growth stocks of companies that do not pay dividends. Investors are attracted to blue-chip stocks because they not only provide a store of wealth in anticipation of capital appreciation but also deliver regular dividend income.

Income Stocks

Income stocks have high dividend payouts, and the companies are typically in the mature stage of their industry life cycles. Stocks of companies that have established a pattern of paying higher than average dividends can be defined as income stocks. Income stocks tend not to appreciate in price as much as blue-chip stocks do because income stock companies are more mature and are not growing as quickly as blue-chip companies are. This statement does not mean that income stock companies are not profitable or are about to go out of business. On the contrary, they have stable earnings and cash flow, but they choose to pay out much higher ratios of their earnings in dividends than other companies do. Utility companies and real estate investment trusts (REITs) are examples of income stocks. Examples include American Electric Power (ticker symbol AEP) with a dividend of $1.40 and a dividend yield of 3.97 percent, Ameren Corp. (ticker symbol AEE) with a dividend of $2.54 and a dividend yield of 5.1 percent, and NiSource (ticker symbol NI) with a current dividend of $0.92 and a dividend yield of 4.11 percent. These dividends and dividend yields, quoted as of December 23, 2004, were based on the stock prices on that day. The average dividend yield for stocks on the standard and poor's (S&P) 500 Index was 1.46 percent as of December 22, 2004. Annaly Mortgage Management Trust, a mortgage REIT, paid a dividend of $2.00 per share with a yield of 9.4 percent. REITs are required to pass on most of their earnings to shareholders because they are pass-through entities for tax purposes.

Growth Stocks

Growth stocks are issued by companies expected to have sustained high rates of growth in sales and earnings. These companies generally have high price-earnings (P/E) ratios and do not pay dividends. Companies such as Home Depot (ticker symbol HD) and Intel (ticker symbol INTC) grew at high double-digits rates during the 1990s; the growth in these companies was curtailed shortly after that for different reasons. Home Depot faces increased competition from Lowes, which has newer, smaller, and more manageable stores. Intel saw sharp declines in its sales because of reductions in capital equipment spending by business and a decline in computer replacement sales by consumers. Nevertheless, Intel still managed to keep its gross profit margins above 50 percent for most quarters during the early years of the decade of 2000.

An indication that these two companies have passed through their sustained high-growth periods is that they no longer retain all their earnings. Both pay out small amounts of their earnings in dividends. In addition, because of their leadership positions in their respective industries, they also could be classified as blue-chip companies. Most growth companies pay no dividends, such as Cisco Systems (CSCO), which saw annual sales in the 30 to 50 percent range during the 1990s technology boom. Cisco's stock price soared around 130,000 percent from its IPO in February 1990 to March 2000. Cisco expects growth to continue in the high single digits to low teens for revenue and earnings over the next five years. Rather than pay out their earnings in dividends, growth companies retain their earnings and reinvest them in the expansion of their businesses. Lowes, eBay, and Starbucks are some other examples of growth companies.

Growth stocks are often referred to as *high-P/E-ratio stocks* because their greater growth prospects make investors more willing to buy them at higher prices. Investors do not receive returns in the form of dividends, so they buy these stocks for their potential capital appreciation.

Value Stocks

Value stocks are low-P/E-ratio stocks that are out of favor with investors. One reason might be disappointing quarterly earnings. For example, at the end of the economic expansion period, automobile companies trade at lower P/E ratios than the stocks of other companies because investors' expectations for the companies' growth prospects are low. Because investors have relatively low expectations for the companies' immediate growth, these stocks trade at lower prices relative to their earnings and dividends. Patient investors with longer time horizons are willing to purchase these stocks and wait for their prospective earnings to increase.

Table 6-4 compares some of the characteristics of growth stocks and value stocks. Investors are willing to pay 107 times earnings for eBay, Inc., an Internet company, because of its potential future sales and earnings growth. EBay Inc. had significant three-year annual earnings growth of 117 percent, whereas Google, Inc., had annual earnings growth for the two-year period since its IPO of 1,321 percent, justifying it P/E ratio of 225. Starbucks Corporation had significant three-year annual growth in earnings of 43 percent from same-store and new-store sales, justifying its high P/E ratio of 63. However, if growth stocks cannot sustain their high growth rates, their stock prices fall by greater amounts than the corresponding fall in value stocks.

The potential strengths of value stocks are not as evident or visible. Pfizer, the pharmaceutical company, saw its earnings grow over the past three years because of sales of its blockbuster drugs Lipitor, Viagra, and Celebrex. However, the possible linkage of heart attacks to Celebrex and Lipitor facing patent expiration brought Pfizer's P/E ratio down, making it a value stock. Washington Mutual has a low P/E ratio because of fears that rising interest rates will cause a drop in mortgage financing. Interpublic Group's stock price has been depressed because of a drop in business advertising during the recession, causing losses in earnings over the past three-years.

TABLE 6-4

Growth Stocks Versus Value Stocks

Company	Symbol	Stock Price	P/E Ratio	1-year Earnings Growth	3-year Earnings Growth
		Growth Stocks			
EBay, Inc	EBAY	$113.25	107	185%	117%
Google, Inc.	GOOG	$187.90	225	5%	1321%*
Starbucks Corp.	SBUX	$ 60.62	63	26%	43.2%
		Value Stocks			
Pfizer	PFE	$ 26.07	21	-57%	23%
Washington Mutual	WM	$ 41.97	14	0.5%	29%
Interpublic Group	IPG	$ 13.34	12	-354%	-156%

Note: Prices as of December 23, 2004.

* 2-year earnings growth.

TABLE 6-5

How to Use the Internet to Find Value and Growth Stocks

Use a stock screener on www.finance.yahoo.com or www.moneycentral.msn.com to see a list of some current growth and value stocks. For growth stocks, enter higher P/E ratios and higher earnings per share growth estimates. For value stocks, enter low P/E ratios and lower earnings per share growth estimates.

As business spending on advertising increases, Interpublic Group's future earnings are expected to grow. Value investors are looking for stocks whose prices are not reflective of their intrinsic worth and are willing to buy stocks issued by companies experiencing temporary setbacks in the hope that they will overcome their earnings and asset-valuations setbacks. Table 6-5 shows how you can use the Internet to find value and growth stocks.

Cyclical Stocks

Cyclical stocks are those that move with changes in economic activity. Cyclical stocks often reach their high and low points before the respective peaks and troughs of the economy. When the economy is in recession, these stocks see a decline in sales and earnings. During periods of expansion, these stocks grow substantially in sales and earnings. Examples of cyclical stocks are stocks issued by capital equipment companies, home builders, automobile companies, and other sectors tied to the fortunes of the economy. Before an expected downturn in economic activity for 1999, analysts downgraded stocks such as John Deere (DE), the farm equipment maker, and Cummins Engine (CMI), the diesel engine manufacturer; this resulted in a fall in their stock prices as investors sold their stocks. This type of down-beaten stock is considered a value stock for patient investors who are willing to buy it and hold it until the next economic turnaround. Cyclical stocks appeal to investors who like to trade actively by moving in and out of stocks as the economy moves through its cycle.

Defensive Stocks

Defensive stocks tend to hold their price levels when the economy declines. Generally, these stocks resist downturns in the economy; they tend to move up more slowly than other stocks during periods of economic expansion. Defensive stocks are the stocks of companies whose prices are expected to remain stable or do well when the economy declines. Defensive stocks are immune to the changes in the economy and are not affected by downturns in the business cycle. Examples of this type of stocks are drug companies, food and beverage companies, utility companies, consumer goods companies, and even auto parts manufacturers. In a recession, people generally wait to replace their cars and are more likely to spend money to repair them. Similarly, during periods of inflation, the prices of gold stocks tend to rise. Drug companies have predictable earnings, which puts them in the defensive category as well as the growth stock category because of their pipelines of new drugs. If the economy goes into a deflationary environment, the stocks of some supermarket chains, which are viewed as defensive-type stocks, might fall out of this category because supermarket chains generally have low profit margins and cannot pass higher prices on to consumers.

Some investors are willing to buy defensive stocks ahead of an economic downturn and hold them until better economic times.

Speculative Stocks

Speculative stocks have the potential for above-average returns, but they also carry above-average risk if a company folds or something less extreme occurs. Speculative stocks are stocks issued by companies that have the potential for large increases in the prices of their stocks. These companies do not have earnings records and are considered to have a high degree of risk. These companies are quite likely to incur losses and not as likely to experience profits, so they have a higher possibility of larger price gains or losses than other types of shares. Speculative stocks are more volatile than the other stock types.

Speculative stocks are often issued by new companies with promising ideas that are in the development stages. In the late 1990s and early 2000s, Internet companies and technology and biotechnology companies were considered to be speculative. Many Internet companies had no earnings, but their stock prices soared into the stratosphere with the expectation of potential profits. For example, within the first week of launching its Web site, the book seller Books-A-Million saw its stock price rise from $3 to $38 per share—a more than twelve fold increase for a company that had no profits.

The requisite quality for buying speculative stocks, because of their high risk, is a strong stomach—you have to be able to sleep well at night under any circumstances. These stocks deliver either large capital gains or large capital losses.

Penny Stocks

Penny stocks are speculative, low-priced stocks that generally trade on the over-the-counter markets and smaller exchanges. Penny stocks are low-priced stocks ($1 or less) of companies whose future operations are in doubt. These companies are extremely speculative. Boiler room (illegal) sales operators promoted many penny stocks by cold calling unsophisticated investors on the telephone to stress how much money they could make by buying these low priced stocks. To paraphrase an old saying, "There are no free lunches on Wall Street." If a share is trading at $0.25, it is probably trading at its fair value and for good reason. If the stock goes up to $0.50, an investor makes a 100 percent return; if the company goes out of business, an investor loses the entire investment.

Foreign Stocks

Foreign stocks are stocks issued by companies outside the country of origin. Although the U.S. stock markets still account for the largest market capitalization of all the stock markets in the world, the foreign

TABLE 6-6

Foreign ADR Stocks

Company	Symbol	Price*	Country	Exchange
Sony Corporation	SNE	$38.41	Japan	NYSE
Royal Dutch Petroleum	RD	$56.97	Holland	NYSE
ASML Holding NV	ASML	$15.76	Holland	NASDAQ
Nokia Corp.	NOK	$15.80	Finland	NYSE

* Prices are as of December 27, 2004.

stock markets are growing in market share. Foreign stocks provide you with the opportunities to earn greater returns and to diversify your portfolios. You can buy foreign stocks directly in the foreign markets or buy the American depository receipts (ADRs) of these foreign companies. An *American depository receipt* is a negotiable receipt on stocks held in custody abroad. These receipts are traded in place of foreign stocks. Many larger foreign companies trade as *American depository receipts* (ADRs) on the U.S. markets (New York Stock Exchange and the over-the-counter market). Table 6-6 provides an example of some of the foreign stocks trading as ADRs in the U.S markets.

Large-, Medium-, and Small-Cap Stocks

You can classify stocks by size; small-cap stocks, medium-cap stocks, and large-cap stocks. *Cap* is short for market *capitalization,* which is the market value of a company. The market value of a company is determined by multiplying its market stock price by its number of outstanding shares. Market capitalization changes all the time, and although the definitions include a market value for each category, these market-value threshold classifications also change over time. Below are the differentiating values for the groupings of companies by size.

Large-cap stocks are the stocks of large companies with considerable earnings and large amounts of common stock outstanding. This group has a market capitalization of greater than $5 billion. Large-cap stocks represent the companies in the Dow Jones Industrial Average and S&P 500 Index. These large-cap companies account for more than half the total value of the U.S. equity markets. These are blue-chip, established companies that can either be growth or value companies. Some examples are Intel, Microsoft, IBM, General Motors, ExxonMobil, and many other large leading companies in their respective industries. During the explosive growth of stock prices of Internet-related stocks in the late 1990s, many of those stocks had market capitalizations that qualified them as large-cap stocks even though many of those companies did not have any earnings.

Medium-cap stocks are the stocks of medium-sized companies with market capitalizations of between $1 billion and $5 billion. Medium-cap companies have the safety net of having significant assets in terms of their capitalization but might not be so well known to the average investor. Some examples of well-known medium-cap companies are Tyson Foods, Outback Steakhouse, Starbucks, and Borders.

Small-cap stocks are the stocks of small-sized companies with a market capitalization of less than $1 billion. Small-cap companies generally are not household names, although they offer the most attractive return opportunities. This group of stocks has, according to studies, outperformed the large-cap stocks over long periods. Small-cap stock prices tend to be more volatile than large and midcaps because of their greater exposure to risk. Some small-cap companies are potentially the Intels and Microsofts of tomorrow. However, many small companies also go out of business, and others grow enough to become the medium- and large-cap companies. Because small-cap stocks are riskier investments, you should diversify your holdings of them to reduce your overall risk of loss.

What becomes apparent from these classifications of common stock types is that companies' stocks can be placed in several classifications. The pharmaceutical company Johnson & Johnson can be classified as a blue-chip stock, a growth stock, a large-cap stock, and a defensive stock. These classifications are useful when you are planning your portfolio to determine the types of stocks you want to own and the percentage of each that you want to hold. Table 6-7 illustrates how to read common stock quotations.

PREFERRED STOCK

What Preferred Stocks Are and What They Can Do for You

Preferred stock is a security that pays a fixed dividend and in the event of bankruptcy is senior to the claims of common stock on the earnings and assets of a company. Preferred stock, like common stock, also represents an equity ownership in a company. *Equity* is defined as

TABLE 6-7

How to Read Common Stock Quotations

The format for reading stock price quotations is much the same for stocks listed on the New York Stock Exchange (NYSE), the American Stock Exchange (AMEX), and the Nasdaq. The amount of company information that is listed varies somewhat; the listings of NYSE companies are the most comprehensive. Market prices of listed stocks are quoted daily in the financial pages of major newspapers. For example, a typical listing of a common stock from the financial pages looks like this:

YTD%			365 Day							
Chg	High	Low	Stock	Sym	Div	Yield %	P/E	Vol 100s	Close	Net. Chg
–7.3	17.34	12.61	Ford Motor	F	0.40	2.7	12	79410	14.83	0.32

As of December 22, 2004

The following list describes what is in the example from left to right across the columns:

- The first column shows the year-to-date change for the stock, which declined by 7.3 percent
- The high and low columns indicate the yearly range of trading of the stock. Ford Motor traded at a 365-day high of $17.34 per share and a low of $12.61 per share.
- The stock column shows the name of the stock, Ford Motor Company, and the symbol column shows that its trading symbol is F.
- The div column indicates the amount of the dividend, $0.40 per share. A corporation might, from time to time, change the amount of dividends it pays, based on its last quarterly or semiannual dividend payment.
- The dividend yield for Ford Motor is 2.7 percent. You can calculate the yield by dividing the expected dividend by the last, or closing, price of the stock (0.40/14.83).
- The P/E (price-earnings) ratio in the P/E column indicates the price investors are willing to pay for a stock in relation to the stock's earnings. In Ford Motor's case, investors buying the stock at $14.83 are willing to pay 12 times Ford's earnings. High P/E ratios indicate that buyers are willing to pay more for a dollar of earnings than low-P/E-ratio stocks.
- The volume column indicates the number of shares traded for that day. In this case, 7,941,000 shares of Ford were traded that day. By following the average daily volume, you can tell if any unusually heavy trading activity has taken place on a particular day.
- The close column indicates the closing price of the stock for that day. Ford closed at $14.83 per share.
- The last column, net change, shows the change in price from the preceding day. In this case, Ford closed up $0.32 from the preceding day's close.

capital invested in a company by its owners; *debt* is capital lent to the corporation, which must be repaid. Preferred stock is a hybrid type of security in that it has characteristics resembling both debt and equity. Preferred stock pays a fixed dividend, and if the preferred stock issue has a call provision, it may be retired by the company.

Although preferred stock is classified as equity, preferred stockholders do not have ownership interest in the company. The failure of a company to pay dividends to preferred stockholders does not result in bankruptcy as it would with the default of interest on bonds. Instead, the company does not pay common stockholders any dividends until the preferred stockholders are paid their dividends. Unlike common stock, the dividend rate on preferred stock is usually fixed. It might be stated as a percentage of the par value of the preferred stock or as a fixed dollar amount. The *par value* is a stated value, and hence a preferred stock issue with $100 par value that has a dividend of 8 percent would pay a dividend of $8 per share (8 percent of $100).

The fixed dividend of preferred stock appeals to investors who seek regular payments of income. In this regard, preferred stock resembles the regular returns of interest on bonds. The downside to a fixed dividend rate is that the price of preferred stock is sensitive to changes in market rates of interest in the same manner as bonds. For example, if you had bought preferred stock for $100 a share that pays a dividend of $4 and market rates of interest subsequently go up to 6 percent, there will be downside pressure on the price of this preferred stock. New investors will not want to buy this preferred stock for $100 when the dividend is only $4 (a return of 4 percent, 4/100) when new preferred stock issues return a higher yield.

To counter these interest-rate swings in preferred stock prices, many financial institutions and utility companies introduced *adjustable-rate preferred stock* in the early 1980s when market rates were high. Dividend payments fluctuated with changes in market rates of interest as measured by the changes in a combination of U.S. Treasury securities. Dividends moved up and down within a stipulated minimum and maximum limit. For example, Bank of America Corporation's 9.25 percent (at offering) adjustable-rate preferred stock had a 6 percent minimum dividend rate and a 12 percent maximum rate. The rate was adjusted to changes in interest rates on a quarterly basis. The advantage of adjustable-rate preferred stock is that the price of preferred stock does not fluctuate as much with changes in market rates of interest.

There is a greater interest in preferred stock since the changes in the tax code in 2003. Dividends from preferred stock are taxed at favorable rates, 5 percent for taxpayers in the 15 percent or lower marginal tax brackets and 15 percent for all other taxpayers. However, a majority of the preferred stock issues do not qualify for this favorable tax treatment because these issues are trust preferred stock.

These trust preferred stock issues are created by trusts that technically pay interest, and therefore, the payments are taxed at the taxpayers' marginal tax rates (which can be as high as 35 percent).

Multiple Classes of Preferred Stock

Most companies have one class of common stock, but it is quite common to see companies with more than one series of preferred stock. Table 6-8 illustrates some of the different preferred stock issues of Citigroup, Inc., listed on the New York Stock Exchange.

Each class of preferred stock has different features. For example, Citigroup's preferred F series pays a dividend of $3.18 per share, with a yield of 5.9 percent at a closing price of $53.75 per share, and was up $0.25 from the preceding day's closing price. Citigroup has several *cumulative preferred stock* issues, which give holders the right to receive all missed dividend payments before common shareholders are paid. *Convertible preferred stock* can be converted, by holders, into a fixed number of shares of common stock of the underlying company. A *call provision* gives the issuing company the right to call the preferred stock at a specific price (normally a premium over its par value). These issues also might be differentiated in their priority status with regard to claims on assets in the event of bankruptcy.

Claim on Income and Assets

Preferred stock has a preference over common stock with regard to claims on both income and assets. Companies are required to pay dividends on preferred stock before they pay dividends to common

TABLE 6-8

Different Preferred Stock Issues of Citigroup Inc.

Stock	Div	Yld	Close*	Net Chg	
Citigroup pfF	3.18	5.9	53.75	0.25	Cumulative preferred stock
Citigroup pfH	3.12	5.7	54.50	—	Cumulative preferred stock
Citigroup pfM	2.93	5.5	53.40	—	Cumulative preferred stock
Citigroup pfS	1.50	6.0	25.17	—	Noncumulative preferred stock
Citigroup pfV	1.78	6.7	26.42	0.05	Trust preferred stock

*Prices as of December 29, 2004.

stockholders. In the event of bankruptcy, preferred stockholders' claims are settled before the claims of common shareholders. This makes preferred stock less risky than common stock but more risky in relation to bonds. This is so because bondholders have priority in claims to income and assets over preferred stockholders. Companies must pay the interest on their debt because in the event of a default, bondholders can force the defaulting corporation into bankruptcy, whereas dividends on preferred stock (and common stock) are declared only at the discretion of the board of directors. In the case of multiple classes of preferred stock, the different issues are prioritized in their claims to income and assets.

Cumulative Dividend

Most preferred stock issues carry a *cumulative feature*, which is a provision requiring a company to pay any preferred dividends that have not been paid in full before the company can pay dividends to its common stockholders. In other words, if the company fails to pay dividends to its cumulative preferred stockholders, it will have to pay all the missed dividends before the company can pay any dividends to its common shareholders. A company that fails to pay its dividends is said to be in *arrears*, which is defined as having outstanding preferred dividends that have not been paid on a cumulative preferred stock issue. Before the company can pay dividends to its common stockholders, it would have to pay the dividends in arrears to its cumulative preferred stockholders first. This cumulative feature protects the rights of the preferred stockholders. A preferred issue that does not have a cumulative feature is called a *noncumulative preferred stock*. Their dividends do not accumulate if they are not paid.

Convertible Feature

Some preferred stock issues have a *convertible feature* that allows holders to exchange their preferred stock for common shares. The conditions and terms of the conversion are set when the preferred stock is first issued. The terms include the conversion ratio, which is the number of common shares the preferred stockholder will get for each preferred share exchanged, and the conversion price of the common stock.

For example, Company XYZ issues a new convertible preferred stock that is sold at $100 per share and is convertible into five common shares of XYZ Company. The conversion ratio is therefore 5:1, and the conversion price is $20 per share for the common stock ($100/5 shares). If the market price of the common stock is $15, it is not advantageous for the preferred stockholder to convert because the value after conversion is $75 (5 shares at $15). However, if the price of the common stock rises to $20, there is parity. The preferred stockholder would not convert because the preferred stock pays a dividend. If the common stock rises above $20 per share, the preferred stockholder can share in the capital appreciation of the common stock by converting to common stock.

The decision to exercise the conversion option depends on three factors:

- The market price of the common stock. It must be greater than the conversion price for the holder to share in capital gains.
- The amount of the preferred dividend
- The amount of the common dividend

The conversion feature provides the investor with the possibility of sharing in the capital gains through the appreciation of the common stock, as well as the relative safety of receiving the preferred dividends before conversion. If the preferred dividend is much greater than the common dividend, holders would weigh this into the amount of the appreciation as to whether to hold the preferred or convert to common stock.

Call Provision

A preferred stock issue with a *call provision* entitles the issuing company to repurchase the stock at its option from outstanding preferred stockholders. The call price is generally more than the preferred stock's par value.

The call provision is advantageous to the issuing company and not to the holder of the preferred stock. When market rates of interest decline significantly below the dividend rate of the preferred issue, companies are more likely to exercise the call provision by retiring the issue and replacing it with a new preferred stock issue with a lower dividend rate. Citigroup redeemed for cash all the outstanding shares of its 8.4 cumulative preferred stock series K at a redemption price of $25 per share plus accrued dividends in October 2001. In January 2003, Citigroup called in its adjustable-rate cumulative preferred stock series Q and series R for a cash price of $25 per share plus accrued dividends.

When a preferred issue is called, the savings to the issuing company represent a loss of income to the preferred stockholders. Thus not only do preferred stockholders suffer a loss of income when their high-dividend-rate preferred stock issues are called in, but the call provision also acts as a ceiling limit on the price appreciation of the preferred stock. When interest rates decline, there is an upward push on the price of high-dividend-rate preferred stock issues, but the price of the preferred stock will not rise above the call price. For example, if a preferred stock issue has a call price of $55, potential buyers of the preferred stock would be unlikely to pay more than this amount when interest rates decline significantly. This is so because investors who pay more than this ceiling price would lose money if the issue is called.

To entice investors to buy preferred stock issues during periods of high interest rates, companies include a *call protection feature*. This prevents the company from calling the issue for a period of time, generally for five years, but this varies. After the call protection period, the issue is callable at the stated call price per share.

REFERENCES

Brown, Ken: "Tax-Cut Plans Spark a Rally-Can it Last?" *Wall Street Journal*, January 7, 2003, pp. C1, C3.

Browning E.S.: "Investors Seek Ray of Hope," *Wall Street Journal*, January 2, 2003, pp. R1, R3.

Davis, Bob, and Greg Ip: "Bush Stimulus Package Needs Many Assumptions to Pan Out," *Wall Street Journal*, January 8, 2003, pp. A1, A5.

CHAPTER 7

Bonds

KEY CONCEPTS

- Characteristics of bonds
- The risks of investing in bonds
- Yield types and the yield curve
- Valuation of bonds
- Why bonds fluctuate in price
- The purchase process of bonds

Stock prices are driven by earnings. When the earnings of a company increase over a period of time, the stock price of the company rises. The reactions of bond prices to economic events are mostly different from stock prices. Bond prices generally decrease when news on the economy is good and increase on bad economic news. An understanding of the characteristics of bonds explains this phenomenon.

CHARACTERISTICS OF BONDS

A *bond* is a negotiable debt security whereby an issuer borrows money and in return agrees to pay a fixed amount of interest over a specified period of time and pay back the principal amount when the bond matures. *Principal* is the face value (par value) of the bond, generally, $1,000 per bond.

A bond is similar to an IOU. Bonds also bear certain similarities to certificates of deposit (CDs) and savings accounts. Investors who deposit money in CDs (or savings accounts) are in effect lending money to banks. The banks pay investors interest on their deposits and then repay the principal when the CDs mature. Similarly, investors in bonds make loans to the issuer (corporation or government). This process makes them creditors, not owners, as in the case of common stock investors. In return, the issuer regularly pays a specified amount of interest until the bond's maturity date. Virtually all bonds have a maturity date, at which time the issuer returns to investors the face value of each bond ($1,000).

The major difference between savings accounts, CDs, and bonds is that investors can sell their bonds on the secondary market to others before the bonds mature. Savings accounts and CDs cannot be sold to other investors. Bear in mind that CDs in amounts over $100,000 can be sold before maturity, making them negotiable investments. Bonds are negotiable IOUs, unlike savings accounts and CDs less than $100,000, and the issuers of the bonds pay regular amounts of interest and repay to bondholders the principal at its maturity date. These regular payments of interest make bonds attractive investments to investors seeking fixed amounts of income and the repayment of principal at the maturity date.

Bonds have similar characteristics. A bond has a *face value*, also known as the *par value*, that is the amount of the bond that is repaid at maturity. The par value of bonds is mostly always $1,000, with a few exceptions. The par value is the amount on which interest is determined. For example, if a bond is bought at issuance for $1,000, the investor bought the bond at its par value. At the bond's maturity date, the investor receives $1,000 per bond held. When bonds are issued, a maturity date is determined by which bondholders will receive the par value of their bonds. The *maturity date* is the date on which the issuer of the bond retires the bond and pays the bondholder its par value. Maturity dates for bonds can range from 1 day to 100 years. Bonds with maturities of 1 year or less from the date of issuance are referred to as *short-term bonds* or *debt*. Bonds with maturities of 1 to 10 years are referred to as *intermediate bonds* or *intermediate notes*. *Long-term bonds* are issues with maturities of longer than 10 years, commonly as many as 30 years. Disney Corporation and a few other corporations have issued 100-year bonds, but this is not a common occurrence.

Bonds have two types of maturities. The most common is a *term bond*, in which the bonds of a given issue all mature on the same date. A *serial bond* has different maturity dates within the same issue.

The *coupon rate* of a bond determines the amount of annual interest paid by the bond, which generally is stated as a percent of the face value. If the coupon rate is 5 percent, the issuer of these bonds promises to pay $50 (5 percent × $1,000, the face value) in annual interest on each bond. Many bonds pay interest semiannually. If a bond has a 5 percent coupon paid semiannually, the bondholder receives $25 per bond every six months. Some bonds have adjustable or floating interest rates, which are tied to a particular index. The coupon payments fluctuate based on the underlying index.

A bond's price is affected by the relationship between the coupon rate and market rates of interest. Figure 7-1 illustrates the relationship between bond prices and market rates of interest. Suppose that you purchased a bond last year with a 5 percent coupon rate when market rates of interest were 5 percent, and you paid $1,000 per bond. This year, market rates of interest rise to 6 percent. What price will you receive if you sell this bond? Obviously, new investors would not pay $1,000 for a bond yielding 5 percent when they could buy new bonds with current coupon rates of 6 percent for $1,000. Because the new investor would expect to get at least 6 percent, this bond would sell for less than $1,000 (a discount) in order to be competitive with current bonds.

Conversely, if market rates of interest fall below the coupon rate, new investors are willing to pay more than $1,000 (a premium) for this bond. Thus bond prices are vulnerable to market rates of interest, as well as other factors discussed later in this chapter.

Bond Prices

Bonds do not necessarily trade at their par values. They may trade above or below their par values. Any bond trading at less than $1,000 is said to be trading at a *discount*. For example, Tenet Health Care bonds, with a coupon rate of 6¾ percent and maturing in the year 2012, traded at a discount, $953.75 per bond, on December 19, 2004.

FIGURE 7-1

Bond Prices and Interest Rates

Bonds trading at a *premium* sell for more than $1,000 (par value). IBM has 7½ percent bonds maturing in the year 2013 that traded at $1,183.75 per bond on December 19, 2004. This $183.75 premium per bond is an amount investors were willing to pay in order to receive a 7½ percent coupon rate for this bond.

Call Provision

A *call provision* allows a bond issuer to repurchase a bond at a fixed price prior to its maturity date. Many bonds have call provisions, which allows the issuers of the bonds to redeem them at a specified price before their scheduled maturity dates. After the specific date of redemption, the issuer no longer pays interest on the bonds, forcing holders to relinquish their bonds.

Issuers generally exercise call provisions when market rates of interest fall well below the coupon rate of the bonds. This action deprives bondholders of higher yields on their bonds, although it is advantageous to the issuers who call in bonds with high coupon rates and issue new bonds with lower coupon rates. This strategy lowers the issuer's total borrowing costs. For example, if a corporation issued 10 percent coupon bonds when interest rates were high and then rates dropped to 6 percent, it would be advantageous for the issuer to refund the old bonds with new bonds at a lower coupon rate. However, if the bond issue contains a *refunding provision*, the issuer is prohibited from using the proceeds from a new lower coupon bond issue to refund a higher-coupon bond issue. Thus a refunding provision prohibits a bond issuer from retiring the bonds of an issue with the funds raised from a new issue of bonds.

An investor in bonds should pay particular attention to a bond issue's call and refunding provisions. There are three types of call provisions:

1. A *noncallable* bond is a bond that the issuer cannot redeem before its maturity. Noncallable bonds offer investors the most protection but have many loopholes. The term *noncallable* implies that the bonds cannot be called before maturity. However, noncallable bonds sometimes have been called, such as in the case of a fire or act of God or when a healthy company stops making its interest payments on the bonds, and the trustees call the bonds in and the debt is paid off

early. Noncallable-for-life bonds are listed in the dealer's quote sheets as NCL.

2. A *freely callable* bond is a bond that the issuer can call at any time before its maturity. Freely callable bonds offer investors no protection because issuers can call them at anytime.

3. A *deferred callable* bond is a bond that the issuer cannot call until after a specified period. Deferred callable bonds offer some protection because the bonds cannot be called until after a specified length of time (e.g., 5, 10, or 15 years after issue). A bond that is noncallable until 2009 would be listed as NC09 on the dealer's quote sheet.

Because call provisions negatively affect investors, issuers compensate bondholders with a call price that is higher than the face value of the bond. The *call price* is the price an issuer pays to retire bonds called before maturity. The call price generally is equal to the face value plus a call premium. The *call premium*, specified in the call provision, is the amount an issuer adds to the bond's face value.

Callable bonds generally are issued with higher coupon rates than noncallable bonds of similar risk and maturity to compensate their holders for the risk of having to forfeit their higher yields if the bonds are called. You should check the call provision of a bond issue before buying.

Put Provision

A *put provision* allows bondholders to sell their bonds back to the issuer at a specified price (usually at par value) before their maturity dates. A put provision in a bond's *indenture*, the legal contract between the issuer of the bonds and the trustees of the bonds who represent the bondholders, is relatively unusual and is the opposite of a call provision in that the holder makes the decision whether to exercise the put option.

The put provision provides a floor price for the bonds in that issue in that bondholders know that they can resell their bonds to the issuer at par. This provision gives bondholders protection against rising interest rates and any deterioration in the credit quality of the issue. However, the price for these advantages is higher bond prices. Bonds with put provisions sell at higher prices than comparable bonds without put provisions.

Sinking-Fund Provision

A *sinking-fund provision* allows an issuer to set aside funds for the orderly retirement of the bonds in the issue. In one type of sinking-fund, an issuer randomly selects bonds to be retired and then calls them for redemption. After the bonds are called, they no longer earn interest. The other type of sinking-fund allows an issuer to make payments to a trustee, who invests the funds. Then the amount accumulated goes toward retiring the bonds at their maturity dates. Issuers also can repurchase their bonds in the bond market and retire them. This practice occurs more frequently when the bonds are trading at a discount. The difference between a call provision and a sinking-fund provision is that in a sinking-fund provision, the issuer does not have to call the bonds in at a premium price.

The significance of a sinking-fund provision is twofold:

- It provides some security to bondholders because the issuer in a sinking fund sets aside payments to repay bondholders. Depending on the circumstances, this action could lessen the price volatility of the issue.
- With a random sinking-fund plan, bondholders whose bonds are called have their principal repaid before maturity. Thus the sinking-fund provision acts as a ceiling price for the bond issue.

Secured or Unsecured Bonds

Bonds are issued on either a *secured* or *unsecured* basis. A *secured bond* is backed by the pledge of specific assets as collateral. For secured bonds, bondholders can seize the assets after proceeding to court in the case of a default. Examples of secured bonds are mortgage bonds (bonds secured by real estate), collateral trust bonds (bonds secured by assets owned by the issuer but held in trust by a third party), and equipment trust certificates (bonds secured by equipment). How safe should you feel holding a mortgage bond issued by a utility company that is backed by the collateral of a power plant? During a utility bankruptcy, do bondholders have the expertise to operate the power plant? Or can they sell off the parts on a piecemeal basis? Although the pledging of assets increases the safety of the principal of the bonds, bondholders should hope that the utility company does not default on its interest and principal payments. Generally, investors in bonds should be more concerned with the issuer's ability to service its debt (creditworthiness) rather than with security alone. In case of bankruptcy, pledged property may not be marketable, and it may involve litigation, which can be time-consuming and costly.

An *unsecured bond* is backed only by the promise of its issuer to abide by the commitments of the bond issue. The ability of the issuer to pay its fixed interest and repay principal at maturity is based on the issuer's creditworthiness. An issuer of bonds can have several different issues of bonds at any time. These bonds can have different features. When an issuer has many different bonds outstanding, *seniority* becomes important, particularly during bankruptcy, because *senior bonds* are the first to be repaid. *Junior bonds* are unsecured bonds, and in bankruptcy, bondholders' claims are secondary to secured bonds and senior bonds.

Debenture bonds are unsecured bonds issued by corporations. In a bankruptcy, debenture bondholders become general creditors of the company. Consequently, debenture holders assess the earnings power of the company as their primary security, which typically results in only well-established and creditworthy companies issuing debenture bonds. *Subordinated debentures* are bonds whose claims are paid only after the claims of secured bonds and other debenture bonds are honored in a bankruptcy. *Income bonds* are the most junior of all bonds, in that the issuer is only obligated to pay interest when earnings are sufficient to cover its interest payments.

Bond Indenture

A *bond indenture* is a legal document specifying the terms of the bond agreement. Bond securities have similar characteristics, which are summarized below.

- *Maturity date.* The date on which the bonds in the issue are paid off.
- *Interest payments.* The amount the issuer promises to pay in return for use of the money that is loaned.
- *Repayment of principal.* The amount the issuer promises to pay back at the maturity date.

All bond issues have a master loan agreement called a *bond indenture* that contains the information for the issue. The issuer is required to meet all the terms and conditions of the indenture agreement. A failure to meet any of the terms of the indenture, especially the timely payment of interest and repayment of principal, can result in the issuer being in default. The following terms of a bond issue are commonly included in the indenture:

- The amount of the bond issue
- The coupon rate
- The frequency of interest payments (annual or semiannual)
- The maturity date
- The call provision, if any (This provision allows the issuer of the bonds to call them in and repay them before their maturity dates.)
- The refunding provision if any (This provision does not allow the issuer to obtain the proceeds from a new debt issue to repay the bondholders of an existing issue before maturity.)
- The sinking-fund provision, if any (This provision offers bondholders greater security in that the issuer sets aside earnings to retire the issue.)
- The put option, if any (This provision allows the bondholders to sell the bonds back to the issuer at par value.)

THE RISKS OF INVESTING IN BONDS

Investing in bonds is not without risk. All bond investments carry risk, although the degree of risk varies with the type of debt and the issuer. The following list describes the potential risks facing bondholders:

- The interest on the bonds might not be paid (credit and default risk).
- The principal might not be repaid.
- The price of the bond might decline to less than the purchase price before maturity (interest-rate risk).
- Interest rates might fall, resulting in less interest income when the proceeds received (interest and principal) are reinvested (reinvestment-rate risk).
- Inflation might rise, causing an erosion of purchasing power of the interest and principal payments received (inflation risk).
- Bonds may be called before maturity.

You should be aware of how these different types of risk affect bond investments.

Interest-rate risk is the risk that interest rates will rise, thereby reducing the market prices of bonds. Interest-rate risk refers to changes in market rates of interest, which have a direct effect on bond prices. The prices of fixed-income securities change inversely with changes in interest rates. During periods of rising interest rates, investors holding fixed-income securities experience losses in the market prices of their bonds because new investors in these bonds want a competitive yield. Similarly, in periods of declining interest rates, the prices of existing fixed-income securities rise. The longer the time to maturity, the greater is the potential interest-rate risk. Investors can lessen interest-rate risk in a portfolio with different maturities by reducing maturities and staggering their bond investment maturities. As an investor, you minimize interest-rate risk if you hold onto your bonds until maturity.

Credit risk (default risk) is the risk that an issuer might be unable to pay the interest and principal payments at their due dates. Credit risk is a function of the creditworthiness of the issuer of debt. *Creditworthiness* refers to the ability of the issuer to make scheduled interest payments and repay the principal when bonds mature. Credit risk varies with bond issuers. U.S. Treasury issues carry virtually no risk of default because the full faith and credit of the U.S. government guarantees interest and principal payments. U.S. agency debt has a slightly increased risk of default depending on the financial strength of the issuer. Not all U.S. government agencies have the backing of the U.S. government. Bonds issued by state and local governments depend on the financial health of the particular issuer and its ability to raise revenue. For corporate issuers, credit risks are linked to the strength of the issuing companies' balance sheets, income statements, and earnings capacities. The price of Enron bonds, for example, plummeted when Enron declared bankruptcy. The restructured Enron Corporation settled with its creditors, paying around $0.14 on the dollar. For bondholders, this settlement paid $140 on a $1,000 face value of each bond.

Credit rating is a grading of the issuer's ability to service its interest and principal obligations when they become due. Independent ratings services evaluate the credit risk of municipal and corporate bonds. Table 7-1 provides a list of credit ratings ranging from the best credit quality for issuers with the strongest financial status to the lowest ratings for issuers in default. A financially strong company or municipality generally has low business and financial risk.

Moody's and Standard & Poor's (S&P) are two of the best-known ratings agencies, and their ratings are similar, though not identical. Ratings of AAA, AA, A, and BBB from S&P are considered to be investment-grade quality. Bonds with ratings lower than BBB are considered to be junk bonds and are speculative. Because these junk bonds have lower ratings, their issuers are more likely to default on their interest and principal repayments.

These ratings provide only a relative guide to assist potential bond investors because the financial status of an issuer can deteriorate over time and result in the bonds being downgraded to a lower rating. A downgrade usually causes a decline in the market price of the bond. The opposite effect occurs when a bond issue is upgraded. The same issuer with many different bond issues outstanding can have different ratings for each issue. You need not be duly alarmed if your bonds are downgraded from AAA to A, for example, because this grade still indicates good quality. However, if an issue is downgraded to lower than BBB, you should review whether to continue owning that bond.

You can minimize credit risks by buying good-quality bonds with ratings of A and above (by S&P), which have a reduced likelihood of default, and by diversifying your investments. In other

TABLE 7-1

Bond Ratings

Moody's	Standard & Poor's	Interpretation of Ratings
Aaa	AAA	Highest-quality obligations
Aa	AA	High-quality obligations
A	A	Bonds that have a strong capacity to repay principal and interest but that may be impaired in the future
Baa	BBB	Medium-grade quality
Ba	BB	Interest and principal that is neither
	B	highly protected nor poorly secured; lower ratings in this category have some speculative characteristics
B	CCC	Speculative bonds with great
Caa	CC	uncertainty
Ca	C	
C	DDD	In default
	DD	
	D	

words, rather than invest all your money in the bonds of one issuer, buy bonds of different issuers in different sectors of the bond market.

Call risk is the risk that a bond issue might be called before its maturity. Bonds with a call provision have call risk. Many corporate and municipal bond issues have call provisions, allowing issuers to repurchase their bonds at a specified (call) price before maturity, which is beneficial to the issuer and detrimental to the investor. Whenever interest rates decline to a few percentage points below the coupon rate of the bond, the issuer more than likely will call in the bonds. The issuer then can reissue new bonds at a lower coupon rate.

Call risk poses a potential loss of principal to the investor whenever bonds are purchased at a premium price that is greater than the call price. You can anticipate the call risk by estimating the level to which interest rates must fall before the issuer would find it worthwhile to call the issue. Callable bonds are not as advantageous as noncallable bonds. Consequently, a callable bond with the same level of risk and comparable features trades at a lower price (higher yield) than a noncallable bond.

To minimize call risk, you should examine the call provisions of the bond and choose bonds that are unlikely to be called. This advice is particularly important if you are contemplating the purchase of bonds that are trading above their par values (at a premium).

Purchasing-power risk is the risk that inflation will erode the returns from holding bonds. Purchasing-power risk is the unexpected change in inflation that diminishes an investor's real rate of return. Purchasing-power risk occurs during periods of inflation that affects bond prices. Because bond interest payments generally are fixed, the value of the payments is affected by inflation. When the rate of inflation rises, bond prices fall because the purchasing power of coupon payments received is reduced. To combat purchasing-power risk, you should invest in bonds whose rates of return exceed that of anticipated inflation. If you anticipate inflation in the future, invest in floating-rate bonds and Treasury inflation protection securities whose coupon rate adjusts up and down with market interest rates and inflation rates.

Reinvestment-rate risk is the risk that payments received from an investment might be reinvested at a lower rate of return. All coupon bonds are subject to reinvestment-rate risk. Interest payments received may be reinvested at a lower interest rate than the coupon rate of the bond, particularly if market rates of interest decline or have declined. Zero-coupon bonds, which make no periodic interest payments, have no reinvestment risk.

Liquidity risk is the risk of selling an investment at a price that is a significant concession from the market price. A bondholder who is selling bonds always runs the risk of having to make significant price concessions from the market price. This risk is prevalent for inactively traded bonds, where a large spread occurs between the bid price and the ask price. Thus, if liquidity is important, you should invest in actively traded bonds. Bear in mind that bonds are not liquid investments like money-market securities.

YIELD TYPES AND THE YIELD CURVE

A relationship exists between bond prices and yield, as illustrated in Fig. 7-2. When bond yields increase, prices of existing bonds decrease. Similarly, when bond yields decrease, prices of existing bonds increase. A bond's cash flows and an investor's required rate of return or interest rate are two components that are used to determine a bond's price. Four basic types of yields exist, which are explained is this section.

Coupon Yield

The *coupon yield* is the stated rate of return on a bond and is determined when the bond is issued. The coupon yield is the specified amount of interest that the issuer of a bond promises to pay to the bondholder each year. This annual amount of interest may be stated as a percentage of the par value of the bond or as a dollar amount. For instance, a bond with a par value of $1,000 that pays $40 in annual interest has a 4% coupon yield. The coupon yield is fixed throughout the lifetime of a bond issue unless it is a variable-interest coupon, which fluctuates throughout the lifetime of the bond.

FIGURE 7-2

Bond Prices and Yields

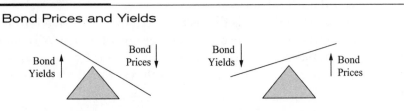

Current Yield

The *current yield* is the annual rate of return from a bond based on the income received in relation to the purchase price of the bond. The difference between the coupon yield and the current yield is that the divisor for the current yield is the purchase price of the bond rather than the face value of the bond. The following equation shows how the current yield is determined:

$$\text{Current Yield} = \frac{\text{coupon interest amount}}{\text{purchase price of the bond}}$$

For example, if a bond is purchased at par, $1,000, and the coupon is 5 percent (the interest paid is $50 per year), the current yield is 5 percent (the same as the coupon yield). However, most bonds trade above or below par. For a bond purchased at $1,100 with a 5 percent coupon, the current yield is 4.54% (50/1,100).

A relationship exists between bond prices, current yields, and coupon rates. Bonds trading at a discount to their par values have current yields that are higher than their coupon rates. Similarly, bonds trading at a premium to their par values have current yields that are lower than their coupon rates. Table 7-2 summarizes these relationships. For investors who are concerned with high current income, the current yield is a useful measure of return.

Yield-to-Maturity

The *yield-to-maturity* is the annual (discounted) rate of return earned on a bond held to maturity. The yield-to-maturity is the discount rate calculated by mathematically equaling the cash flows of the interest payments and principal received with the purchase price of the bond. This term is also referred to as the *internal rate of return* or

TABLE 7-2

The Relationship Between Bond Prices, Current Yield, and the Coupon Yield

Bond Price			
Discount	Current yield	>	coupon yield
Face	Current yield	=	coupon yield
Premium	Current yield	<	coupon yield

TABLE 7-3

Using Microsoft Excel to Compute a Bond's Yield to Maturity

The yield-to-maturity of a bond that was purchased for $770.36 that pays a coupon of 5 percent ($50 annually) with a maturity of 10 years can be solved as follows:

Click on "f*", which is on the top row of the toolbar in the Excel spreadsheet program. A list of functions pops up. Highlight "*financial*" in the box on the left and "rate" in the box on the right, and then click "OK." A box with five rows in it is displayed:

Nper		Enter the total number of payments.
PMT		Enter the interest payments.
PV		Enter the purchase price of the bond.
FV		Enter the face value of the bond.
Type		Enter 0 for payment received at the end of the period.

Nper	10
PMT	50
PV	−770.31
FV	1000
Type	0
Formula result = 0.085	

---

the *expected rate of return* of the bond and is the yield most investors in a bond are interested in. Table 7-3 illustrates how you can calculate the yield-to-maturity of a bond using Microsoft Excel software.

The yield-to-maturity is 8.5 percent. If you do not have Microsoft Excel software on your computer, you can use the following approximation formula to determine the yield-to-maturity (YTM) for the same example:

$$YTM = \frac{\text{coupon payment} + [(1{,}000 - \text{purchase price})/\text{periods to maturity}]}{(1{,}000 + \text{purchase price})/2}$$

$$YTM = \frac{50 + [(1{,}000 - 770.36)/10]}{(1{,}000 + 770.36)/2}$$

$$= 8.24 \text{ percent}$$

Using the approximation formula, the 8.24 percent yield understates the true yield-to-maturity that is calculated using a computer. The reason is that the approximation formula does not use the time value of money for compounding of the coupon payments.

The yield-to-maturity hinges on two assumptions:

- The bonds are held to maturity.
- The interest payments received are reinvested at the same rate as the yield-to-maturity.

If the bond is not held to maturity, you can calculate the internal rate of return of the bond by substituting the sale price of the bond for the maturity value and the period held to the sale date for the period to maturity.

The yield-to-maturity rate assumes that the bondholder reinvests the interest received at the same yield-to-maturity. If this does not occur, the holder's rate of return will differ from the quoted yield-to-maturity rate. For example, if the interest received is spent and not reinvested, the interest does not earn interest; the investor earns much less than the stated yield-to-maturity. Similarly, if the stated yield-to-maturity is 8 percent and the investor reinvests the interest at lesser (or greater) rates, the 8 percent is not achieved. In reality, matching the yield-to-maturity rate for the interest received is difficult because interest rates are changing constantly. The interest received is usually reinvested at different rates from the stated yield-to-maturity rate.

The yield-to-maturity is useful, however, in comparing and evaluating different bonds of varying quality with different coupon rates and prices. For example, by comparing the yield-to-maturity of an AAA-rated bond with a BBB-rated bond, you can see easily how much the increment in yield would be in choosing the lower-rated bond. You also can see the yield differential between bonds with different maturities.

The relationship between the coupon yield, current yield, yield-to-maturity, and bond price is summarized below:

Bond Price

Discount	Coupon yield	<	current yield	<	yield-to-maturity
Face	Coupon yield	=	current yield	=	yield-to-maturity
Premium	Coupon yield	>	current yield	>	yield-to-maturity

Yield-to-Call

The *yield-to-call* is the annual rate of return a bondholder receives to the date on which the bond is called. When a bond has a call feature, the bondholder can calculate the yield-to-call by substituting the call price for the maturity price in the equation discussed in the yield-to-maturity section. Both the yield-to-call and the yield-to-maturity should be determined, because if the bond is called, the yield-to-call is the yearly total return that the bondholder receives on the bond.

The Yield Curve

The yield curve shows the relationship between bond yields and the term to maturity of bonds with the same level of risk. Figure 7-3 shows the yield curve for U.S. Treasury securities as of June 21, 2000, June 19, 2003, and December 31, 2004. Yields for the 3-month, 6-month, 2-year, 5-year, 10-year, and 30-year Treasury securities are plotted.

	June 21, 2000	June 19, 2003	December 31, 2004
3-month Treasury bill	5.63%	0.82%	2.28%
6-month Treasury bill	5.92%	0.83%	2.56%
2-year Treasury Note	6.43%	1.17%	3.04%
5-year Treasury Note	6.20%	2.28%	3.58%
10-year Treasury Note	6.02%	3.37%	4.21%
30-year Treasury Bond	5.89%	4.42%	5.00%

FIGURE 7-3

Treasury Yield Curve

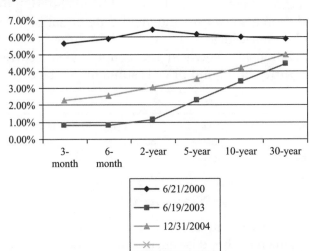

An examination of the yield curve on any particular day gives you a snapshot of the different yields of various maturities for a bond security. Figure 7-3 shows the yield curve for Treasuries, but you can create a yield curve for other bond types, such as municipal bonds, corporate bonds, and agency bonds.

Note the shape of the yield curve for June 21, 2000. It has an upward slope from 3 months to 2 years and then a declining curve for longer maturities through 30 years. This inverted curve is generally atypical. An inverted yield curve indicates that by extending maturities, investors are taking greater risks for smaller returns. Yield curves typically assume four general shapes: rising, flat, falling, and humped, such as the one for June 21, 2000. The most common type is the rising yield curve, as depicted on June 19, 2003. You might expect an upward-sloping curve because the longer the maturity, the greater is the bondholder's exposure to risk. For this reason, bond issuers tend to pay more to compensate investors for the risk involved with longer maturities. With interest rates at a 45-year low, this steeply positive yield curve points to higher future rates. The December 31, 2004, yield curve shows how yields have increased 18 months later.

On a few occasions, the yield curve has had a downward slope where short-term yields have exceeded long-term yields. In other words, yields decline as maturities increase. This situation happened in 1979, 1981, and 1982.

The shape of the yield curve changes daily with the changes in yield because of fluctuations in market rates of interest. The yield curve can assist you in choosing which maturities of bonds to buy. Table 7-4 illustrates how to use the Internet to obtain information to graph a yield curve.

TABLE 7-4

How to Obtain Bond Yields to Construct a Yield Curve

Using the Internet, obtain yields for the different Treasury securities to construct a yield curve. Based on the shape of the yield curve, decide whether you would invest in long- or short-term maturity bonds. You can obtain information from www.tradebonds.com. On its home page is a ticker tape that posts the daily prices and yields of Treasury securities.

Keep in mind the following generalities about yield curves:

- Most of the time the yield curve is upward-sloping, where yields on long-term securities are greater than the yields of short-term securities.
- Changes in the yield curve generally take the form of shifts up and down over time. When short-term yields are rising, generally long-term yields also rise. Similarly, when short-term yields are falling, long-term yields also fall.
- During a recession, short-term yields fall faster than long-term yields; during a period of economic expansion, short-term yields rise faster than long-term yields.

VALUATION OF BONDS

Bond prices fluctuate because of the relationship between coupon rates, market rates of interest (required rate of return), the bond's creditworthiness, and the length of time to maturity. After bonds are issued, they rarely trade at their par values ($1,000) in the secondary markets because interest rates are always changing. Certain bonds sell at premium prices and others sell at discounted prices.

The market price of a bond is determined using the bond's coupon payments, the principal repayment, and the investor's required rate of return, as illustrated in Fig. 7-4. Using the time value of money, this stream of future interest payments and principal repayment is discounted at the investor's required rate of return or the market rate of interest to its present value in today's dollars.

FIGURE 7-4

Market Price of a Bond

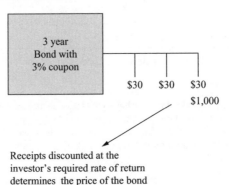

3 year
Bond with
3% coupon

$30 $30 $30
                 $1,000

Receipts discounted at the
investor's required rate of return
determines the price of the bond

Most corporate bonds pay interest semiannually, which means that the coupon rate is halved and the length of time to maturity is multiplied by 2 to convert to six-month periods. Using these modifications, the price of a bond is determined easily using Microsoft Excel.

What is the price of a bond that has a 10 percent coupon rate, pays interest semiannually, and matures in three years time? The investor's required rate of return for this bond is 6 percent.

A 10 percent coupon payable semiannually results in a coupon payment of $50 per six-month period, and the 6 percent annual discount rate is halved to 3 percent for six semiannual periods until maturity.

Using Excel to find the price of a bond, click on "PV" in the right-hand box, and enter the data as illustrated:

Rate	0.03
Nper	6
PMT	50
FV	1000
Type	0

Formula result = 1108.34

The price of the bond is linked to its coupon payment, market rates of interest or investor's required rate of return, risk of the bond, and the length of time to maturity. If you compare the price of a U.S. Treasury note with the same coupon rate and maturity as that of a corporate bond, you notice that they have different prices. The Treasury note trades at a higher price than the corporate bond because a greater risk of default exists with the corporate bond; the price therefore is calculated with a higher discount rate (or yield-to-maturity). You then require a greater coupon yield (and required rate of return) on the corporate bond for assuming a greater risk of default. This description confirms why an AAA-rated corporate bond trades at a higher price than a BBB-rated corporate bond if the coupon and maturity are the same. The difference in yield between the AAA- and BBB-rated bonds is referred to as the *excess yield*, which issuers must pay for the extra grade of credit risk. Bond prices fluctuate depending on investors' assessments of the bonds' risk. The relationships can be summarized this way: The greater the risk of a bond, the greater is its yield, and the lower is its market price.

WHY BONDS FLUCTUATE IN PRICE

Several factors account directly for fluctuations in bond prices. These factors include the relationships between bond prices, coupon rates, market yields, maturities (Malkiel, pp. 197–218), and risk assessment. The following axioms illustrate these relationships:

- *The coupon rate relative to market rates of interest.* When market rates of interest rise and exceed the coupon rate of a bond, the price of the bond will decline in order to relate the current yield to the market rate of interest. When interest rates fall, the price of the bond will rise. The smaller the coupon rate of the bond, the greater will be the fluctuations in price.
- *The length of time to maturity.* The longer the maturity, the more volatile will be the price fluctuations.
- *For a given change in a bond's yield.* The longer the maturity of the bond, the greater will be the magnitude of change in the bond's price.
- *For a given change in a bond's yield.* The size of the change in the bond's price increases at a diminishing rate the longer the maturity of the bond.
- *For a given change in the bond's yield.* The magnitude of the bond's price is inversely related to the bond's yield.
- *For a given change in a bond's yield.* The magnitude of the price increase caused by a decrease in yield is greater than the price decrease caused by an increase in yield.
- *Changes in risk assessment by the market.* The lesser the quality of the bond, the lower is the price; the greater the quality of the bond, the higher is the price. The greater the risk of the bond, the more volatile will be the bond's price fluctuations.

Interest Rates and Bond Prices

The first reason that bond prices fluctuate has to do with the inverse relationship between bond prices and market rates of interest. When market rates of interest rise, the prices of existing bonds fall; when interest rates fall, prices of existing bonds rise. The extent of this change in bond prices is determined by the coupon rates of the bonds. This relationship between interest rates and the coupon rates of bonds determines whether bonds trade at a discount or at a premium price, as shown below:

- *Discount.* Bonds trade at a discount when their coupon rates are lower than market rates of interest.
- *Discount.* When the yield-to-maturity of the bond (ask yield or bid yield) is greater than the coupon rate, the bond generally trades at a discount.
- *Premium.* Bonds trade at a premium when their coupon rates are higher than market rates of interest.
- *Premium.* A bond generally trades at a premium when its yield-to-maturity is lower than its coupon rate.

Interest Rates and Maturity

A second reason for the fluctuations in bond prices is the relationship between interest rates and the length of time to maturity. Some bonds are more sensitive to changes in interest rates than other bonds because of their different maturities. For example, two bonds with the same coupon rate but different maturities react differently to changes in interest rates. Not only is the longer-maturity bond more volatile than the shorter-maturity bond, but the magnitude of price changes is also greater for bonds with longer maturities. Figure 7-5 summarizes some of the major factors that affect bond prices.

THE PURCHASE PROCESS OF BONDS

Price Quotes

Bonds are quoted in hundreds but trade in denominations of thousands. A bond price quote of $86¾ indicates that the bond is trading not at $86.75 but rather at $867.50 per bond.

FIGURE 7-5

Factors that Affect the Price of a Bond

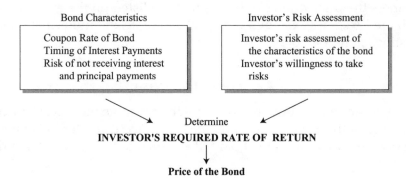

The *bid price* is the highest price a buyer will pay for a bond. For example, when someone sells a bond that is quoted at a bid of 94½, the highest amount buyers will offer is $945.00 per bond. The *ask price* is the lowest price offered by a seller of a bond. For example, an investor buying a bond with a bid of $94½ and an ask price of $94⅝ would pay $946.25 per bond (the lowest price that a seller of this bond will accept). The *spread* is the difference between the bid and ask prices of the bond, part of which is a commission paid to the broker or dealer. A large spread indicates that the bond is inactively traded.

Bonds are purchased the same way stocks are. Although most bonds are bought and sold through brokerage firms, you can purchase some bonds through banks or directly from their issuers. The different types of purchase orders (market and limit orders) used for stocks also apply to the purchase of bonds. The major difference between buying stocks and buying bonds is the lack of pricing transparency for bonds. Current price quotes indicating the bid and ask prices for bonds during the trading day are not quoted on the Internet. When you want to buy the stock of a company, you call your broker or search the Web for the current price. You can obtain the current bid and ask prices easily for a stock. Finding the current bid and ask prices for a bond can be difficult because the bond market is a dealer market, where the same bonds could be offered at different prices. For example, one dealer offered a General Motors bond maturing in 2028 at $867.50, and another dealer asked $900.00 for the same bond (Norris, p. C1). Individual investors are unlikely to receive not only the best prices but also the bid and ask prices of bonds in order to ascertain their spreads.

Although some corporate bonds are listed on the New York and American stock exchanges, the vast majority of bonds are traded in the over-the-counter markets. You can easily find in the daily newspapers the price quotes of bonds that are listed on the exchanges. Figure 7-6 shows examples of typical corporate and municipal bond listings in newspapers.

Accrued Interest

An investor who is buying a bond might pay more than its ask price because of the *accrued interest* on the bond. Accrued interest is interest that is owed but not yet paid. It is added to the price of a bond.

FIGURE 7-6

Corporate and Municipal Bond Quotation

Corporate Bonds

Name	Coupon	Maturity	Last Price	Last Yield	Est. Spread
General Motors	8.375	July 15, 2033	101.452	8.242	346

After the name of the bond, General Motors, is the coupon yield of 8.375 percent. Bondholders receive $83.75 in interest each year per bond held until maturity.	This bond matures on July 15, 2033.	The last price indicates that this bond traded at $1014.52 at the close of the preceding day Jan. 11, 2005	The last yield of 8.242% is the percentage yield a bondholder would receive if this bond was bought and held to maturity	The estimated spread is 346 basis points, or 3.46 percent. The spread is the difference between the bid and ask price

Municipal Bonds

ISSUE	COUPON	MAT	PRICE	BID YIELD
NYC gen oblig bond	5.00	11-01-34	101.778	4.77

The name of the issuer is New York City New York general obligation bonds.	These bonds pay 5.00 percent of par ($1000) which is $50.00 per bond per year.	The maturity date is November 1, 2034.	The price of the bond was $1017.78. as of the preceding day.	The bid yield is the percentage yield if the bond was purchased at the bid price and held to maturity.

Although a bond earns interest daily, the issuer of the bonds pays out the interest once or twice a year. Therefore, if a bond is purchased between the dates on which the interest is paid, the buyer owes the seller the accrued interest for the number of days the seller owned the bond. The amount of accrued interest is added to the purchase price of the bond. The accrued interest is stated separately on the confirmation statement the brokerage firm sends when the bonds are bought and sold. The following example illustrates how accrued interest is calculated.

Jason bought a bond with a coupon of 6 percent payable annually on June 30. He purchased the bond on December 31 of the preceding year. How much must he pay the seller in accrued interest?

Jason owes the seller for the interest accrued from July 1 to December 31 (six months of the previous year):

$$\text{Accrued interest} = \text{length of time the seller owned the bond}$$
$$\text{before interest is paid} \times \text{coupon}$$
$$= 6/12 \times \$60$$
$$= \$30$$

Bonds that are in default and no longer paying interest are said to trade *flat*. Flat bonds do not trade with accrued interest and in the bond quotes in the financial pages of the newspapers have an *f* next to the bond signifying that it is trading flat.

REFERENCES

Faerber, Esmé: *Fundamentals of the Bond Market*. New York: McGraw-Hill, 2001.

Malkiel, Burton C.: "Expectations, Bond Prices, and the Term Structure of Interest Rates," *Quarterly Journal of Economics*, May 1962, pp. 197–218.

Norris, Floyd.: "Putting Sticker Prices on Corporate Bonds," *New York Times*, June 27, 2003, p. C1.

CHAPTER 8

Treasury, Government, Mortgage-Backed Securities, Corporate, and Municipal Bonds

KEY CONCEPTS

- Treasury securities
- Government agency and pass-through securities
- Corporate bonds
- Municipal bonds

Although all bonds have similar features such as a coupon rate, a face value, and a maturity date, the types of bonds in the market have many differences between them. Treasury notes and bonds are free of credit and default risk; in addition, some Treasury notes and bonds offer protection from inflation; municipal bonds provide interest income that is exempt from federal taxes; mortgage bonds provide regular payments of interest and principal; and junk bonds have the capability of returning double-digit returns likes stocks. Not only do these types of bonds differ, but you also must investigate the varying characteristics of each bond issue before purchasing them.

In deciding which types of bonds to buy, you must be aware of your reasons for investing in them. Bonds generally are safer than stocks and provide regular payments of income. Bonds, however, do not double their value overnight like some Internet and biotechnology stocks did in the late 1990s. Bonds provide protection for your portfolio if the stock market declines. You buy bonds, therefore, to provide insurance against large losses in the value of your portfolio and to provide a fixed stream of income.

TABLE 8-1

Characteristics of the Different Types of Bonds

Treasury securities
        Safest bond type
        Interest exempt from state taxes
        Easiest to buy directly without commissions
        Active secondary market with the lowest spreads
Treasury inflation-indexed securities
        Return rises with inflation
        Safety of interest and principal
        If no inflation occurs, lower returns than with other bond types
Municipal bonds
        Interest exempt from federal income taxes
        Varying credit quality depending on issuer
        Higher transaction costs when buying and selling
Federal agency securities
        Higher yields than Treasury securities
        Potential government backing in the event of default
Mortgage-backed bonds
        Higher yields than Treasury securities
        Income payments possibly erratic depending on market rates of interest
Corporate bonds
        Higher yields than agency and Treasury securities
        Greater risk of default on interest and principal
Corporate junk bonds
        High-yield, high-risk bonds
        Low-rated bonds with regard to ability to service interest payments
        and repay principal

Which bonds should you buy? Municipal bonds offer tax advantages for taxpayers in high marginal tax brackets, and Treasury bonds are the safest in terms of credit and default risk. Although corporate bonds provide higher yields, their credit quality varies. Corporate junk bonds provide the highest yields but also involve greater risk. Table 8-1 outlines some reasons for buying different types of bonds.

TREASURY SECURITIES

The U.S. government issues Treasury bills, notes, bonds, inflation-protected securities, and savings bonds.

Treasury Notes and Bonds

Treasury notes and *bonds* are coupon securities issued by the Department of Treasury and backed by the U.S. government. Treasury notes are intermediate-term (1 to 10 years) coupon debt, and Treasury bonds are long-term (more than 10 years) coupon debt issued by the U.S. Treasury. Because Treasury notes and bonds are coupon securities, they differ from Treasury bills. Coupon securities pay interest every six months, whereas Treasury bills are discount securities on which periodic interest payments are not made.

U.S. Treasury notes are issued with original maturities ranging from two, three, and five years, and U.S. Treasury bonds have maturities of ten years or more. Treasury notes and bonds are issued in denominations of $1,000 to $1 million. These issues are the safest intermediate- and long-term bonds available. Consequently, yields on these issues are lower than those of comparable-maturity agency and corporate bonds.

Treasury notes and bonds issued since 1985 are not callable, and interest payments are made semiannually (beginning six months from the date of issue). Interest payments from Treasury securities are exempt from state income taxes.

Buying and Selling Treasury Notes and Bonds

You can purchase new issues at auction or existing Treasury securities trading in the secondary market.

New Issues

You can purchase new issues of Treasury notes and bonds at auction or through brokerage firms and commercial banks. Buying through banks and brokerage firms involves paying commissions, which vary depending on the face value of the securities purchased and the markup charged for the purchase. To avoid having to pay commissions, you can purchase new issues through auctions directly from Federal Reserve banks.

Auctions of new issues take place on a regular schedule. You also can call the Federal Reserve bank and ask to be added to the mailing list for new note and bond issues. A 24-hour Reserve bank information number lists forthcoming auctions. Financial newspapers print the schedules of forthcoming auctions. The U.S. Treasury Department has made Treasury notes and bonds available to investors who want to purchase them online through the Treasury Direct program. You can find information, updates on auctions, and news on all Treasury

TABLE 8-2

A Sample 5-Year Treasury Note Auction
Result

Applications	$35,386,040,000
Accepted bids	$14,826,895,000
Date of issue	01-15-2005
Maturity date	01-15-2010
Accepted noncompetitively	$5,895,040,000
Auction price (rate)	99.52073 (3.731%)
Interest rate	3.625%
Cusip number	912828DG2

Note: The auction results for Treasury notes auctioned January 12, 2005 (which mature January 15, 2010) show the dollar amount of applications, accepted noncompetitive bids, and the average accepted auction price ($995.207 per note) with a yield of 3.731percent if held to maturity. The coupon rate is 3.625 percent. The cusip number is a unique identification number assigned to each bill, note, and bond issue.

Source: Bureau of Public Debt.

securities on this Web site: www.publicdebt.treas.gov. Table 8-2 shows an example of an auction result.

When buying directly, you first must open an account with the Federal Reserve. By completing a new account request form (see Fig. 5-1), you establish a Treasury Direct account, where Treasury securities are held in book form. Treasury certificates are no longer issued. After submitting this form to the Federal Reserve bank or branch in your area, you receive confirmation of your account with a unique account number pertaining to the information in the account. This account number is used for your purchases of Treasury securities (bills, notes, bonds, or indexed-inflation securities) and is maintained for free up to $100,000. Security amounts over this amount incur an annual $25 fee.

You are now ready to fill out a tender form to buy Treasury notes or bonds at auction from the Federal Reserve bank. See Fig. 5-2 for a copy of the Treasury note and bond tender form. This form is the same form used for Treasury bills and the new inflation-indexed Treasury securities.

Fill in the personal information on the tender form. The nine-digit *routing number* identifies your financial institution. This number appears in front of your account number in the lower corner of a check from your bank.

You have a choice on the form to buy Treasuries by using either a competitive or a noncompetitive bid. More sophisticated investors use a competitive bid, where a yield bid to two decimal places (e.g., 4.06 percent) is submitted for the issue. You can get a clue about the probable range of the yield to submit by watching the preauction trading of that issue. Dealers begin trading these securities a few days before the auction on a "when issued" basis, and the when issued yield is often reported in the financial section of the *Wall Street Journal* and *New York Times*.

Investors submit sealed, written bids, and the Treasury accepts bids with the lower yields than the stop-out yield until the supply is sold. All the winning bidders receive a single price. If you bid too aggressively, you run the risk of not having your bid accepted in the auction.

If you do not want to run the risk of having your bid rejected, or if you do not know what to bid, you can submit a noncompetitive bid. You then can buy Treasury notes and bonds at the stop-out yield for as much as $5 million.

You can submit bids on tender forms by mail or in person before the close of an auction. Competitive bids must be received by the time designated in the offering circular. Noncompetitive bids that are mailed must be postmarked no later than midnight the day before the auction and received on or before the issue date of the securities.

Payment must accompany the tender form, and the amount of the check should be for the face value of the securities. If the auction price is lower than the face value, you receive a check for the difference. If the auction price of the note or bond is higher than its face value, you receive an amount due notice for the difference.

After your bid is accepted, you receive a confirmation receipt from the Federal Reserve. The Treasury pays interest on notes and bonds every six months.

About 45 days before maturity of the notes or bonds, a reinvestment option notification is mailed to all note and bondholders giving them the option to reinvest their principal in a new issue. If you decline the reinvestment option, the redemption payment is made directly into your bank account on the maturity date.

If you decide to sell your Treasury notes or bonds before maturity, you can use the secondary market composed of dealers. Before selling, you must fill out a transfer request form (PD 5179) if you bought the notes or bonds directly from the Federal Reserve. The account is then transferred from the Treasury Direct book-entry system to the commercial book-entry system. Then you can sell the Treasury notes or bonds. The commercial book-entry system records Treasuries bought through financial institutions and government security dealers. You must sell Treasuries in the secondary market through a bank or brokerage firm

Existing Issues

Investors buy (and sell) existing issues through banks or brokerage firms. Many issues are available with a wide range of maturities trading at discounts or premiums depending on their coupon rates and length of time to maturity. As with corporate bonds, Treasury notes and bonds are quoted in the financial sections of newspapers under the "Treasury Issues" heading. Treasury note and bond prices are quoted as a percentage of par basis, and the fractions of the percentage are of a point. For example, a quoted price of $101:16 is $101, or $1015.00.

The secondary market for Treasuries is an over-the-counter market, where dealers quote bid and asked prices. The spreads on Treasuries are the smallest (rarely more than a few cents) of all the fixed-income securities because of the liquidity of many of the issues. The market is active, with huge quantities of Treasuries traded.

The Risks of Treasury Notes and Bonds

Because Treasuries are a direct obligation of the federal government, they have no credit risk and no default risk. Treasuries issued after 1985 are free from event risk and call risk, but they are subject to interest rate risk and inflation risk. Avoid longer-term maturities unless you are confident that both inflation and market rates of interest are headed downward.

Treasury Inflation-Protection Securities (TIPS)

Treasury inflation-protection securities (TIPS) are securities issued by the Treasury whose interest and principal payments are adjusted for changes in inflation. Treasury inflation-indexed bonds offer protection against rising inflation. Because inflation has been low historically in the early years of this decade, these bonds have not generated much enthusiasm.

TIPS are issued with a fixed coupon rate plus an amount that is indexed for inflation. The coupon rate is set at auction and remains fixed throughout the term of the security. The principal amount of the security is adjusted for inflation, but this inflation-adjusted premium is paid only at maturity. For example, if you purchase a bond with a 3½ percent coupon rate at $1,000 and inflation averages 2 percent for the year, the price of the bond is adjusted for this inflation to $1,020. The 3½ percent coupon rate is paid on the adjusted value of the bond (3½ percent × $1,020). The opposite is true if inflation falls. The price of the bond is adjusted downward, and the interest payments are calculated against the lower bond price. Semiannual interest payments are based on the inflation-adjusted principal amount at the time the interest is paid.

Yields on Treasury inflation-indexed securities generally are lower than those on regular bonds during periods of low inflation, and you should compare yields and your expectations for inflation before investing. For example, if a 10-year Treasury bond is yielding 4.875 percent and a 10-year inflation-indexed bond is yielding 4.25 percent, in order to exceed the regular Treasury bond, inflation will have to increase by more than 0.625 percent (4.875 percent − 4.25 percent) over the next 10 years.

The auction process uses the single-priced, or Dutch, auction method for these securities. The securities are eligible for stripping into principal and interest components in the Treasury's Separate Trading of Registered Interest and Principal of Securities (STRIPS) program (discussed in Chapter 9).

At maturity, TIPS are redeemed at the greater of their inflation-adjusted principal or par value.

The downside to an inflation-indexed Treasury is that its holders must pay federal income taxes on the interest plus the inflation adjustment, even though the inflation adjustment is paid out only when the bond matures. In other words, a negative cash flow takes place on this "phantom" adjustment income, which makes this type of investment more suitable for a tax-deferred account. Like all other types of Treasury securities, interest income is exempt from state and local taxes. You purchase these issues in the same way as you purchase regular Treasury notes and bonds. Because of the newness of this type of security, you do not have many issues to choose from on the secondary markets.

This type of security, like all other fixed income securities, is subject to interest rate risk. Yields on these securities are much lower than on regular Treasury issues, and if inflation remains low, any changes in interest rates will make the prices of these securities more volatile, especially for issues that have longer periods until maturity.

However, this type of security protects against the ravages of inflation. But the opposite is true: If inflation remains low, holders of TIPS receive lower returns than they would receive with regular Treasury notes and bonds that have the same maturities.

GOVERNMENT AGENCY AND PASS-THROUGH SECURITIES

Government agency bonds are debt securities issued by agencies of the government. *Government pass-through securities* are debt securities issued by government agencies that pass through to investors the payments received from borrowers. Certain government agencies and federally sponsored corporations issue debt. Agency bonds are issued by major federally sponsored agencies, such as the Federal Home Loan Mortgage Corporation (FHLMC), the Federal National Mortgage Association (FNMA), the Federal Home Loan Bank (FHLB) System, Farm Credit Banks, and the Student Loan Marketing Association (SLMA). The first three of these agencies (FHLMC, FNMA, and FHLB) provide funds to the mortgage and housing sectors of the economy. The Farm Credit Banks provide funds for the agricultural sector, and SLMA ("Sallie Mae") provides funds for higher education. Agencies of the government issue traditional debt securities (agency bonds), in addition to mortgage pass-through securities. *Government mortgage-backed securities* (pass-throughs) are debt issues whose interest and principal payments made by borrowers are passed through to investors after a fee is deducted. Government agency bonds and pass-through securities appeal to investors who are interested in investing in high-quality bonds with higher yields than Treasury securities.

Government Agency Securities

Many different government agencies issue securities, and the characteristics of these securities can vary considerably. However, they do have many common features:

- New issues of agency securities are sold through a syndicate of dealers. These dealers also buy and sell these securities in the secondary markets.
- Large agency issues are marketable and fairly liquid.
- Agency securities are exempt from registration with the Securities and Exchange Commission (SEC).

- Some agency issues have tax advantages in that interest income is exempt from state and local taxes.
- Agency securities have either *de facto* or *de jure* (actual or by right) backing from the federal government, making them safer than corporate bonds.

Agency securities tend to offer greater yields than Treasuries with comparable maturities but lower than the yields of most Aa- or Aaa-rated corporate bonds. The different agency securities with their wide range of offerings and maturities appeal to investors who like the slightly higher yields than those offered by Treasuries without sacrificing much credit risk. The federal government does not guarantee agency bonds, but it is not likely to allow any of its agencies to default on their interest and principal obligations.

Mortgage-Backed or Pass-Through Securities

Mortgage pass-through securities are much more complex than regular fixed-income securities. Mortgage pass-through securities are created from mortgage transactions. Most home purchases are financed with borrowed funds from financial institutions, such as banks and mortgage companies that issue mortgages. Borrowers promise to repay, in monthly payments throughout the life of the mortgage loans, the amounts that are loaned. However, most banks and mortgage companies do not hold these mortgages to maturity. Instead, they sell the mortgages to other (government and private) institutions that package the mortgages into pass-through securities and then sell them to investors. Homeowners continue to make their same monthly payments to the newly assigned financial institutions.

These financial institutions pool their mortgages and sell shares in those pools to investors. *Mortgage pools* are collections of similar mortgages. Mortgage pass-through securities are shares in pools or collections of similar mortgages. The investor then receives monthly interest and principal repayments (minus a modest fee, normally about one-half of 1 percent), hence the term *pass-through securities*. The size of mortgage pools varies, with some consisting of several thousand mortgages and others having just a few mortgages. These pools normally are issued with a minimum of at least $1 million.

You can better understand pass-through securities by examining how mortgages work. Suppose that a $1 million mortgage pool consists of a single conventional 30-year mortgage of $1 million at 9 percent. The monthly payment the homeowner makes to the mortgage lender is $8,046.23. This payment consists of interest and a portion that goes toward the reduction of the principal balance. Table 8-3 shows the amortization schedule for the first 12 months of this mortgage. In the first payment, the amount of interest is $7,500 ($1 million × 9 percent/12), and $546.23 ($8046.23 − $7,500) is applied to the principal balance, reducing it from $1 million to $999,453.77. The interest rate is 9 percent per year, and the interest rate per month is 9 percent/12, or 0.0075. You calculate the interest expense by multiplying the monthly rate by the mortgage balance. The interest for the first payment, therefore, is $7,500 (0.0075 multiplied by $1 million).

The monthly payments are designed to reduce the mortgage balance to zero at the end of the mortgage term (30 years, or 360 payments). As you can see from the first 12 payments, the amount of interest expense declines each month, which means that more of the monthly payment is applied to reducing the outstanding loan (mortgage) balance. In other words, the fixed amount of the payment is the same, but the proportionate amount of interest received declines and the proportionate amount of the principal repayment increases.

TABLE 8-3

Amortization Schedule: $1 Million Mortgage (30-Years, 9 Percent)

Month/Year	Payment	Interest (9.00%)	Principal	Loan Balance
—	—	—	—	$1 million
1/2005	8046.23	7500.00	546.23	999,453.77
2/2005	8046.23	7495.90	550.32	998,903.45
3/2005	8046.23	7491.78	554.45	998,349.00
4/2005	8046.23	7487.62	558.61	997,790.39
5/2005	8046.23	7483.43	562.80	997,227.59
6/2005	8046.23	7479.21	567.02	996,660.57
7/2005	8046.23	7474.95	571.27	996,089.30
8/2005	8046.23	7470.67	575.56	995,513.75
9/2005	8046.23	7466.35	579.87	994,933.87
10/2005	8046.23	7462.00	584.22	994,349.65
11/2005	8046.23	7457.62	588.60	993,761.05
12/2005	8046.23	7453.21	593.02	993,168.03

In this case, an investor in this pass-through security receives his or her share of the pass-through interest and principal minus servicing fees and any other charges by the servicing institution. You cannot always count on the monthly amount being the same because mortgage borrowers have the option to prepay their mortgages. The payment might be the entire amount of the mortgage or only a part of it. For example, if the mortgage borrower in this example prepays an additional $1,000 per month, the mortgage pass-through security investor receives a proportionate share of this additional payment, which is, in essence, a return of the pass-through investor's principal or investment capital.

For many reasons, mortgage borrowers prepay the entire amount of their mortgages before their maturity dates. Homeowners sell their homes or refinance their mortgages when interest rates decrease, or in the case of fire and other casualties in which the property is destroyed, insurance proceeds are used to pay off the mortgage.

Consequently, in a mortgage pool, if numerous mortgages are prepaid, the amounts of the cash flows to investors are not regular (they may fluctuate from month to month), and neither is there certainty about the length of time to maturity of the pool. Investors cannot be certain about the timing of monthly cash flows. Suppose that mortgage payments are due on the first day of the month. If borrowers are late in sending in their payments and the processing of those payments is delayed, payments to investors are also delayed. The length of the delay also varies according to the type of pass-through security. In addition to the level-payment conventional mortgage described (see Table 8-3), which is the most common type of pass-through security, other types of mortgages (e.g., adjustable-rate mortgages and graduated-payment mortgages) are available to be used for pass-through securities.

Various types of mortgage pass-through securities are available, each with its own nuance. Despite these differences, investors in all mortgage pass-through securities are concerned with the following criteria:

- The safety of the issue
- The liquidity and marketability of the issue
- The overall rate of return of the issue
- The expected maturity of the issue

Government National Mortgage Association

The majority of pass-through securities are issued by three government agencies, the Government National Mortgage Association, the Federal National Mortgage Association, and the Federal Home Loan Mortgage Corporation. A marked growth also has taken place in the number of mortgage pass-through securities issued by private issuers since the mid-1980s.

The Government National Mortgage Association, or "Ginnie Mae," is a wholly owned agency of the Department of Housing and Urban Development (HUD). Hence the timely interest and principal payments of Ginnie Mae pass-through securities are guaranteed by the full faith and credit of the U.S. government. They have zero credit risk, therefore, which is appealing to investors.

The agency does not issue pass-through securities but rather insures them. These securities are issued by mortgage bankers and thrift institutions. Many of these institutions bundle their mortgages into pools of at least $1 million. These mortgage bankers apply to the Government National Mortgage Association for backing and, if accepted, get a pool number. Shares of these pools are sold to investors, consisting mainly of banks, pension funds, and insurance companies. The minimum purchase amount is $25,000, which explains why the majority of investors in these pools are institutions. After all the shares of the GNMA pool are sold, the GNMA securities are traded on the security markets.

A number of Ginnie Mae pools exist. The major pools are GNMA I and GNMA II. GNMA I has fixed-rate 20- to 30-year mortgages totaling a minimum face value of $1 million, all with the same interest rates. GNMA II pools are larger than GNMA I pools and have mortgages with a variety of interest rates and maturities.

There are a number of different GNMA pools, such as midgets (mortgages with 15-year terms), GNMA graduated-payment mortgages, (GPMs) GNMA adjustable-rate mortgages (ARMs), GNMA mobile home pools, GNMA buy-downs, and GNMA, Federal Housing Authority (FHA) projects. The different types of mortgages, maturities, interest rates, and pool sizes make the analysis more difficult for each type of pool. Generally, larger pool sizes have more liquid payments and are less affected by prepayments. The shorter the term of the mortgages, the shorter is the average life and half-life of the pool of pass-through securities.

Average life, defined as the weighted-average time that each dollar of principal is outstanding, is a measure of the investment life of mortgage-backed securities in a pool. The pool's average life depends on the prepayment rate. The greater the number of prepayments in the pool, the shorter is the average life and the weighted-average life, and the lower is the volatility in price of the GNMA security. GNMA and other types of mortgage securities are traded on their assumed average life, as opposed to their maturity dates, as with other bonds.

Half- life is the time it takes to return half the principal in a pool. The average life and half-life are useful measures for comparison purposes because you would use these concepts, not the length of time to maturity, to compare GNMA securities with other fixed-income investments. For example, if you want to compare the yield on a GNMA security with a 5-year half-life and a maturity of 12 years with a Treasury note, you compare it with Treasury notes with 5-year maturities.

GNMA investments are much more complex than other fixed-income investments because of the uncertainties about not only the length of time to maturity for that investment but also the amount and timing of the cash flows. GNMA provides statistics about prepayment histories for each GNMA pool, but these statistics are not cast in stone and can vary. The estimated payments, therefore, are revised continually.

Yields on GNMA securities are also difficult to determine accurately, as you might expect. If you are not sure about the size, frequency, or regularity of the cash flow, you cannot determine the investment's precise yield. However, various calculation methods have been developed based on different assumptions of prepayment speed (fast, average, or slow). On an offering sheet, a number of yields are quoted depending on the FHA-estimated experience of prepayment speed. The slowest speed offers the highest yield. From a safety point of view, therefore, whenever you buy GNMA securities, assume that you will earn the lowest of the predicted yields.

When you are comparing the estimated yields on GNMA securities with yields on other fixed-income securities, keep these issues in mind:

- Reinvestment risk is greater for GNMA securities than for other fixed-income securities because interest and the return of principal payments are made monthly for pass-through securities, as opposed to semiannually or annually for regular bonds. For example, if a significant downturn occurs in market rates of interest, the returned interest and principal are reinvested at lower rates, and the total return is lower for the GNMA investment than the quoted yield-to-maturity, assuming reinvestment at the quoted yield.

- Exact rates of return cannot be determined because of the uncertainty of reinvestment risk.
- If the monthly interest and principal payments are spent rather than reinvested, the total rate of return is even lower.
- Principal repayments should not be included in the cash flow yield because they are a return of the investor's initial investment.

GNMA securities and all pass-through securities, like all other fixed-income securities, are sensitive to changes in market rates of interest. When market rates of interest rise, bond prices decline. When market rates of interest decline, many homeowners will prepay their mortgages and then refinance them with mortgages at lower rates. This process acts as a ceiling on GNMA prices, so they do not increase as much, generally speaking, as regular bond prices when market rates decline. You not only receive your principal earlier, but you are also faced with reinvesting the proceeds in investments with lower yields.

You can purchase GNMA securities directly from the issuer through dealers or brokers. Minimum purchase amounts are $25,000. However, you can buy GNMA mutual funds or unit investment trusts (discussed in Chapter 4) by investing as little as $1,000 to $2,500 (the minimum amount specified by the GNMA mutual fund or investment trust). You can buy or sell existing GNMA issues on the secondary market. GNMA securities are both marketable and liquid because of the large volume of issues traded. When you are buying from a broker or bank, you should be aware of these guidelines:

- Prices quoted in financial newspapers or offering sheets are for large buyers (institutions), small investors are quoted larger spreads (difference between bid and ask prices).
- The yields that are quoted are based on prepayment assumptions. If only one yield is quoted, ask your broker for the different prepayment assumptions and their corresponding yields. Use the most conservative yield because even then it may not be realized.
- The remaining term of the mortgage pool or length of time until maturity is not as important as the weighted-average

life because the former assumes no prepayments. The assumption in the secondary market is that a 30-year GNMA will be repaid, on average, in 12 years.

- Price is important. If the GNMA is trading at a premium, you might be more inclined to suffer a capital loss. If interest rates decline, homeowners might prepay their mortgages in the pool faster than estimated. Then you might not recover the premium you paid over the face value, and you also have to reinvest the money at lower interest rates. Buying at a discount offers the opportunity of capital gains, but the coupon yield for the GNMA is lower than coupons offered at that time.

Federal Home Loan Mortgage Corporation (FHLMC)

The Federal Home Loan Mortgage Corporation, or "Freddie Mac," is the second largest issuer of pass-through securities. Shares of Freddie Mac, a government-sponsored agency, are traded on the New York Stock Exchange under the ticker symbol FRE.

The participation certificates offered by Freddie Mac are similar in many ways to GNMA securities. The major differences are as follows:

- Participation certificate pools contain conventional mortgages (most are single-family loans with 30-year terms) that are underwritten and purchased by Freddie Mac. These pools tend to be larger than GNMA pools.
- Freddie Mac guarantees the timely payment of interest and, ultimately, the repayment of principal (within a year). Because Freddie Mac is an agency, its guarantee is weaker than the federal government's full faith and credit provision for GNMA securities. Some participation certificates guarantee only the timely payment of interest.
- Participation certificates are not as marketable as GNMA securities because fewer participation certificates are traded in the secondary market. To improve the marketability of its participation certificates, Freddie Mac buys them back directly from holders.
- Yields on participation certificates are slightly higher than the yields on GNMA securities because of the slight discrepancy

in safety and the slightly lesser degree of marketability. This statement does not mean that participation certificates are not safe or marketable. Compared with GNMA securities, their level of credit risk is slight (far less than a corporate issue), and they are marketable (and liquid), but because GNMA securities have a greater presence in the marketplace, they are not as marketable or liquid.

The Federal Home Loan Mortgage Corporation has, in addition to participation certificates, a mortgage pass-through security called a *guaranteed mortgage certificate* (GMC). The GMC was designed for institutional investors with minimum amounts of $100,000 (as opposed to $25,000 for GNMA securities and participation certificates), and it pays out interest and principal semiannually. Freddie Mac guarantees its interest payments and the full payment of principal.

Federal National Mortgage Association (FNMA)

The Federal National Mortgage Association (FNMA), also known as "Fannie Mae," is a quasi-private organization whose common stock is traded on the New York Stock Exchange. Fannie Mae was established by Congress in 1938 but then was rechartered by Congress to become a private corporation in 1968 with a mandate to assist in the development of a secondary market for conventional mortgages.

Some of the features of Fannie Mae pass-through securities are

- FNMA guarantees timely interest and principal payments—a weaker guarantee than the one given for GNMA pass-through securities.
- FNMA pools tend to be larger than GNMA pools.
- FNMA securities are not as marketable as GNMA securities, and yields on FNMA securities tend to be higher than those offered on GNMA securities.

Table 8-4 lists the Web sites where you can obtain more information about GNMA, FNMA, and Freddie Mac pass-through securities.

To offset prepayment and cash-flow uncertainties of agency pass-through securities, collateralized mortgage obligations were developed in the private sector.

TABLE 8-4

Web Sites of Pass-Through Securities

Visit the GNMA, FNMA, and FHLMC Web sites to determine information about new
  issues, mortgage rates, and information pertaining to the issuers at

www.ginniemae.gov

www.fanniemae.com

www.freddiemac.com

Collateralized Mortgage Obligations

Collateralized mortgage obligations (CMOs) are mortgage pass-through
securities that provide more predictable interest and principal payments than do GNMA, FNMA, and Freddie Mac pass-through
mortgage securities. CMO pools are split into *tranches*, which are
classified according to expected maturities of the securities and
specific payment rules. The first CMO was issued in 1983. The main
innovation of the CMO is that it provides investors with a steady
stream of income for predictable terms. A CMO is a debt security
based on a pool of mortgages (like GNMA securities). Mortgage borrowers make monthly interest and principal payments. However,
the return of principal payments is segmented and paid sequen-
tially to a number of different portions of the pool's investors.

   CMOs are created when CMO pools are divided into tranches
(or slices) ranging from 3 to 17. Investors buy bonds with varying
maturities in these tranches. For example, the classic CMO has four
tranches; the first three (class A, class B, and class C) pay interest at
the stated coupon rate to bondholders of each tranche. The fourth
tranche (often referred to as a class Z or a Z-bond class) resembles
a zero coupon bond where interest is accrued. The last tranche is
always the Z tranche.

   The cash flows received are used first to pay the interest on the
first three classes of bonds and then to retire the bonds in the first
tranche at maturity. All prepayments are applied to the first tranche,
class A; then, when all the bonds are retired, the prepayments continue to the next tranche, class B. This process continues until class
B bonds are aid off, and then class C bonds follow. Z bonds receive
no payments (interest and principal) until all the other tranches are
paid off. Subsequent cash flows are used to pay off the accrued
interest and then the return of principal to retire the Z bonds.

Z bonds are much more complex than A, B, or C bonds in CMOs for a number of reasons. First, the length of time until maturity cannot be predicted accurately (for Z bonds), whereas regular A, B, and C tranches have stated maturities. Second, because Z bonds are long-term bonds, people investing in them face greater risks than with shorter-term securities. For this reason, Z bonds can be quite volatile, and you should understand the risks before buying Z-tranche bonds in a CMO. Your credit risks vary, depending on the backing of the CMO pool. If GNMA or FNMA backs CMO pools, then the credit risk is minimal. The risks rise for private issuers, who are not as creditworthy. Some characteristics of private CMO pools are as follows:

- Greater certainty exists for cash flows (quarterly or semi-annually) of earlier tranches than for tranches with longer terms to maturity.
- Earlier tranches have shorter and more predictable maturities and, consequently, less exposure to interest-rate risk.
- Later tranches have greater prepayment risk than earlier tranches (because they cannot receive any principal payments until the earlier tranches have been paid off).
- CMO pools are much larger than GNMA pools.
- Depending on the backing of the mortgages, CMOs can have little to no credit risk. Some pools are backed by GNMA, FNMA, or FHLMC, which have no credit risk. Privately backed pools have pool insurance, but they also may have greater credit risks.
- Depending on the brokerage firms selling CMOs, minimum investment amounts can be as low as $10,000.
- Yields on Z-tranche bonds are higher than the yields of GNMA securities, but risk is also much greater for Z-tranche bonds.
- CMOs are less liquid and might be less marketable than GNMA, FNMA, and Freddie Mac securities.
- Z-tranche bonds can be quite volatile when market rates of interest change.
- Yields on the earlier tranches tend to be lower than those on GNMA securities.
- Z-tranche bonds have more complicated tax aspects in that interest is taxed as accrued even though holders do not

receive interest payments in the early years (only when the Z tranche pays out).

Many different classes of CMOs have evolved. The complexities of each specific class have increased with the evolution of CMOs. CMOs offset some problems of the traditional pass-through securities by providing a stream of cash flows for a relatively predictable length of time to maturity (particularly for early tranches).

CORPORATE BONDS

Corporate bonds are issued by corporations and represent the promises by those corporate issuers to make periodic interest payments and to return the principal at maturity to bondholders. Many types of corporate bonds are available, such as mortgage bonds, debenture bonds, variable-interest bonds, convertible bonds, and zero-coupon bonds. These bonds are either secured or unsecured.

A junk bond is not a special type of bond but is a regular high-risk, low-rated bond. This type of corporate bond has a rating of BBB (by Standard & Poor's) and Baa (by Moody's Investor Services, Inc.) or less, which consist of a range of poor-quality debt that is close to default. Some of these bonds have no ratings. To entice investors, coupon rates of junk bonds are higher than the coupon rates of investment-grade bonds.

The Risks of Corporate Bonds

The *risk of default* is more of a concern for investors in corporate bonds as a group than for other types of bonds, such as U.S. Treasury bonds and government agency bonds, where the risk of default is much lower. U.S. Treasuries are considered to be free of credit and default risk. For this reason, corporate bonds offer higher yields than Treasury notes and bonds and government agency bonds. The greater the risk of default, the higher is the coupon rate for that issue. For the risks of credit and default on individual corporate bond issues, most investors rely on the ratings of the issues given by the commercial rating companies such as Standard & Poor's, Moody's, and Fitch.

Another risk that affects bond prices of existing issues is *event risk*, which is the risk that large corporations will issue large amounts of debt to finance their takeovers of other corporations (also known as a *leveraged buyout*). This strategy causes the price of existing bond issues of those takeover corporations to plummet because the corporations significantly increase the amount of their debt, which can result in downgraded ratings. Consequently, to entice investors to buy these new issues, corporate issuers introduced provisions that made takeovers more expensive. These "poison puts" allow bondholders to sell their bonds back to their issuers at par in the event of a takeover or when the bond's ratings are downgraded.

The advantage of a *put feature* in a bond's indenture is often paid for by a lower bond coupon than other comparable bonds without put features. Regardless, a put feature is attractive because it protects against the *risk of a rise in interest rates and inflation*. When interest rates or inflation increase (or both), the price of bonds falls, and holders of bonds with put features can sell their bonds back to the issuers at face value before maturity.

All bonds, except for floating-rate bonds, are subject to interest-rate risk. Citicorp was the first corporation to introduce floating-rate bonds in the 1970s. They were unique at the time in that the coupon rate fluctuated with the rate of Treasury bills, and after a two-year period (after issuance), bondholders could redeem the bonds at par value. Therefore, the prices of floating-rate bonds do not fluctuate much because of changes in interest rates, unlike the prices of regular fixed-income bonds. As pointed out in Chapter 7, bond prices fluctuate inversely with market rates of interest. The longer the maturity of a bond, the greater is the price fluctuation in relation to changes in interest rates.

Many corporate bonds have call features, which means that they are subject to *call risk*. This call feature allows an issuer to retire their bonds before their maturity. When a bond is called, interest no longer accrues, which forces bondholders to retire their bonds. The call feature benefits the issuer rather than the bondholder. Table 8-5 describes some options to lessen the impact of interest-rate risk.

Purchasing Corporate Bonds

Corporate bonds can be bought through brokerage firms. When a new issue of bonds is sold for the first time, the issuing corporation absorbs commissions. Existing corporate bond issues trade on the over-the-counter market, and a number of corporate issues are listed on the New York Stock Exchange (NYSE) and American Stock Exchange (AMEX). The trading of listed bonds does not take place in the same location as common stocks on these exchanges. Actively listed bonds

TABLE 8-5

Lessening the Effects of Interest-Rate Risk

Bond investors can lessen the impact of changes in interest rates by adhering to the following investment strategies:

- Vary the maturities of the bond issues in your portfolio to even out the effect of changing market rates of interest. (Rather than investing only in bonds with 20-year maturities, for example, ladder the maturities between 2, 5, 10, 15, and 20 years.) A *bond ladder* consists of investing equal amounts of money in bonds with different maturities.
- Diversify the bond portfolio by buying different types of bonds.
- Purchase good-quality bonds.
- Lessen the length of the maturities.
- Buy bonds with a put feature, which allows you to sell your bonds back to the issuer at face value when interest rates rise.

The downside to this strategy is that these bonds have lower coupon rates and shorter maturities. However, the optimal strategy, in theory, is to invest in short maturities when market rates of interest are increasing and then, when they peak, to buy long-term bonds to lock in to the higher coupon rates. The obvious question is how do you know when market rates of interest will peak? Locking in at the peak of market interest rates is not as important as at least trying to follow the strategy.

on the NYSE are traded in the Bond Room, where members announce their bid and ask prices. Other members either accept these prices or make counteroffers. Buying and selling are done through these members, therefore, and not through specialists, as in the case of common stocks. Inactively listed bonds are traded through the computer system in the Bond Room. Members respond by entering their orders through a computer terminal.

The advantage of buying listed bonds is that their prices appear in the daily newspapers, which gives you some idea of the prices traded. The actual bid and ask prices are not disclosed in newspapers. Bonds that trade over the counter are unlisted, and bond price quotes can vary considerably from dealer to dealer—especially for lower-quality, inactively traded bonds, where the size of the spread between the bid and ask prices can be quite large. In fact, pressure exists to regulate unruly trading in the junk bond market by instituting a price quotation system for the most actively traded junk bonds. This system would have to be approved by the SEC before being implemented. Until that happens, individual investors continue to be disadvantaged by these abusive trading practices. When dealers have to report their prices, many of these inefficiencies will disappear.

Thus, when buying unlisted bonds, therefore, you must shop around for the best quotes from different brokers.

Investors should always ask for both the bid and ask prices of the bonds that they are interested in buying because the size of the spread tells much about that bond issue. A large spread (4 percent or more) indicates that the bond is more than likely illiquid (it cannot be resold quickly) or inactively traded and possibly has some other bad news attached, such as a potential downgrading in ratings (Thau, p. 13). A small spread indicates the opposite: active trading with little risk of resale. Higher transactions costs are charged if investors buy or sell a small number of bonds (fewer than 10 bonds).

Several brokerage firms and online trading companies have addressed some of these difficulties. The Discover Brokerage System of Morgan Stanley allows investors access to the bid and ask spread on any bond. Electronic bond trading might take off in the future, but even with electronic trading, you should pay attention to finding the lowest costs for your transactions (Zuckerman, pp. C1 and C15). Table 8-6 assesses the risks of buying new corporate bond issues.

To summarize, before buying existing corporate bonds, check these factors:

- The issuer's credit ratings
- The issue's seniority
- The call and refunding provisions. You can avoid losses of principal by not buying premium-priced bonds with higher coupon rates than market rates, which could be called at lower prices. In other words, check whether the premium price exceeds the call price.
- The sinking-fund provision
- Whether you have a "poison put" protection against event risk
- Whether the bonds are part of a small issue (less than $75 million). Avoid buying bonds of small issues.
- Whether the bonds are listed or trade over the counter
- The maturity of the bond. The longer the maturity, the greater is the risk. Every now and then, corporations issue bonds with 50- and 100-year maturities. Within this time period, much can happen to affect a company's ability to repay the issue. Disney Corporation issued a 100-year bond, for example, that matures for the next generation's children and grand-children. With this time span, stocks are a better investment.

TABLE 8 - 6

Assessing the Overall Risks of New Corporate Issues

Before investing in a new issue, examine the company's prospectus to assess the overall risks. From the balance sheet, you can determine the level of debt and the number of debt issues that are senior to the one offered. In the event of bankruptcy, the greater the number of senior issues to this one, the lower is the priority of this bond investor's claims.

From the income statement, assess whether the level of earnings will provide adequate coverage for the interest payments on all outstanding debt issues, including the issue to be financed. If a downturn in sales takes place, you want to see how much interest cover the company has before the earnings become insufficient to service its debt.

From the statement of changes in cash position, assess whether the company has been selling off assets to generate funds and whether the ratio of debt to total assets is high. If the answer to both is yes, warning flags should go up concerning the issue. This process of analyzing the financial statements is particularly important when you are considering the purchase of lower-quality new corporate issues. You can obtain the financial statements of listed companies on the Internet or on the government Web site (www.freeedgar-online.com.)

- Risk-averse investors should buy good-quality corporate bond issues.

Investing in corporate bonds requires large sums of money to achieve a diversified portfolio to lessen the risks of default. If you invest in junk bonds, you should not invest a large portion of your investment funds in this category.

Compare the corporate issue coupon yield with the yields offered on Treasuries and government agency bonds with similar maturities to see if the spread warrants the additional risk of exposure to corporate bonds. If you are risk-averse, you should avoid junk bonds and choose high-quality corporate bonds.

MUNICIPAL BONDS

Municipal bonds are bonds issued by state, county, city, or other political entities. Interest paid by most municipal bond issuers is exempt from federal income taxes and from state and local taxes if the bonds are issued in the state and local tax area. This exemption from federal taxes is the most important feature of municipal bonds.

Municipal bonds that are issued and backed by the full faith and credit of states and municipalities are called *general-obligation bonds*. General-obligation bonds are municipal bonds on which the interest and principal are backed by the financial resources and taxing power of the issuing authority. In other words, the interest paid to bondholders comes from unlimited taxing authority, but in reality, it might not be easy to enact their "unlimited" taxing powers. For example, New York City defaulted on its general-obligation notes in 1975. Not all general-obligation bonds are equal. Their safety in terms of credit and default risk depends on the economic and financial strengths of the issuers.

Revenue bonds are municipal bonds whose interest and principal payments are paid only if there is sufficient revenue generated by the issuing authority. Revenue bonds are issued by enterprises such as hospitals, universities, airports, toll roads, and public utilities, whereby the revenues generated by these enterprises or their projects are used to pay the interest on the debt. For example, airport revenue bonds might generate revenues based on traffic use at the airport or revenues generated by the use of the airport facilities, such as leasing a terminal building. In the former case of revenue collection, bondholders should determine whether a growing demand exists for both passenger and airline traffic use of the airport; in the latter form of revenue collection, bondholders should determine whether the lease payments are sufficient to service the debt.

Proceeds from highway revenue bonds might be used to build toll roads or bridges or to make improvements to the highway infrastructure. Bondholders have a claim to tolls collected on the roads and bridges, but what about the improvements to the highways? Improving a highway does not generate revenue. Revenue bonds, which are not self-supporting, have revenues earmarked to secure the debt. Some examples are gasoline taxes, license fees, and automobile registration fees.

The security or safety of revenue bonds depends on how essential the services are that the enterprise provides, the flow of revenues, whether these revenues are increasing or decreasing, and whether any other claims to the revenues are made before those of the bondholders. The relative strength of the issuer of the revenue bonds to generate revenues and the ease with which the issuer can cover the interest payments determine the rating of the revenue bonds.

The Risks of Municipal Bonds

Although the number of defaults on municipal issues has been small historically, some highly publicized examples have made investors quite conscious of the *risk of default*. Table 8-7 outlines some steps you can take to reduce the risk of default.

Interest-rate risk can be greater than the risk of default for quality tax-exempt issues. This situation is not unique to municipal bonds but applies to all fixed-income securities. The longer the term to maturity, the greater is the price volatility because of fluctuations in interest rates. Although you receive greater yields from longer-term

TABLE 8-7

Reducing the Risk of Default for Municipal Bonds

The following steps might reduce the risk of default for municipal bonds:

Ratings. You should consider the ratings of a bond offering. Moody's and Standard & Poor's rate these offerings based on a substantial amount of financial information. Because municipal bonds do not have to be registered with the SEC, little information about the issuer's financial status is available for investors. States and municipalities might not publish their annual financial statements. To minimize your risk of default, therefore, limit purchases to bonds with AAA or AA ratings. Ratings are not cast in stone and can change over time. Do not, therefore, base your decision on ratings alone.

Insurance. Determine whether the issue is insured. Bond insurance can increase the ratings of an issue. When a bond is insured, it is given an AAA rating even if the bond had a lower rating before the insurance was issued. A bond issue that has a rating of AAA or AA without insurance is a stronger offering than an insured bond with AAA ratings. Insurance corporations, such as the Municipal Bond Insurance Association (MBIA) and the Financial Guaranty Insurance Co. (FGIC), sell insurance policies guaranteeing the interest payments and the return of principal. The quality of the insurance company also affects the ratings of the issue.

Credit enhancements. Some issuers have, rather than insurance, letters of credit from banks and insurance companies. A letter of credit does not guarantee interest payments by a bank or insurance company. Rather, it offers the issuer a line of credit. If the issuer does not have enough cash to cover the interest payments, the bank or insurance company lends the issuer the money. Because this method offers a lower degree of protection than insurance does, you should check the ratings of the bank or insurance company providing the line of credit.

Official statement. Obtain a copy of the official statement or offering circular, which is similar to a prospectus for a corporate security. In the statement, review these elements:

- *The legal opinion.* If you have any doubt about the tax exemption, avoid the issue.
- *A statement of how the issue will be repaid.* This ought to be fairly clear.
- *Qualifying phrases.* If you read phrases that make you nervous, such as "no assurance can be given," find another issue to invest in.

Diversification. Purchase bonds of different issuers, which spreads the credit and default risks associated with any single issuer.

(30-year) than shorter-term municipal bonds, you face increased volatility and must consider the fact that yield spreads between maturities tend to be wider for municipal bonds than they are for bonds in the taxable-bond market.

The *risk of a municipal bond being called* is a common risk. Most municipal bonds have call or refunding provisions that allow issuers to call in the bonds when interest rates decrease significantly. You should read the call provision before a purchase to see whether it has any unusual terms. Because housing revenue bonds, for example, might not stipulate a call date, they can be called anytime after they are issued. Be careful if a premium is paid on these bonds because if they are called, you may not recoup your premium price.

Because municipal securities are not as actively traded as government bonds, the spreads between the bid and ask prices tend to be relatively wide, even for the most actively traded issues. This *wide spread* makes municipal bonds less liquid than Treasury issues and agency bonds. The larger issues of general-obligation bonds and the well-known authorities tend to be marketable, but the smaller, thinly traded issues are less marketable. For some small issues, in fact, the only market that exists might be the issuing locality.

You run the risk of paying excessive markups on the pricing of individual municipal bonds. Under current pricing practices, you do not know whether you are being charged an excessive markup by your brokerage firm when you buy individual municipal bonds because these bonds are traded on the over-the-counter markets where the prices are not publicized. When you call your broker and ask for a price quote, the broker can quote any price (because the prices are not quoted in the newspapers, as they are for stocks). Shopping around at other brokerage firms is difficult unless investors have accounts at these firms. A brokerage firm might not quote its prices for the same bond issues unless the investor has an account. For example, a brokerage firm might buy a particular bond issue at $90 per bond and sell it to investors for $99 per bond. This is a $9 markup, or 9.89 percent. This price is in lieu of commissions because the brokerage firm owns the bonds, and it bears the risk of the bond prices falling. Another brokerage firm might have bought the same issue of bonds at $89 and is offering it to investors at $93 per bond. Lack of pricing information is a big disadvantage because investors never know whether they are paying excessive markups on the individual municipal bonds that they purchase and sell. You should buy municipal bonds and hold them to maturity, therefore, rather than use them as trading vehicles for capital gains because this lack of pricing also affects the sale of the bonds. The SEC is hoping to rectify this problem of a lack of pricing information in the corporate bond and municipal bond markets.

Purchasing Municipal Bonds

Investors buy municipal bonds at issue or on the secondary market. Financial newspapers, *Barron's*, the *Wall Street Journal*, and the *New York Times* publish weekly the forthcoming sales of new municipals. *The Bond Buyer*, a trade publication about municipal bonds, also provides information about forthcoming sales, in addition to the results of the preceding week's sales of municipal bonds.

State and local governments market their issues directly in some cases by placing them privately in the market, usually directly to institutional buyers. Mostly, new municipal bonds are placed through investment bankers who offer them for sale to the investment community (the public). The investment banker forms a syndicate of brokerage firms to sell the new issue. Investors place orders through their brokerage firms for these new issues. If their brokerage firms are part of the syndicate, they earn no sales commission on the purchase. The other advantage of buying at issue is that the bonds are priced uniformly (at the syndicate offering price) until all the orders for the syndicate have been filled. Only then can the bonds trade at market prices.

Buying municipals on the secondary market is slightly more difficult because the financial newspapers only print the prices of some popular revenue bonds. The prices of government-obligation bonds are not quoted in the newspapers. To learn which bonds are available in the secondary market, you can get a copy of the *Blue List*, published daily by Standard & Poor's. It lists the bonds that dealers own in their portfolios and want to sell. The listings of each bond generally include this information:

- The number of bonds for sale in each issue
- The name of the issuer
- The coupon rate and maturity date
- The price (not including the bid and ask spread)
- The name of the dealer selling the bonds

Because a subscription to the *Blue List*, which is the best source of information, is quite costly for most individual investors, ask your broker for a copy. You should not be surprised to find that by the time you see the *Blue List*, some bond issues already might be sold. Because the bid and ask spreads are not quoted, expect some deviation from the prices quoted in the *Blue List*.

Some Internet sites provide daily information about municipal bonds. The Web site www.bondmarkets.com has many municipal bond links. Another site, www.investinginbonds.com, lists the municipal bond prices, yields, and credit ratings of the bonds that are traded.

Many municipal bond dealers throughout the United States support the municipal bond secondary market. Brokers serve as intermediaries between dealers, and institutional and individual investors for municipal bond issues. Many brokerage firms maintain markets in their local and regional issues.

The pricing of municipal bond issues can vary significantly from dealer to dealer, so when you are buying (or selling), you should get several quotes from different brokerage firms. The bottom line: Shop around because paying high commissions and wide spreads lowers overall returns.

Municipal bonds on the secondary market can trade at either a discount or a premium depending on a number of factors, such as quality, coupon yield, financial strength of the issuer, and length of time to maturity. When you buy municipal bonds at a discount or premium, be aware of the likelihood of incurring capital gains when the bonds are sold or called. For example, if you bought 50 municipal bonds with a face value of $50,000 at a discount of $45,000 in 2005, and you buy another 50 municipal bonds with a face value of $50,000 at a premium of $55,000 with both issues maturing in 2005, $5,000 is subject to capital gains in 2005. (Puzzled? Most people are.)

According to the Internal Revenue Service Tax Code (Section 171), tax-exempt bonds offer no allowable deduction for amortization of the premium. In other words, you cannot offset your $5,000 gain against your $5,000 loss because the loss is not recognized (the loss cannot be deducted). The premium is amortized over the life of the bond to maturity or until it is called, which results in municipal bondholders being penalized twice:

1. You can buy coupon bonds at a premium, only to find that the bonds could be called at a lower price (than the premium purchase price paid).

2. The loss is not deductible against other capital gains.

The nondeductibility of the amortization is unique to tax-exempt bonds, and you should be aware that you might be liable for taxes because of gains from buying bonds at a discount and through the process of amortization of a premium. To illustrate the latter process, suppose that you buy a tax-exempt bond at a premium of $1,200 and sell the bond five years later for $1,200. As a result of having to amortize or "write down" the premium over time, the adjusted basis of the tax-exempt bond is less than $1,200. A taxable gain occurs, therefore, between the adjusted basis and the selling price.

Municipalities often issue serial bonds, which are groups of bonds with different maturities within an issue. Bear in mind that with a serial issue, you can choose the maturity when the issue is originally sold in the market.

If you are a taxpayer in a lower marginal tax bracket, you should first compare the yields of taxable bonds with those of municipal bonds before investing, as described in Table 8-8. Table 8-9 shows how to compare the returns of municipal bonds with those of dividend-yielding stocks.

The Bush Jobs and Growth Tax Relief Reconciliation Act of 2003, signed into law on May 28, 2003, reduced the amount of taxes that shareholders pay on the receipt of corporate dividends. Shareholders are taxed on their dividend income at a rate of 5 or 15 percent, depending on their marginal tax bracket. The prospect of reduced taxes on corporate dividends has had a marked effect on the bond markets, especially municipal bonds.

Municipal bonds, whose interest is tax-exempt, are most directly affected by the dividend tax reduction because the tax-exempt advantage that municipal bonds offer is sharply reduced (Ablan, p. MW10). Municipal bond investors usually are attracted to the contractual tax-free interest payments and the return of principal at maturity. In other words, municipal bond investors seek income and capital preservation. Stocks paying dividends offer yields that may be as attractive as the yields offered by municipal bonds, along with the possibility of capital appreciation (or, on the downside, capital loss).

Some other advantages of common stocks over municipal bonds might not be as obvious. Transaction costs are higher for municipal bonds than for stocks, making bonds more conducive to buy and hold to maturity rather than as a trading investment. Spreads (the difference between bid and ask prices) on stocks have narrowed to pennies on the dollar, whereas the spreads on municipal bonds are

TABLE 8-8

Determining the Taxable Equivalent Yield of a Municipal Bond

To compare municipal bonds with taxable bonds, you must convert the tax-exempt yield of a municipal into the equivalent of a taxable bond. The formula is

$$\text{Taxable equivalent yield} = \frac{\text{tax free yield}}{1 - \text{tax rate}}$$

If you buy a municipal bond with a 6 percent coupon and you are in the 35 percent marginal tax bracket, the bond has a before-tax return of 9.23 percent:

$$\text{Taxable equivalent yield} = \frac{6\ \text{percent}}{1 - 0.35}$$

$$= 9.23\ \text{percent}$$

The equivalent yield of a taxable bond in the investor's tax bracket is the yield that you would have to earn on a taxable bond to equal the yield on a municipal bond. For example, if you are an investor in the 15 percent tax bracket and are purchasing a taxable bond with a 7.65 percent coupon yield, you would earn the equivalent from a 6½ percent tax-exempt municipal bond. Put another way, if you are in the 15 percent tax bracket, you would purchase a municipal bond yielding 6½ percent only if taxable bonds of similar maturities were yielding less than 7.65 percent. If you could earn more than 7.65 percent on taxable bonds, you would not want to consider municipal bonds. However, if you are in a higher tax bracket, your taxable equivalent yield is much greater. If you are in the 35 percent tax bracket, the taxable equivalent yield on a 6½ percent municipal bond is 10 percent. As tax brackets (rates) increase, therefore, the taxable equivalent yields increase, and municipal bonds become more attractive. For taxpayers in the highest marginal tax bracket (35 percent), a 5 percent coupon on a municipal bond is the equivalent of a 7.69 percent taxable-bond coupon.

considerably larger. Consider the following spreads on two municipal bonds sold in January and February of 2003, respectively (Foust, p. 91):

Calvert County Pollution Control 5.55% 2014	Bought $60, sold $100
Boston Water & Sewer 10.875% 2009	Bought $100, sold $129

In addition to excessive markups in price, the municipal bond market is both less liquid and less marketable than the stock market.

Many municipal bonds have call features that allow issuers to buy back bonds early, before maturity and often at the par price. Any municipal bonds bought at a premium price (above $1,000) with this type of call feature pose a risk for investors. If the bonds

TABLE 8-9

Comparing Yields of Dividend-Paying Stocks and Municipal Bonds

Qualified dividends from stocks (both common and preferred) are taxed at lower rates than ordinary income. The maximum tax rate for qualified dividends is 15 percent for taxpayers in marginal tax brackets greater than 15 percent and 5 percent for taxpayers in lower tax brackets. The equation for converting dividend yields into after-tax yields is

$$\text{After-tax dividend yield} = \frac{\text{dividend}}{\text{purchase price of stock}} \times (1 - \text{investor's dividend tax rate})$$

A stock purchased at $19 pays a dividend of $1.08 per year. The after-tax dividend yield for a taxpayer in the 35 percent marginal tax bracket is 4.83 percent:

$$\text{After-tax dividend yield} = \frac{\$1.08}{19} \times (1 - 0.15)$$

$$= 4.83 \text{ percent}$$

If you are seeking investments yielding income, you can compare this after-tax dividend yield with municipal bond yields. A municipal bond with a yield-to-maturity of 4.5 percent, therefore, might not look as attractive as the yield from this stock, assuming that the risk of the company issuing the stock and the authority issuing the municipal bond is similar.

are called at par, investors do not receive the interest to cover the premium, leaving them short of their principal investments.

With these potential pitfalls in the municipal bond market, dividend-paying stocks with the new reduction in federal taxes on dividends become much more attractive if you are seeking income and the potential for capital growth.

REFERENCES

Ablan, Jennifer: "Bonds Bushwhacked," *Barron's*, January 13, 2003, p. MW10.

Faerber, Esmé: *All About Bonds and Bond Mutual Funds*. New York: McGraw-Hill, 2000.

Faerber, Esmé: *Fundamentals of the Bond Market*. New York: McGraw-Hill, 2001.

Foust, Dean. "Munis: What's a Fair Price?" *Business Week*, July 14, 2003, pp. 90–91.

Hayre, Lakbir S., and Cyrus Mohebbi: "Mortgage Pass-Through Securities," in Frank J. Fabozzi (ed.), *Advances and Innovations in the Bond and Mortgage Markets*. New York: McGraw-Hill, 1989.

Thau, Annette: *The Bond Book*. New York: McGraw-Hill, 1992.

Zuckerman, Gregory: "Online Push Barely Budges Bond Trading," *Wall Street Journal*, December 28, 1998, pp. C1 and C15.

Convertible Bonds and Zero-Coupon Bonds

KEY CONCEPTS

- What you should know about convertible and zero-coupon bonds
- Convertible bonds
- Zero-coupon bonds

WHAT YOU SHOULD KNOW ABOUT CONVERTIBLE AND ZERO-COUPON BONDS

Convertible bonds and zero-coupon bonds have features that are common to both stocks and bonds. You buy bonds primarily for the regular payments of income that they pay and the return of principal at maturity, and you invest in stocks primarily for capital appreciation and income generation if the stocks pay dividends. Convertible bonds provide income and capital appreciation if the stock of the company (issuing the convertible bonds) increases in value. Zero-coupon bonds are the most volatile of all the different types of bonds. Prices of zero-coupon bonds can soar and plummet in the same manner as a rollercoaster when market rates of interest fluctuate.

The downside to convertible and zero-coupon securities is that if the bond and stock markets decline, these securities are hit even harder than individual stocks and bonds. AMR Corporation, the parent company of American Airlines, had to withdraw a $250 million 20-year convertible bond offering from the market because of a combination of a weak bond market and the company's poor credit quality.

With the rise and fall of the stock markets, many mutual funds have looked for innovative ways to insulate investors from losing money. This action resulted in the growth of "principal protected" mutual funds, which might protect principal but also might deny any potential capital gains. Some of the investments that these funds chose were zero-coupon bonds because of the low yields on Treasury notes and bonds.

The European semiconductor company ST Microelectronics NV issued $1.2 billion in convertible zero-coupon bonds maturing in 2010. Because this issue straddles both the zero-coupon and convertible bond markets, as well as involving the equity markets, investors would need to understand the combination of factors in the respective markets, in addition to the specific terms of the issue that can affect returns on that investment.

CONVERTIBLE BONDS

A *convertible bond* is an unsecured corporate bond that can be converted at the convertible bondholder's option into a specified number of common shares of stock of the issuing company. A convertible bond is a debenture bond with a conversion feature whereby the bond can be exchanged for a specified number of common shares of the issuing corporation at the option of the convertible bondholder. In a few cases, convertible bonds have been exchanged for preferred stock or other bond issues.

The issuance of convertible bonds provides a popular source of funding for corporations. Because of the conversion feature, convertible bonds generally are subordinate to the company's other bond issues, and companies can offer lower coupon rates than they would on nonconvertible bonds. This means that companies can issue lower-quality debt at a lower interest cost.

The following definitions can help you to make sense of the mechanics of a convertible bond. The *conversion price* is the price per share of the common stock at which the convertible bond can be exchanged for common shares. The *conversion ratio* is the number of shares of stock into which a convertible bond can be exchanged. The *conversion value* is the market price of the underlying stock times the number of shares obtained in the exchange.

Suppose that a corporation wanting to raise funds decides that it does not want to issue more common stock because the market price of the stock is too low. To raise enough cash, it would have to issue many more shares of common stock (at the low stock price), which would dilute earnings per share for existing shareholders. A straight debt issue also would be too costly because the company would have to match the coupon rate of comparable existing corporate debt issues with similar risk and maturities. Instead, the company can issue convertible bonds, and because of the conversion feature, investors would accept a lower coupon rate on the issue. The company would need to consider the current market price of its common stock to determine the number of shares that each bondholder would receive on conversion. For example, if the company's stock is currently trading at $18 per share, the company may decide on a conversion price of $25 to make the bonds more appealing to investors. The conversion price is the price of the underlying common stock at which the convertible bond will be exchanged. The conversion ratio is the number of common shares received for each bond, which in this example is 40 shares per bond ($1,000/25). The conversion ratio is the face value of the bond divided by the conversion price. The conversion value, therefore, is the market price of the underlying stock into which the convertible bond is exchanged multiplied by the conversion ratio ($25 × 40 shares, which equals $1,000). The following equations show the relationships among the defined terms.

Conversion ratio = number of common shares exchanged for each bond

$$\text{Conversion ratio} = \frac{\text{face value of bond}}{\text{conversion price}}$$

$$\text{Conversion price} = \frac{\text{face value of bond}}{\text{conversion ratio}}$$

Conversion value = price per share of common stock × conversion ratio

Convertible bonds are valued either in relation to the conversion value of the stock or as straight debt. In reality, both these factors are taken into account in valuation of the convertible security

The Value of a Convertible Bond as Stock

The value of a convertible security as stock depends on the market price of the common stock. Using the conversion equation, the value of the convertible bond is the number of shares into which the bond is convertible multiplied by the market price of the stock. In the example quoted, if the market price of the stock is $18, the convertible can be exchanged into 40 shares, which is then multiplied by $18, to equal the value of the convertible bond at $720.

The relationship between the value of the convertible bond as stock and the price of the common stock is illustrated in Table 9-1.

From Table 9-1, as the market price of the stock rises (column 2), the value of the convertible increases. The value of the convertible is obtained by multiplying the conversion ratio by the market price of the stock. When the price of the common stock is below the conversion price of $25, the value of the convertible is less than the face amount of the bond ($1,000).

- When the stock price is greater than the conversion price ($25), the value of the convertible is greater than the face value of the bond. Thus the conversion feature allows for the upside potential of capital gains through appreciation of the stock price.

- Moreover, there is a floor price below which the price of the convertible will not fall, and this is the straight value of the bond.

For example, assume that using the preceding illustration, the market price of the common stock falls to $10 per share. The conversion value is $400, but the market price will not fall below the value of the bond owing to the value of the coupon interest payments on

TABLE 9-1

Value of Convertible Bond as Stock

Conversion Ratio*	Market Price of Stock	Value of Convertible as Stock
40	$10	$ 400
40	18	720
40	25	1,000
40	30	1,200
40	35	1,400
40	40	1,600

*The number of shares the convertible is exchanged into.

FIGURE 9-1

Pricing of a Covertible Bond

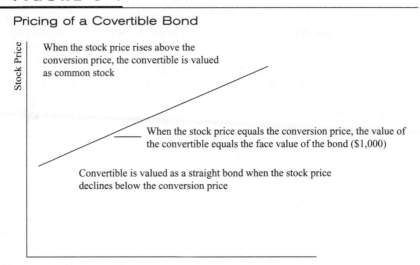

the bond. Similarly, the market price of the convertible will not be less than the conversion value of the security. This is due in part to the activity of arbitrageurs, who buy and sell the same security in two different markets to take advantage of price differentials. This is discussed in the next section. A graphic explanation of the dual pricing concepts of a convertible bond is given in Fig. 9-1.

Value of the Convertible Bond as Debt

The value of a convertible as debt is determined by the coupon rate, credit quality of the issuer, length of time to maturity, the call provision, and market rates of interest. Most convertible bonds have call provisions. The investment value of the bond is determined by discounting both the coupon interest payments of the convertible and the face value of the bond at maturity (assuming that it is not converted) at a comparable rate of return used on similar debt. In other words, the value of the convertible bond is the present value of the cash flows of the coupon payments and the face value of the bond at maturity discounted at an interest rate that includes a risk premium for investing in the security.

As with regular bonds, the value of a convertible bond as debt fluctuates with changes in market rates of interest. When interest rates increase, the price of the convertible bond declines, and conversely, when interest rates decline, the price of the convertible rises.

This inverse relationship occurs because the coupon rate on a convertible bond is fixed.

The value of a convertible bond as straight debt is important because it sets a floor price. When the stock price is trading below the conversion price, the straight-bond value provides the floor value, and the convertible bond will not fall below this value because the convertible option is of no consequence at lower stock prices. When stock prices rise above the conversion price, the price of the convertible bond is the conversion value as stock. The convertible bond is equity in disguise.

Value of the Convertible Bond as a Hybrid Security

At low stock prices (below the conversion price), the floor price of the convertible is no lower than its value as a straight bond, and at sufficiently high stock prices (above the conversion price), the price of the convertible is the same as the conversion value into stock. In between these extremes in stock prices, the convertible security generally trades at a premium price over its value as equity and over its value as debt.

These relationships are examined in Table 9-2 using the example of a 6 percent 20-year convertible bond with a conversion ratio of 40 shares. The market rate of interest (or required rate of return) used is 8 percent.

The price of the convertible bond is determined as follows:

$$\text{Convertible bond price} = \sum_{T=1}^{20} \frac{\$60}{(1 + 0.08)^{20}} + \frac{\$1,000}{(1 + 0.08)^{20}}$$

$$= \$803.59$$

The price of a convertible bond can be determined using Excel software.

The conversion value as stock is determined using the following equation:

$$\text{Conversion value} = \text{price per share of common stock} \\ \times \text{conversion ratio}$$

At low stock prices ($5 and $10 per share), the market price of the convertible bond is the same as its value as straight debt, and the premium over the stock price is large. At $25 per share, the conversion

TABLE 9-2

Premiums on Convertible Bonds

Share Price	Conversion Ratio	Value of Bond as Stock	Value as Straight Debt	Market Price of Convertible Bond*	Premium of Bond over Stock Value	Premium of Convertible Bond over Non-convertible Bond
$ 5	40	$ 200	$803.59	$ 803.59	$603.59	$ 0
10	40	400	803.59	803.59	403.59	0
18	40	720	803.59	820.00	100.00	16.41
25	40	1,000	803.59	1,020.00	20.00	216.41
35	40	1,400	803.59	1,410.00	10.00	606.41
40	40	1,600	803.59	1,600.00	0	796.41

*In reality, it is difficult to calculate the market price of the convertible security owing to its hybrid nature and the many factors affecting the market price. Therefore, the market prices between the extremes in stock prices in this example are hypothetical and in reality fluctuate around these values.

price, the market price for the convertible is $1,020, which exceeds both the value of the debt by $216.41 and the value as stock by $20. At a significantly high stock price of $40 for this company, the market price of the convertible is the same as the value as stock, and the premium over the value as debt is very high ($796.41).

This example illustrates that when the stock price rises, the premium paid over the value of the convertible bond as straight debt increases. This increase in premium occurs because of the importance of the conversion feature on the convertible and the fact that the straight debt becomes less important as the stock price increases.

There is also the probability that the bond could be called, which would force conversion when the stock price is greater than the conversion price. For example, suppose that the convertible bond was bought at $1,410, and the company calls in the bonds when the stock price is trading at $35. Convertible bondholders would not turn in their bonds for $1,000 per bond. Instead, they would convert their bonds into equity, receiving $1,400 per bond (40 shares × $35), which results in a loss of $10 per bond for the bondholder. Thus, as the stock price rises, downward pressure is exerted on the premium over the stock price, and the market price for the convertible converges with the stock value of the convertible.

Most convertible securities trade at a premium over either the stock value or the value as a straight bond.

Risks of Convertible Bonds

As with any debt security, the *risk of default* is a major concern. This is especially so for convertible bonds because they are subordinate to the other debt issues of the issuing company. Consequently, convertible bonds are not as safe as the company's senior debt, and in the event of bankruptcy, convertible bondholders stand behind the other bondholders in the collection line. Hence convertible bondholders might only receive a fraction of their invested principal at best.

Convertible bonds are affected by *interest-rate risk*. Convertible bonds are fixed-income securities with coupon rates that tend to be lower than those of conventional debt issues. Consequently, an increase in market rates of interest causes a greater decline in the price of convertible issues than nonconvertible bonds. Generally, high interest rates tend to depress stock market prices, and a convertible bond is doubly cursed if the issuing company's stock price is depressed. Stock prices and stock markets can be both uncertain and volatile, which do not ensure appreciation of the convertible. There is the risk that if the stock price never rises above the conversion value, the convertible bond will not be converted, and the convertible bondholder will receive a lower return through the life of the bond than he or she would on a regular bond. This lower return is due to the lower coupon yields of convertible bonds than those of comparable nonconvertible bonds.

Convertible bonds mostly have call provisions, so there is always the *risk of call*. Corporations might call in bond issues when interest rates decline so that they can issue new bonds at lower coupon rates and save money.

Purchase and Sale of Convertible Bonds

Convertible bonds are bought and sold in the same way as corporate bonds. New issues are bought through an underwriter or participating syndicate broker, where investors are not charged a fee or markup.

Convertible securities trading on the secondary market are purchased (sold) through full-service brokerage firms, discount brokers, brokerage services offered by banks, and online brokers. Most of the convertible bonds are listed on the over-the-counter markets, whereas convertible bonds of larger, well-known companies are listed on the New York Bond Exchange.

Brokerage fees for purchasing convertible bonds are similar to those charged for buying regular bonds. Markups charged per bond vary depending on several factors, such as the number of convertible bonds purchased and the total value of the purchase and the type of broker (full-service or discount). It is important to shop around to find the lowest markups and dealer spreads before buying. Investors have the same difficulties obtaining prices on convertible bonds as they do on other types of bonds, such as corporate, agency, and municipal bonds.

The Advantages of Convertible Bonds

Convertible bonds offer upside potential through capital gains when the stock price of the underlying company rises above the conversion price and downside protection when the market price of the stock falls below the conversion price because the convertible would be valued at no less than the value of the bond. Convertible bond prices generally rise when interest rates decline, which also could coincide with increasing stock prices. This action happened in 2003 and 2004 when convertible bonds outperformed the stock market indices. On an individual basis, much depends on the fundamental financial factors of the issuing company and the features of the convertible bond. Generally, however, if the stock price of the issuing company keeps increasing, investors will not do as well with convertible bonds as they would have had they bought the common stock of the company instead of the company's convertible bonds.

Some companies do not pay dividends, and by investing in the convertible bonds of these companies, investors receive a regular stream of income from the fixed interest payments before conversion.

Convertible securities offer some protection against inflation because market prices of both common stocks and convertible bonds rise with inflation. However, if the market price of the common stock does not reach the conversion price and conversion never occurs, then investors receive no protection from inflation because the amount of the interest payments on bonds is fixed.

Experienced investors can use convertible bonds to profit from diverging prices of the convertible in the bond and stock markets. This action involves the use of arbitrage activities, buying one security and simultaneously selling short the related security. For example, buying the convertible bond and selling short the related stock can result in profits when there are price discrepancies. A definition of arbitrage may help you to understand how exploitation of the pricing of convertibles in two different markets works. *Arbitrage* takes place when a similar security is bought and sold in different markets in order to exploit price differentials.

For example, if the market value of a convertible bond is $900 (same example used in the preceding section), when the stock price moves to $24, arbitrageurs will exploit this price differential for their own profit. The conversion value is $960 (40 shares × $24 per share), and arbitrageurs would sell short the stock. To sell short is to borrow a security and sell it on the market. Arbitrageurs simultaneously buy the convertible bond for $900 while selling short 40 shares of the stock for $960. The conversion option on the convertible bond is exercised, and the shares that were borrowed are tendered. The resulting profit is $60 per bond before taking into account commissions charged for buying and selling the securities. Through this action, arbitrageurs bid up the price of the bonds until there is no longer a price differential. In reality, the price of a convertible bond is rarely the same as its conversion value into stock. Mostly, the price of the convertible exceeds that of the conversion value owing to the bond's value. In addition to the upside appreciation owing to the conversion value, the value of the bond as debt provides a floor price for the convertible bond. Table 9-3 presents another arbitrage example.

Disadvantages of Convertible Securities

In the event of liquidation or bankruptcy of the issuing company, convertible bondholders' claims to the assets are subordinate to the claims of the company's other holders of debt. Convertible securities, like all fixed income securities, are sensitive to changes in interest rates. Convertible bonds generally have call provisions, and when market interest rates fall, there is an increased risk that the issuing company calls the convertible bonds. The issuing company then can refinance the convertible bonds with cheaper debt.

Yields on convertible securities generally are lower than yields on straight bonds, which is advantageous for corporations looking for a cheaper source of funds than issuing straight bonds. If the bonds are never converted, investors would have received lower coupon yields for the life of the bonds than they would have had they had invested in comparable nonconvertible bonds.

TABLE 9-3

Convertible Bond Arbitrage

What would an arbitrageur do to exploit the differential in this situation?

Convertible bond price: $1,000
Conversion price: $35
Conversion ratio: 28.57 shares
Stock price: $37

1. Buy the convertible bond at $1,000 per bond.
2. Convert the bond into common stock worth $1,057.09 (28.57 × 37= $1,057.09).
3. Sell the stock, which results in a profit of $57.09 per bond purchased ($1,057.09 − $1,000).
4. The greater the number of bonds purchased, the greater is the total profit.

or

1. Sell the stock short (receive $1,057.09).
2. Buy the convertible bonds at $1,000 per bond.
3. Convert the bond into stock, and then close out the short position.
4. Realize a profit of $57.09 for each convertible bond or batch of 28.57 shares of the stock.

This example ignores transaction costs.

When to Buy Convertible Securities

Convertible securities offer the potential for both appreciation and a steady stream of income, but they may not be the best of both worlds. They certainly allow you to hedge your bets in both the debt and equities markets. However, under certain conditions, they might not be the best investments, and you would have been better off owning either regular debt or equity securities.

Generally, convertible securities do well when interest rates are falling and the stock market is rising. This was the case in 1992, 1999, 2003, and 2004 when convertible securities outperformed the stock market indices. However, on an individual basis, much depends on the fundamentals of the issuing company of the convertible. If investors like the common stock of a particular company but are not sure whether the stock market is going to go up, they could buy the company's convertible bonds, which would potentially be less volatile in price swings than the common stock while receiving a regular stream of interest income. However, if the stock price of the company increases, investors would not do as well with convertibles as they would have had they bought the stock instead of the convertible.

The downside to convertible bonds is that they can be complicated in structure with call provisions, which could result in holders losing money if they had bought the convertible bonds at a premium price. Similarly, if convertible bonds are not converted into equity, investors generally would have been better with regular bonds, which tend to pay higher coupons.

Convertible securities are suited to investors who have the knowledge of the workings and intricacies of these specialized securities and who can hedge their bets in the bond and equity markets.

What the Conversion Premium or Discount Means

A *conversion premium* is the excess amount at which a convertible bond sells above its conversion value. A convertible bond generally sells at a premium price over its straight-bond value and conversion value into equity. For example, Navistar International issued senior convertible bonds in a private placement in December 2002 at a conversion premium of 30 percent on a closing equity price of $26.70. The price of a convertible bond is usually quoted as a percentage of its conversion value, which is also known as the *conversion premium*. For example, a convertible bond selling at $1,000 with a straight-bond value of $798 and a conversion value of $852 is trading at a conversion premium of 17.4 percent:

$$\text{Conversion premium} = \frac{\text{price of bond} - \text{conversion value}}{\text{conversion value}}$$

$$= \frac{\$1,000 - 852}{852}$$

$$= 17.4 \text{ percent}$$

In 1999, Amazon.com, Inc., sold $1.25 billion in convertible bonds at a 27 percent conversion premium. Several years ago, Battle Mountain, a gold mining company, had 6 percent convertible bonds trading at a 141 percent premium over its equity value, whereas another mining company, Couer d'Alene, had 7 percent convertible bonds trading at a 31 percent premium over the equity value. So what does the conversion premium mean, and how is it interpreted? The conversion premium is affected by several factors. A company with a volatile stock price has a greater conversion premium (owing to the fact that conversion is more likely with a volatile stock). After a convertible is issued, the conversion premium decreases if the stock price rises. For example, Couer d'Alene's convertible bond, with a lower premium over its equity value, offers greater appreciation potential than Battle Mountain's higher-conversion-premium bonds. The length of time to maturity also affects the conversion premium. Convertible bonds with long maturities have higher conversion premiums owing to the greater likelihood of the stock price being able to rise above the conversion price. The shorter the time left to maturity, the smaller is the conversion premium. See the Table 9-4 for a discussion of the hazards of investing in convertible bonds and the downside risk of not being able to convert the bonds to equity.

ZERO-COUPON BONDS

Zero-coupon bonds are the most volatile of all the different bond types. Zero-coupon bond prices are most sensitive to changes in interest rates and swing up and down resembling a rollercoaster ride. Zero-coupon bonds are more complex than regular bonds, and you need to understand how they work.

What Are Zero-Coupon Bonds?

A *zero-coupon bond* pays no coupon interest and is issued at a deep discount to its face value. The bond increases in value until maturity, when it is equal to its face value. Zero-coupon bonds are debt securities that are issued at deep discounts from their face values, pay no periodic interest, and are redeemed at face value ($1,000) at maturity. For example, a 10-year zero-coupon bond (with a face value of $1,000) yielding 5 percent would cost about $613.91 at issuance. In other words, you would buy this zero-coupon bond for $613.91, receive no interim interest payments, and at the end of the tenth year receive $1,000, the face value of the bond. Since zero-coupon bonds do not pay interest, they do not have a current yield like regular bonds.

TABLE 9-4

The Hazards of Convertible Bonds

Convertible bonds offer potential capital appreciation in rising stock markets and protection of a portion of invested capital owing to the underlying floor price of the straight value of the bond in down markets. However, investing in convertible bonds is not without risk.

At the peak of the stock market in 1999, many technology and Internet companies raised new sources of funds by issuing convertible bonds. In that year, a record 144 convertible issues came to the market, with 25 of them over $500 million per issue (Avital Louria Hahn). Amazon.com, Inc., raised $1.25 billion with a convertible bond issue despite the fact that its bonds had a rating of CCC+. What was even more remarkable was that the coupon rate was only 4¾ percent, and the issue sold at a 27 percent conversion premium to equity. This issue was priced when Amazon's stock was $61 per share and a conversion price of $78 per share. In the bear market that followed in 2000, the stock price of Amazon (and other Internet and technology companies) plummeted. When Amazon's stock price was $16 per share, the value of the straight bond was $530. Consequently, investors in this issue had little choice but to wait until maturity in 2009 to receive their invested principal. Some time later Amazon's stock price slid into the single digits, when many investors feared that Amazon might default on its bond obligations. If a bankruptcy occurred, convertible bond holders would have received nothing. Convertible bonds do not offer the same protection in bankruptcy as straight bond issues because convertible bonds are subordinate to regular bond issues of a company.

The choices for Amazon convertible bondholders were to sell their bonds at significant losses to their purchase prices (the convertibles were trading well below their straight bond values) or to hold them and hope that Amazon would not default on its debt obligations. Of course, there is always the hope with convertibles that the underlying stock price will rise above the conversion price, resulting in capital appreciation. In Amazon's case, this would be a meteoric rise to above $78 per share.

The hazards of convertible bonds are greater than those of straight debt if the underlying stock price never goes above the conversion price. In the event of bankruptcy, convertible bondholders are the last in the line of debt holders to claim on assets. Second, if there is no conversion, convertible bondholders receive lower yields than they would have on comparable straight debt.

Sources: Avital Louria Hahn, "'Tech-communica-dia' Propels Convertible Issuance to new Heights," June 10, 2000, www.findarticles.com; "No Protection on Converts: Moody's Says the Hot Hybrids Are Risky," July 23, 2001, www.findarticles.com.

The price of a zero-coupon bond is the present value of the face value of the bond at the maturity date discounted at its internal rate of return. In other words, the investor's funds grow from $613.91 to $1,000 in 10 years. The initial price is compounded at a rate of return to equal $1,000 in 10 years. The rate of return, or yield, on a zero-coupon bond can be solved mathematically or using compound-interest tables, a financial calculator, or a personal computer.

The yield on a zero-coupon bond is determined using Microsoft Excel software:

1. Click on the "*f**" key on the toolbar.
2. Highlight "*rate.*"
3. Fill in the information in the following box:

Nper	10
Pmt	0
PV	−613,91
FV	1000
Type	1
Formula result (rate) = 0.05	

Nper = total number of payments
Pmt = payment (interest) each period
PV = present value of bond (needs a
    negative sign before the amount)
FV = future value (face value) of bond
Type = 1 for payments at the end of
    each period
Formula result = rate

Knowing the yield on the bond is helpful not only for federal tax purposes but also for calculating the price of the bond. Even though zero-coupon bondholders receive no interest payments, bondholders are required to pay federal income taxes on their accrued interest as if it had been paid. In the example used, the accrued interest for the first year is $30.70:

$$Interest = \$613.91 \times 0.05$$

$$= \$30.70$$

The zero-coupon bondholder pays taxes on this amount of $30.70 even though it has not been received, thereby creating a negative cash flow. The bondholder pays cash out of pocket for the taxes without receiving the $30.70. Instead, the interest is added to the principal price of the zero-coupon bond so that at the end of the first year, the price of the bond increases to $644.61 ($613.91 + 30.70).

The accrued interest for year 2 is $32.23:

$$Interest = \$644.61 \times 0.05$$

$$= \$32.23$$

The price of the bond at the end of the second year is $676.84 ($644.61 + 32.23). Theoretically, the price rises with accrued interest until the price reaches $1,000 at maturity. This theoretical price

FIGURE 9-2

Price of a 10-Year Zero-Coupon Bond

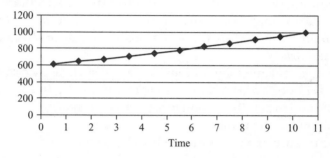

structure is illustrated in Fig. 9-2. There are other factors, besides accrued interest that affect the price of a zero-coupon bond. For example, if interest rates increase, the price of the bond would fall below the theoretical prices shown in the graph.

Owing to negative cash flows from paying taxes on accrued (phantom) interest during the life of the bond, zero-coupon bonds are better suited for investment accounts that are not subject to taxes. These are pension funds, individual retirement accounts (IRAs), 401(k)s, and SEP accounts. In these plans, accrued interest is taxed only when the funds are withdrawn. Investing in municipal zero-coupon bonds can eliminate the phantom interest tax problem.

Relationships Influencing the Price of Zero-Coupon Bonds

The price of a zero-coupon bond is affected by the quality of the bond, length of time to maturity, call provision, market rates of interest, and yield. The *quality* of a zero-coupon bond is important because the return depends on

- The ability of the issuer to redeem the bonds at maturity
- Whether the bondholder is able to sell the bonds before maturity at a higher price than the purchase price

A zero-coupon bondholder has more to lose in the event of a default than a conventional bondholder because with the latter, bondholders receive some interest payments that reduce the original principal invested in the bonds.

The quality of a zero-coupon bond is an assessment of the issuer's ability to pay off the bond at maturity. A good-quality zero-coupon bond has less risk of default than a speculative low-quality zero-coupon bond. Investors are willing to pay more for a good-quality bond. Thus there is a positive relationship between *quality and price.*

Ratings assigned by ratings agencies such as Moody's and Standard & Poor's are yardsticks as to credit quality, but you always should be aware that these ratings are subject to changes in the financial positions of the issuing entity.

The quality of a zero-coupon bond is also related to its *yield.* A low-quality zero-coupon bond offers a higher yield than a good-quality zero-coupon bond to entice investors. The flip side of the coin is that investors pay less for a low-quality zero-coupon bond than for a high-quality zero-coupon bond. Price, therefore, is inversely related to yield.

Zero-coupon bond prices are sensitive to *fluctuations in market interest rates.* The purchase price of a zero-coupon bond determines the yield over the life of the security because interest is paid only at maturity, and interest accrues at that fixed yield. If market rates of interest rise above the fixed yield of a zero-coupon bond, investors would want to sell the zero-coupon bond and reinvest in a bond with a higher yield. This action has the effect of depressing the price of existing zero-coupon bonds more than conventional type bonds, which pay interest annually or semiannually. Zero-coupon bonds are more volatile in price than regular fixed-interest-payment bonds because zero-coupon bondholders do not receive any interest payments until the zero-coupon bonds mature. Similarly, when interest rates fall, zero-coupon bonds appreciate more than existing conventional bonds owing to the fixed yield on the zero-coupon bond.

Market factors also have a bearing on price. An actively traded zero-coupon bond is priced differently from an inactively traded zero-coupon bond with the same maturity and yield.

Types of Zero-Coupon Bonds

Besides conventional zero-coupon bonds issued by corporations and government entities, there are different types of zero-coupon bonds. Several brokerage houses introduced derivative zero-coupon bonds during the early 1980s primarily for use in retirement accounts.

They are called *derivative securities* because these securities obtain their value based on another underlying security.

A stripped security is an example of a derivative security. A *stripped security* is a zero-coupon bond that is created and sold by brokerage firms that are based on the separated interest and principal payments of Treasury notes or bonds that are held in escrow.

Stripped Government Securities

In 1982, Salomon Brothers and Merrill Lynch both created *zero-coupon stripped Treasury securities*. To create their respective securities, the brokerage firms bought long-term U.S. Treasury bonds and held them in escrow. They then sold zero-coupon bonds representing an ownership interest in the underlying Treasury bonds (held in escrow) and their interest payments. Stripping the coupon payments on the U.S. Treasury bonds created these securities. An important distinction to make with stripped zero-coupon securities is that they are not backed by the faith and credit of the U.S. Treasury. Treasury bonds are backed by the faith and credit of the U.S. government, but the zero-coupon securities are merely the products of the brokerage houses.

Salomon's product was marketed under the name Certificates of Accrual on Treasury Securities (CATs), and Merrill Lynch's stripped zero-coupon security went under the name Treasury Income Growth Receipts (TIGRs). Other brokerage firms followed with their stripped zero-coupon securities under other feline acronyms.

The major disadvantage to these stripped zero-coupon securities of the brokerage firms is the lack of liquidity. Competing dealers did not trade the securities of other brokerage firms, so to improve liquidity of the stripped zero-coupon bonds, a group of primary dealers in the Treasury bond market decided to issue generic securities. These securities were called *Treasury Receipts,* and they were not associated with any of the participating dealers (Fabozzi and Fabozzi).

In 1985, the U.S. Treasury announced its own Separate Trading of Registered Interest and Principal (STRIP) program. Designated Treasury bonds could be stripped to create zero-coupon Treasury bonds. STRIPs are Treasury securities that have had their coupons and principal payments separated, which form the basis for the creation of zero-coupon bonds.

Since these securities are the direct obligations of the U.S. government, they tend to have slightly lower yields than brokerage firm's stripped zero-coupon securities. Moreover, Treasury's STRIP securities offer greater marketability than the generics offered by the brokerage firms.

Salomon Brothers created stripped federal agency zero-coupon bonds in the late 1980s. The brokerage firm purchased $750 million of FICO (Financing Corporation) bonds, stripped them of their interest, and sold them as zero-coupon FICO strips. Congress had created FICO with the purpose of raising money for the financially strapped Federal Savings and Loan Insurance Corporation (FSLIC).

The FICO zeros were not assigned credit ratings by the rating companies but were believed to be relatively safe because of Congress' commitment to FICO and the FSLIC. Hence yields on FICO zeros were slightly higher than those on Treasury STRIPs. Agency strips, such as FICO zeros, can be bought through brokers and trade over the counter in the secondary market.

Mortgage-Backed Zero-Coupon Bonds

Ginnie Mae, Fannie Mae, and Freddie Mac offer mortgage-backed zero-coupon bonds that are fully backed by their issuers. However, owing to prepayment risk, investors may find that these zeros could be paid off before their stated maturities.

Municipal Zero-Coupon Bonds

These securities are issued by state and local governments and are advantageous in that the accrued interest is exempt from federal income taxes and generally from state taxes (if issued in the state of the taxpayer).

Municipal zero-coupon bonds come in two types: *general-obligation zero-coupon bonds* issued by states and *project zero-coupon bonds* issued by highway authorities for highway projects, public projects for sewer systems, and other municipal projects. General-obligation issues are backed by the taxing power of the states issuing them, whereas project securities are backed by the revenues generated from the projects. Hence project zero-coupon bonds are less secure.

The quality of a zero-coupon bond issue is important for the reason stated earlier in this chapter, namely, that the holder receives no payments other than the payment of principal and interest at maturity. Consequently, you should not settle for lower-quality zero-coupon municipal issues because there are many good-quality issues. This point is especially relevant for long-term issues (over 15 years to maturity), where anything could happen to affect the issuer's ability to repay the bonds. For higher-quality zero-coupon bond issues, you will sacrifice slightly on yields.

Many municipal zero-coupon issues are callable, and you should check the call provisions before buying. If there is a choice between a callable and a noncallable issue of similar quality and maturity, avoid the callable issue.

Both the call price and the call date listed in the bond's indenture are important. The call price could be less than the market price, resulting in a loss if the issue is called, so it is wise to check out the call provision first. An issue might have a serial call, which means that some bonds in the issue could be called earlier than other bonds in the issue.

Although municipal zero-coupon bonds are exempt from federal income taxes, investors might want to find out how their states tax the accrued interest on the securities. Some states tax the phantom interest as it accrues, and other states tax the interest at maturity or when the securities are sold. Investors can get this information from their state revenue offices. Before selling a zero-coupon bond, you should consult with your tax advisor or accountant as to the tax consequences of gains and losses.

Zero-Coupon Corporate Convertible Bonds

These securities are deeply discounted bonds with conversion provisions. The yields of these securities tend to be lower than those of conventional bonds, and they do not pay annual interest. Holders are required to accrue the interest for federal tax purposes, and as with regular zero-coupon bonds, they are suitable for tax-deferred accounts such as IRAs, 401(k)s, and pension plans.

Like convertible bonds, these securities can be exchanged into a predetermined number of the issuing corporation's common stock. ST Microelectronics NV, the largest European semiconductor maker, issued $1.2 billion in zero-coupon convertible bonds in July 2003 due in 2010.

Some zero-coupon convertibles have put options, which allow holders to sell their securities back to the issuer at the original issue price plus accrued interest after a certain date (usually 5 or 10 years). Call provisions on many zero-coupon convertible securities have worked to the detriment of investors. Walt Disney's zero-coupon convertible securities, which were scheduled to mature in the year 2005, were called several years after issuance at a price that was lower than what many investors had paid in the secondary market to purchase the zero-coupon convertibles. The conversion feature did not help the holders of those Disney zero-coupon convertible bonds because the securities were tied to Euro Disney stock, traded on the Paris Exchange, which was depressed and trading well below the conversion price.

When market rates of interest decline, many companies redeem their zero-coupon convertible issues and issue new regular bonds with lower coupon yields. The advantage of zero-coupon convertible bonds is the upside potential for appreciation if the common stock rises above the conversion price. However, if conversion does not occur, the holder receives a lower return than with similar-maturity "plain vanilla" bonds (regular bonds).

What Are the Risks of Zero-Coupon Bonds?

The *risk of default* of an issue is directly related to the financial position of the issuer and is of great importance to the zero-coupon bond-holder because interest and principal are paid in a single payment at maturity, and if the issuer is not able to make this single payment, the bondholder receives no payments. With regular bonds, the holder would have received some interest payments during the life of the bond before default. Consequently, the quality of the zero-coupon bond is an assessment of the likelihood of the issuer's ability to be able to pay off the bondholder at maturity. The risk of default can be lessened by choosing high-quality zero-coupon bond issues and/or government stripped bonds.

Interest-rate risk has a greater impact on zero-coupon bonds than on regular-coupon bonds. This increased volatility of zero-coupon bond prices to changes in interest rates is due to the fact that the entire amount that a zero-coupon bondholder receives is a single payment at maturity, whereas for regular interest-bearing bonds the price is the discounted cash flows of the interest payments and principal at maturity. Generally, with coupon interest-paying bonds, the lower the coupon rate of the bond, the greater is the price volatility owing to changes in market rates of interest. This explains the price volatility of zero-coupon bonds, which have no coupon payments. Some zero-coupon bonds are more volatile in price than other similar-yielding zero-coupon bonds as a result of different trading activity, quality differences, call features, and length of time to maturity.

When interest rates decline, many outstanding bond issues are *called*, and zero-coupon bonds are no exception. Zero-coupon bonds also have call provisions, which is a lesson many zero-coupon bondholders have learned the hard way. When interest rates decline, higher-yielding zero-coupon bonds appreciate significantly owing to the fact that these bonds are locked into an above-market-rate yield. However, issuers of these bonds are not thrilled at paying above-market rates, and if their bonds have call provisions, they would call them.

Zero-coupon bonds have no *reinvestment risk* because the yield is determined by the purchase price and then locked in over the life of the bond. With a regular-coupon bond, the holder is faced with the uncertainty of having to reinvest the interest payments at fluctuating market rates of interest. Moreover, the disadvantage occurs when interest rates rise, zero-coupon bondholders are locked into their existing lower yields.

If zero-coupon bonds are sold before maturity, there is always the risk of a loss in principal owing to the extreme volatility of zero-coupon bonds. Zero-coupon bonds are the most volatile of all bonds. In addition, markups in the pricing of zero-coupon bonds are large, and prices of bonds vary from dealer to dealer, making zero-coupon bonds expensive to buy and sell over short periods of time.

Advantages and Disadvantages of Zero-Coupon Bonds

The major advantages of zero-coupon bonds are as follows:

1. They appreciate more than conventional fixed coupon bonds when interest rates decline. However, when market rates rise, prices of zero-coupon bonds generally decline by amounts greater than those of conventional bonds.

TABLE 9-5

Are Contingent Convertible Bonds the New Magic Securities?

Investment bankers historically have been quite innovative in creating new types of investment securities that are always one step ahead of financial rules and regulations. The contingent convertible is one such security. Tyco International, Ltd., is believed to be one of the first companies to have issued contingent convertible securities in order to take advantage of an omission in a Financial Accounting Standards Board proposed rule that did not include contingent convertibles.

Companies issuing regular convertible bonds are required to count the shares that might be converted (if conversion takes place) in their computation of earnings per share using generally accepted accounting principles (GAAP). However, if a condition or a contingency is added to the convertible bond issue, then the company does not have to count the shares as if converted in the earnings per share calculation, thereby avoiding the disclosure of any potential dilution affecting earnings per share. David Henry estimated the hidden dilution of earnings for the following companies that issued contingent convertibles for 2004 to be

Cephalon	15 percent
Lattice Semiconductor	13 percent
Converse Technology	11 percent
General Motors	10 percent
Mercury Interactive	10 percent

Thus, by adding a contingent clause to its convertible bond issue, Cephalon, a biotech company, could exclude the additional shares that would be converted and avoid the revelation of a 15 percent dilution to its earnings in 2004. The terms of the contingent convertible are particularly interesting. Only half of Cephalon's contingent convertible bonds could be converted into common stock when the price of the common stock surpassed 20 percent of the conversion price. The conversion price is $56.50, which means that conversion can only take place if the stock trades above $67.80 (20 percent above $56.50) and for only half the bondholders. Investors also were not deterred by the 0 percent coupon on Cephalon's contingent convertibles, which the company sold easily.

The winner in this type of security is not the bondholder or shareholder of the company, but the company itself. Raising money by paying no interest or in other cases below-market coupons and then being able to postpone the conversion with a condition requiring an additional premium to the conversion price is not advantageous to contingent convertible bondholders. Common stockholders are also in for a nasty surprise. The companies do not have to reveal the amount of dilution to earnings per share if the bonds are exchanged for stock. Thus, with contingent convertible bond issues, there is a cloud over the real amount that a company can earn per share.

Investors should scrutinize the characteristics of other hybrid securities. The tax law of 2003, which cut the maximum tax on dividend income to 15 percent, does not

TABLE 9-5 (Continued)

apply to most preferred stock issues such as trust preferreds. Brokerage firms created these with acronyms such as MIPS, TOPRS, and QUIPS, which are quasi-debt and preferred stock. They have par values of $25, trade on the stock exchanges, and have call provisions and maturity dates. Since the dividends that companies pay on these are a deductible expense, the dividends are taxed at shareholders' marginal tax rates instead of the maximum 15 percent rate.

With any investment, it is "buyer beware," and you should be even more cautious with these "newly minted securities" that investment bankers create.

Source: Henry, David. "The Latest Magic in Corporate Finance," *Business Week*, September 8, 2003, pp. 88 and 90.

2. Investments in zero-coupon bonds require less capital than other fixed-income securities because they are sold at a deep discount. For example, a purchase of 10 regular bonds at face value requires an outlay of $10,000, whereas 10 zero-coupon bonds selling at $180 require a capital outlay of only $1,800.

The major disadvantages of zero-coupon bonds are as follows:

1. The consequences of paying taxes annually on accrued (phantom) interest, which is not received until maturity, creates negative cash flows over the life of the bond.
2. Zero-coupon bond prices are extremely volatile; when market rates of interest rise, zero-coupon bond prices plunge significantly, resulting in large capital losses if the investor sells the bonds before maturity. For zero-coupon bondholders, there is no benefit from an increase in interest rates because there is no coupon interest to reinvest.
3. Many zero-coupon bonds have call provisions, which allow issuers to redeem the bonds before maturity when interest rates decline.
4. If a zero-coupon bond issuer defaults, investors have more to lose than with conventional bonds because with the latter they would have received some interest receipts, which could have been reinvested.

Table 9-5 discusses contingent convertible bonds, a new type of security, explaining why it is so important to understand everything about an investment before investing.

REFERENCES

Faerber, Esmé. *All About Bonds and Bond Mutual Funds.* New York: McGraw-Hill, 2000.

Fabozzi, Frank J., and T. Dessa Fabozzi. "Survey of Bonds and Mortgage-Backed Securities," in Frank J. Fabozzi (ed.), *Portfolio and Investment Management.* New York: McGraw-Hill, 1989.

Options

KEY CONCEPTS

- Options and how they work
- Call options and how to benefit from them
- Put options and how to benefit from them
- Writing options
- Should you invest in stocks or options?
- Use of a combination of puts and calls

This chapter focuses on options, which are stock derivative investments. A *derivative security* is a financial security that derives its value from another security. Stock derivatives, such as options and futures, are securities that offer investors some of the benefits of stocks without having to own them. Futures contracts are discussed in Chapter 11.

OPTIONS AND HOW THEY WORK

An *options* contract gives the holder the right to buy or sell shares of a particular common stock at a predetermined price (strike price) on or before a specified date (expiration date). An option is a right, not an obligation, to buy or sell stock at a specified price before or on an expiration date. The *strike price* is the price at which the holder of the option can buy or sell the stock. An option expires on its *expiration date*. A stock option is a derivative security because its value depends on the underlying security, which is the common stock of the company. For example, the value of an option to buy or sell Intel stock depends on the market price of Intel stock. Other underlying securities for option contracts besides common stock are stock indices, foreign currencies, U.S. government debt, and commodities.

Options are traded on the Chicago Board Options Exchange (CBOE), as well as on the New York Stock Exchange (NYSE), the American Stock Exchange (AMEX), the Philadelphia Exchange (PHLX), and the Pacific Exchange (PSE). Options also can be traded in the over-the-counter (OTC) market.

Understanding how options contracts work can provide you with additional tools that can be used successfully in volatile markets. Options are used to speculate on the movement of future stock prices and to reduce the impact of the volatility of stock prices. In some respects, options are similar to futures contracts. One of these similarities is that option holders with a small investment can control a large dollar amount of stock for a limited time. However, the risk of loss is much less for option holders than it is for futures holders.

An options contract gives the owner the right to buy or sell a specified number of common shares (generally 100) of a company at a specified price within a time period. The two types of contracts to buy and sell stocks are calls and puts. A *call option* gives the option owner the right to buy shares of the underlying company at a predetermined price (strike price) before expiration, and a *put option* gives the option owner the right to sell shares of the underlying company at the strike price before expiration. The option holder has the right to convert the contract at his or her discretion. It is not an obligation. In other words, holders of the option can exercise the option when it is to their advantage. There are six items of note in an options contract:

1. The name of the company whose shares can be bought or sold
2. The number of shares that can be bought or sold, generally 100 shares per contract
3. The exercise or strike price, which is the stated purchase or sale price of the shares in the contract
4. The expiration date, which is the date when the option to buy or sell expires
5. The settlement procedure
6. The options exercise style

As in any contract, there are at least two parties: buyers and sellers. The option buyer is also referred to as the *option holder*, and the seller of the original contract is referred to as the *option writer*. Table 10-1 presents a summary of the features of options buyers and sellers.

TABLE 10-1

Characteristics of Options Contracts for Buyers and Sellers

Option	Buyer's Obligation	Right	Seller's/Writer's Obligation	Right
Call option	Buys at the option price	Owner can buy the underlying stock at the strike price before expiration from the writer	Required to sell the underlying stock at the strike price to the buyer, at the buyer's option, before expiration	Receives the option
Put option	Buys at the option price	Owner can sell the underlying stock at the strike price before expiration to the writer	Required to buy the underlying stock at the strike price before expiration from the buyer, at the buyer's option	Receives the option price

The settlement procedure is stipulated for stock options, which indicates when delivery of the underlying common stock takes place after the holder exercises the option. There are two basic exercise styles that determine when the option can be exercised. Options on individual stocks can be exercised any time before the expiration date (*American style*), whereas stock index options can be exercised only on the expiration date (*European style*). The expiration date is also important because it specifies the life of the option. The expiration dates are standardized for options contracts listed on the exchanges. There are three cycles for listed option expirations, and each option is assigned to one of these cycles:

> January cycle: January – April – July – October
> February cycle: February – May – August – November
> March cycle: March – June – September – December

How Options Work

The following example illustrates how options contracts work. Investor A thinks that the stock of Exxon Corporation is going to go up but does not want to invest the large amount required to buy 100 shares. Investor A can buy a call option contract for 100 shares of Exxon Corporation with a strike price (or exercise price) of $35 per share. Investor W wrote this contract to sell 100 shares of Exxon Corporation stock with a strike price of $35 per share. At the time, Exxon stock was trading around $38 per share. Both investors have different outlooks as to the direction of Exxon's share price. Investor A believes that the share price will go up, whereas Investor W anticipates that the share price is going to decline in the near future.

Investor W bears the risk of loss if the price of Exxon stock goes up instead of down. If Investor A exercises the option to call in the stock, then Investor W will have to buy Exxon stock at a higher price and deliver it to Investor A. Investor W is compensated for this risk by charging the buyer of the contract an amount of money called a *premium* or *option price*. If the premium is $3 per share, Investor A pays $300 to Investor W to buy the call option contract giving Investor A the right to buy 100 share of Exxon stock at $35 per share before the expiration date of the contract.

If the price of Exxon stock rises above $35 per share within the time period before the expiration date, Investor A will profit by exercising the option. Assume that Exxon stock rises to $42 per share within the time period, and Investor A decides to exercise the option. Under the call option terms, Investor A has the right to buy 100 shares of Exxon stock at $35 per share. Investor A pays Investor W $3,500 for 100 shares of Exxon. If Investor W does not have 100 shares of Exxon, he or she would have to buy the stock at $4,200 (100 shares at $42) and transfer it to Investor A.

Investor A paid a total of $3,800: $300 for the option (premium price) plus $3,500 for the stock. The costs for Investor W resulted in a total loss of $400, composed as follows: an outlay of $4,200 that was partially offset by the receipt from Investor A of $3,500 for the stock plus $300 for the option contract. This example is illustrated in Figure 10-1.

FIGURE 10-1

How a Call Option Works

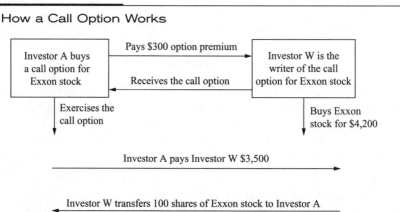

If, on the other hand, the price of Exxon stock declines to $32 and remains at that price throughout the duration of the contract, Investor A will have lost the amount of the contract premium ($300). Thus the greatest amount that an investor can lose buying an option is the cost of the option contract. The advantage of a call option is that the investor has a high degree of leverage (a small amount of money, $3 per share, that controls a larger sum, $35 per share). The option buyer also can profit from selling the option if there is an increase in the premium price.

Investor W also has some alternatives. If Investor W wants to get out of this contract, he or she can buy the contract from someone else. The trading of options is greatly facilitated by the Options Clearing Corporation (OCC), which, besides maintaining a liquid marketplace, also keeps track of the options and the positions of each investor.

Buyers and writers of options do not deal directly with one another but instead deal with the Options Clearing Corporation. When an investor buys a contract, the OCC acts as an intermediary and ensures that the provisions of the contract are fulfilled. When the contract is exercised, the OCC guarantees that the option buyer receives the stock even if the writer defaults on delivery.

Similarly, the OCC facilitates the process of buyers and writers closing out their positions. When a buyer of an option contract sells the contract, the OCC will cancel both entries in the investor's account. The same process is true for a writer of a contract. If a writer wants to get out of his or her position, he or she buys the contract, which then offsets the original position.

The astute reader immediately realizes that in order for the OCC to guarantee this process, there would have to be standardized contracts. Generally, two options on a stock are introduced to the market at the same time with identical terms except for the strike (exercise) price. The contract period for stock options is standardized with three-, six- and nine-month expiration dates. Longer-term options contracts, called *long-term equity anticipation securities* (LEAPS), have been added to the options exchanges. LEAPS can have life spans of up to three years before expiration. They have similar characteristics to the short-tem options contracts, but because of their longer expiration periods they have higher premium prices.

Reading Options Quotes

Newspapers do not list all the stock options available owing to the large number of contracts available. Instead, only the most actively traded stock options are listed in the newspapers. Consequently, if

TABLE 10-2

Example of One of the Most Active Equity Options

Option Name	Strike Price	Volume	Last Price	Net Change	Exchange Close
Nasd 100Tr Mar	37.00	22,491	1.05	0.20	37.62
Nasd 100Tr Mar	37.00 p	22,289	0.35	- 0.30	37.62

February 25, 2005.

you do not see a particular stock option listed in the newspaper, it does not mean that it has expired. It probably was not an actively traded option for that day. Table 10-2 illustrates an example of an actively listed stock option.

The first column in Table 10-2 indicates the name of the option traded, Nasdaq 100 Trust. The month following indicates the expiration, in both cases it is the month of March. The strike price is $37 per share. In the case of the first option, which is a call option, the holder has the right to buy 100 shares of the Nasdaq 100 Trust at $37 per share. In the case of the second option listed, which is a put, denoted by the *p* following the strike price, the option holder has the right to sell 100 shares of the Nasdaq 100 Trust at $37 per share. The next column shows the sales volume of contracts traded for that day (a daily newspaper). For the Nasdaq 100 Trust call option contract, there were 22,491 contracts traded for the day. The last price indicates the price of the last trade of the option ($1.05 per share for the call option and $0.35 per share for the put option). The net change indicates the change in price from the previous day's closing price. The call option increased by $0.20 per share, and the put option decreased by $0.30 per share from the preceding day's closing option prices. The previous day's closing price of Nasdaq 100 Trust's common stock was $37.62 per share.

Different Web sites on the Internet provide more comprehensive listings of options and trading information. Table 10-3 provides an example of online quotes for Cisco stock options. The *call* information is displayed on the first line, and the information on the *put* option is shown on the second line. The Cisco call option has a *strike price* of $17.50 per share and an *expiration* in March. The *last sale* indicates the price of the last transaction of this call option, $0.35

TABLE 10-3

Delayed Option Quotes for Cisco Corporation, February 28, 2005

		Last Sale	Bid	Ask	Vol	Open Interest
Calls	Mar 17.50	0.35	0.30	0.35	1515	57669
Puts	Mar 17.50	0.35	0.30	0.40	3245	42677

Source: http://quote.cboe.com.

per share. In this last trade, a buyer or seller of this call option paid (received) $0.35 per share for this option for the right to call in 100 shares of Cisco stock at $17.50 per share. The bid/ask quotes reflect the highest price that a buyer is willing to pay for an option and the lowest price that a seller is willing to sell the option. The *bid price* of $0.30 per share is the highest price that a purchaser of this option is willing to pay. The *ask price* of $0.35 per share is the lowest price the seller of this option is willing to accept. An investor buys at the ask price and sells at the bid price. The *volume* indicates the number of contracts traded for the day. In both the Cisco put and call options, the trades for that day were 1,515 and 324 contracts, respectively. *Open interest* indicates the number of outstanding or open contracts. When an investor buys an options contract to take a new position in the company, it increases the open interest. Similarly, if an investor sells an options contract that he or she already owns, that investor is closing out a position, and open interest will be decreased by that contract. There are 57,669 open interest contracts for the Cisco call option and 42,677 open interest contracts for the Cisco put option. Table 10-4 lists various Web sites that quote options and outlines how to obtain option quotes using the Chicago Board Options Exchange.

CALL OPTIONS AND HOW TO BENEFIT FROM THEM

A *call option* gives the holder the right to buy 100 shares of the underlying stock at the exercise or strike price up through the date of expiration of the option. Using the Exxon example cited in the

TABLE 10-4

Options Web sites and How to Obtain Price Quotes

Use the Internet to visit the following options exchanges to obtain options price quotes:

www.cboe.com

www.nyse.com

www.amex.com

www.phlx.com

www.pacificex.com

Using the Chicago Board Options Exchange at www.cboe.com, click on "Market quotes", and highlight "delayed options quotes". The 20-minute delayed quotes are free, as they are with stocks. In the box, enter the stock symbol of the option of interest, for example, MSFT for Microsoft, INTC for Intel, PEP for Pepsi Cola. Click on all exchanges, and list all options and LEAPS. Click on "Submit", and a list of options for the stock you requested will appear.

preceding section, we can see how buying a call option can be beneficial to an investor.

In return for paying the premium of $300 ($3 premium price × 100 shares), Investor A has the right to buy Exxon shares at $35 per share anytime until expiration of the option. The downside risk is that the option is not exercised, and the investor loses the $300 (for the option contract) plus a commission. When buying a call option the investor puts up a fraction of the cost of the stock in order to participate in the appreciation of the stock if it moves above the strike price of $35 per share. Instead of putting up $3,800 to buy 100 shares of Exxon stock when the market price is $38 per share, the investor invests $300. Should the stock rise above $38, the investor can exercise the option and buy the stock at the strike price of $35 per share.

The basic problem is that the stock would have to move up in price above the strike price before the option expires because the option is worth nothing at expiration. It is a wasting asset. There is a time value to the price of an option. The more time before the option expires, the greater is the time value of the option. Similarly, as the option moves closer to its expiration, so the time value of the option decreases in value.

The links to the time value of the option are the underlying price of the stock and the call option's strike price. These relationships affect the *intrinsic value* of the option. The intrinsic value is the difference between the market price of the stock and the strike price.

When the market price is greater than the strike price, the call option is said to be *in the money*. In the Exxon example, if the market price of Exxon stock moves up to $37 per share, the intrinsic value of the call option is $2 per share, and the option holder can acquire Exxon stock for less than the current price. The value of a call option is greatest when it is *in the money*. A call option is said to be *out of the money* when the market price of the stock is less than the strike price. *At the money* is when the market price equals the strike price:

$$\text{Intrinisic value of call option} = (\text{market price of the stock} - \text{strike price})$$

$$= (\$37 - \$35)$$

$$= \$2 \text{ per share}$$

The time until expiration of the option has a direct effect on the valuation of the option. The greater the length of time until expiration, the greater is the chance that the option will be *in the money*. Thus, an option with a longer time until expiration trades at a higher premium than options approaching expiration.

The option premium price fluctuates depending on two factors:

- The underlying price of the stock
- The time left until the expiration of the option

If Exxon's stock moves up to $40 per share, the intrinsic value of the option rises to $5 per share. This increase in the stock price causes the option to trade for much more than the $3 premium price that the option was sold for originally.

Another course of action for the call buyer is to sell the option for a profit rather than exercising it. The leverage that can be obtained explains why so many investors prefer this course of action. See the example in Table 10-5, which illustrates the benefits of leverage from buying and selling the option rather than buying and selling the stock.

Buying and selling the stock, in scenario one, results in a 20 percent return. This is not to be sneezed at; but compared with buying and selling the option, in scenario two, the buying and selling of the stock comes in as a poor second to a return of 230 percent. Comparatively, the third scenario of buying and exercising the option produces the smallest return of 12 percent. Moreover, this third alternative also requires the greatest outlay of capital ($3,750 versus only $250 for the call option and $3,500 to buy the stock). However, if the stock price declines to $30 per share, buying the stock

TABLE 10-5

Leverage: Should You Buy and Sell the Option or the Stock?

Stock price $35   Option price $2.5   Strike price $35
Stock price rises to $42   Option premium price increases to $8.25

Scenario one: Buying the Stock

Buy 100 shares of the stock at $35 per share	Total cost	$3,500
Sell 100 shares of the stock at $42 per share	Total proceeds	$4,200
Profit		$ 700
Return on investment 700/3500	20 percent	

Scenario two: Buying and Selling the Option

Buy stock option	Total cost	$ 250
Sell stock option	Total proceeds	$ 825
Profit		$ 575
Return on investment 575/250	230 percent	

Scenario three: Exercise Option

Buy stock option	Cost	$ 250
Cost to exercise option at strike price	Cost	3,500
Total cost	Total	$3,750
Sell stock at $42 per share	Total proceeds	$4,200
Profit		$ 450
Return on investment 450/3750	12 percent	

at $35 and selling it at $30 results in a $500 loss and a 14.28 percent loss (–500/3500). Buying the stock option and having it expire, results in a 100 percent loss on invested capital and a $250 loss of capital. There is no third alternative because the strike price is above the current price so the option would not be exercised. The maximum loss is the cost of the option, $250. The three profit/loss scenarios are illustrated in Fig. 10-2.

Buying and selling the option not only gives the greatest return on investment but also requires the lowest capital outlay. By buying a call option instead of the stock, the investor invests a small fraction of the cost of the stock. If the stock price rises significantly above the strike price within the period before expiration, the investor can profit by selling or exercising the option. In the latter case, the investor then can sell the stock or hold it for long-term capital appreciation.

FIGURE 10-2

Profit and Loss from Buying the Stock Versus a Call Option

Buy the stock at $35 per share and sell that stock at $42 per share

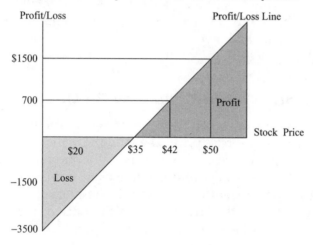

Buying the Call Option at $250 and selling the Call Option at $825

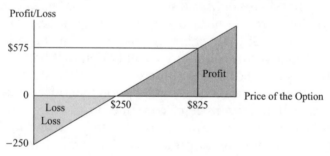

Profit and loss from Exercising Call Option

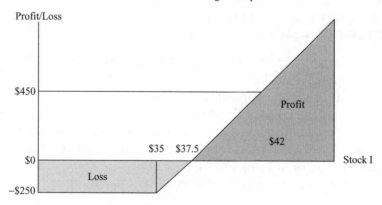

The most that an investor can lose from buying a call option is the cost of the option. Thus the downside risk is limited, as opposed to the potential loss in the case of buying stock. There are many examples of high-flying stocks that have risen to abnormally high prices only to fall back into oblivion, resulting in tremendous losses for those investors who had invested, when the stocks were trading at excessively high prices.

Situations Where Calls May Be Used

Call options benefit buyers when the price of the underlying stock rises above the strike or exercise price. The example in the preceding section shows that if an investor bought the call option instead of the stock, the greatest percentage return would come from selling the option, owing to the concept of leverage. If the market price of the stock declines below the strike price of the option, the most that the investor would lose is the option premium.

Call options also may be used as a hedge against an upturn in the price of a stock on a short position. Assume that an investor had sold short 100 shares of Merck stock when it was $80 per share. When the price of Merck declines to $69 per share, the investor wants to protect the $11 profit per share against a rise in the price of Merck stock. The investor could buy a call option that has a strike price of $70 per share. For every $1 increase in Merck stock above $70 per share, there is a profit on the call option that offsets the loss on the short sale. If, however, Merck continues to go down in price, the investor has lost only the amount paid to buy the option. This strategy allows an investor to protect profits without having to close out his or her position.

PUT OPTIONS AND HOW TO BENEFIT FROM THEM

A *put option* gives the holder the right to sell 100 shares of the under-lying company's stock at the strike price until the expiration date of the option. This is the opposite of a call option. The put option buyer profits when the price of the underlying stock falls below the strike price. A put option increases in value when the price of the under-lying stock declines. Investors buy puts when they are bearish on the stock. The premiums on puts generally are smaller than those of calls for the same stock. This is so because more investors are bullish than bearish, and hence fewer put options are traded than call options.

When to Buy Puts

Put options are used to protect existing profits in stocks and limit the extent of capital losses in existing stock positions. Investors profit from buying puts when the price of the underlying stock declines below the exercise or strike price. Rather than selling a stock short when a decline in the stock's price is anticipated, an investor can buy a put option. For example, if an investor is bearish on a stock that is currently trading at $32 per share, a six-month put option with a strike price of $30 could be bought for about $200 (contract for 100 shares). If the stock does go down in price below the strike price, the investor can either exercise the option by selling 100 shares of the stock at the strike price of $30 per share and buying the stock at the lower market price or sell the put option at a profit.

The use of put options limits the risk of loss as compared with short selling, where the risk of loss is open-ended. When selling a stock short, the price of the stock could increase rather than decrease, thereby increasing the amount of money that would be lost. The greatest amount that can be lost with a put option is the premium paid to buy the option.

The put option holder has various alternatives:

- Exercise the option at the strike price using your own shares, or buy the shares at a lower price and tender them at exercise.
- Sell the option at a profit.
- If the stock price increases above the strike price, the option expires, and the most that can be lost is the amount of the premium paid for the option.

These alternatives are shown in Table 10-6, also illustrating the concept of leverage. Assume that years ago you bought 100 shares of a stock at $30 per share, and the stock price is currently $70 per share. You buy a six-month put option on that stock with a strike price of $70 for a premium of $200.

The put option holder also benefits from leverage in the same manner as for call options. For a small premium, the investor can control the larger dollar value of the stock, as shown by the rate of return of 1,400 percent in alternative C. In alternative A, you have protected your existing capital profit against the decline in market

TABLE 10-6

Returns from Buying and Exercising Put Options or Buying and Selling Puts

---

Present situation

Own 100 shares of the stock at a cost basis of	$3,000 ($30 per share)
Buy a six month put option with a strike price of $70 per share	Premium cost $200

5-months time

Price of the stock declines to $40 per share

A. Exercise the Put Option Using Your 100 shares

Exercise the put option (sell the shares at $70 per share), Gross proceeds$7,000

Tender the shares originally purchased at a cost of		3,000
Profit		4,000
Rate of return on investment $4,000/$3200*	125 percent	

* includes the cost of the option

B. Exercise the Put Option and Buy the Shares at the Lower Price

Sell the shares at $70 per share	Gross proceeds	$7,000
Purchase 100 shares at a cost of $40 per share		4,000
Profit		3,000
Rate of return on investment $3,000/$4200	71 percent	

C. Sell the Put Option

Sell the put option $30 per share	Gross proceeds	$3,000
Cost to purchase the put option		200
Profit		2,800
Rate of return on investment $2,800/200	1,400 percent	

D. Price of the Stock Rises to $90 per Share at the End of Six Months

Value of the put option equals 0 at expiration

Loss is $200, or 100 percent of invested capital.

---

price of the stock through the purchase of a put option. If you did not already own the stock or wanted to retain the shares of the stock that you originally purchased, you could exercise the option and purchase the shares for a 71 percent return, as shown in alternative B.

As with calls, puts are wasting assets and have no value at expiration. The intrinsic value of the put option is determined by subtracting the market price of the stock from the strike price.

$$\text{The intrinsic value of a put option} = \text{strike price} - \text{market price of the stock}$$

The intrinsic value cannot be less than zero (a negative number) by convention. If an option has no intrinsic value, it is said to be *out of the money*. When it is profitable to exercise the put option, it is said to be *in the money* because it does have intrinsic value. If the strike price equals the market price of the stock, the option is said to be *at the money*. Generally, options are not exercised until they are close to expiration because an earlier exercise means throwing away the remaining time value. Another generalization with options (both calls and puts) is that most options are not bought with the intent of exercising them. Instead, they are bought with the intent of selling them.

When an option is *in the money*, the option holder can sell and receive an amount of money greater than the premium paid, whereas if the option is exercised, the put holder has to come up with the money to buy the stocks (if they are not already owned) so that they can then be sold at the strike price. Transaction costs are incurred in both these transactions.

The use of a put option can be viewed as an insurance premium to protect profits against a decline in the price of the stock.

WRITING OPTIONS

Investors also can write or sell options, which provide additional income from the premiums received from the buyers of the option contracts. The upside potential to this strategy for option writers, however, is limited because the most money that the writer can make is the amount of the option premium.

There are two ways to write options. The more conservative method is to write covered options. A *covered option* is an option that is written against an underlying stock that is owned or sold short by the writer. The writer of the option owns the stock against which the options are written. The second method is the writing of a *naked option*, which is an option written on an underlying stock that is not owned or sold short by the writer.

Writing Covered Calls

Investors seeking ways to increase income on stocks that they already own can write covered calls. Using this strategy works the same way as a call, except that the writer owns the stock. An example illustrates how writing covered calls work.

Suppose that an investor has 1,000 shares of Citigroup stock that was purchased some time back at $25 per share. Citigroup is selling around $48 per share. Instead of selling the stock outright, the investor can write call options on Citigroup. If the investor writes 10 call contracts of 100 shares per contract with a strike price of $50 at a premium of $2 per share ($2,000 for 10 contracts) with expiration in September, he or she will receive $2,000 minus commissions. If Citigroup's stock price never goes above $50 per share before expiration of the contracts, the buyer will not exercise the call, and the writer ends up with an additional $2,000 (minus commissions on the options contracts).

If the stock price rises above $50 per share, the buyer exercises the call and buys the stock for $50 per share. The writer makes a profit of $27 per share ($50 minus the $25 cost of the shares plus the $2 per share premium). This is the maximum profit that the writer will get from the covered call option, even if Citigroup rises to $100 per share. This additional appreciation will be lost because the writer must surrender the stock at the strike price of $50.

Summing up, a covered call limits the appreciation the writer can realize. Therefore, it is a good idea to write covered calls on the stocks that you think will not rise or fall very much in price. The other side of the coin is that if the stock falls significantly in price during the option period, the writer will lose money if the writer eventually sells the stock at the low price. The call buyer will not exercise the call because the market price of the stock will be cheaper than the strike price.

Writing Naked Calls

Writing a naked call on a stock is more risky than writing a covered call because of the potential for unlimited losses. A naked call occurs when the writer does not own the underlying stock, which would limit the losses if the stock rocketed up in price. For example, assume that a writer writes a naked call on Citigroup stock for which the writer receives a premium of $2 per share with a strike price of $50 per share. If Citigroup rises dramatically in price to $90 per share and the option buyer exercises the call, the writer will be left with a large loss. The writer receives $50 per share (the strike price) plus the premium price of $2 per share, but he or she also would have to pay $90 per share to buy the stock to deliver to the buyer. Of course, if the writer anticipates the rise in price, he or she would have bought

Citigroup stock earlier at a lower price or bought back the option to close out his or her position.

Writers of naked (or uncovered) options, calls, and puts must deposit the required margins with their brokerage firms, whereas writers of covered options need not deposit any money with their brokerage firms. Investors can profit from writing naked calls on stocks whose prices either decline or remain relatively flat below the strike price for calls.

Writing Covered Puts

A put is the opposite position to a call. The writer of a covered put would sell short the underlying stock and would receive a premium for the covered put. If the option is exercised, the writer would buy back the stock at the strike price and use the shares to close out his or her short position. Writing covered put options is rare because if the writer sells short the stock, the writer expects the stock to go down in price. If the stock goes up in price, it would not benefit the writer to write a covered put because the option would not be exercised, and the writer would have to buy back the stock at a higher price to close out the short sale.

Writing Naked Puts

The writer of a put option expects the stock to rise or at best not fall in price. If the put writer does not own the underlying stock, the contract is a naked or uncovered put, which necessitates that the writer deposit an amount of money with the brokerage firm for the required margin. Thus, without owning the underlying stocks, the potential loss is not cushioned if the price of the stock falls rapidly.

For example, when the market price of Citigroup is at $45 per share, if an investor writes a naked put on Citigroup with a strike price of $45 and receives a $2 premium per share, the writer has the same loss potential as owning the shares. If the shares decline in price, the writer would lose money. For example, if Citigroup shares fall to $40 per share, the writer would have to buy Citigroup at $45 at exercise, resulting in a loss of $300 ($4,500 − $4,000 + $200). The most that can be lost is $43 per share (the price of the stock up to $45 per share if Citigroup declines to $0 before expiration minus the option premium of $2 per share). If the price of Citigroup's stock

FIGURE 10-3

Profit and Loss from Writing a Naked Put on Citigroup Stock

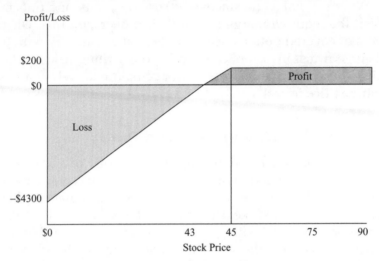

rises above $45 per share, the put option will not be exercised, and the maximum profit that the writer will make is $200. The profit/loss in this example is illustrated graphically in Fig. 10-3.

SHOULD YOU INVEST IN STOCKS OR OPTIONS?

The Advantages of Options

- Options allow investors to speculate on the future direction of the price of a stock by investing a relatively small amount of money.
- Investors can use options as insurance to hedge against large losses from adverse changes in stock prices.
- Writing options provides a source of income for investors.
- The losses from buying options are limited to the amount of the premium.

The Disadvantages of Options

- Options are wasting assets in that they have short lives (up to nine months). LEAPs have longer lives.

TABLE 10-7

Summary of Profit and Loss Potential

Purchase common stock	Unlimited gain; maximum loss is the cost of the stock
Purchase call option	Unlimited gain; maximum loss is the cost of the option
Purchase a put option	Maximum gain is the strike price minus the cost of the option; maximum loss is the cost of the put option
Write a call option	Maximum gain is the premium received on the option; maximum loss limited to no more than the cost of the stock minus the premium
Write a put option	Maximum gain is the premium received on the option; maximum loss is the strike price minus the premium received from the option.
Sell stock short	Maximum gain is the price of the stock; unlimited loss
Covered call	Maximum gain is the strike price minus the cost of the shares plus the premium received on the option; maximum loss is the price paid for the stock
Write a naked put option	Maximum gain is the premium received on the option; maximum loss is the price of the stock falling to $0 minus the premium received on the option

- If the price of the stock does not reach or go beyond the strike price, the option investor loses money.
- Although options can be used to produce relatively large percentage profits from the small amounts invested, you need to be aware that commissions tend to be high on a percentage basis.

Table 10-7 summarizes the potential profits and losses for the different ownership positions in stocks and options.

USE OF A COMBINATION OF PUTS AND CALLS

As investors get more sophisticated in their use of options, there are situations where a combination of puts and calls can be combined for profit opportunities. A *straddle* is the purchase (or sale) of a put and a call with the same strike price and the same expiration date, whereas a *spread* is the purchase or sale of a combination of put and call options contracts with different strike prices.

Using a Straddle

The following example illustrates how an investor can profit from using a straddle. Suppose that an investor is interested in buying some oil stocks. With an economic slowdown in Europe and Asia and the possibility of Iraqi oil coming back into the world markets, the investor is not sure whether the price of oil will go up or down from its current price.

Consequently, instead of buying oil stocks, the investor could buy a combination call and put option on an oil stock. Options on Exxon, whose stock was trading at $39 per share, can be bought as follows:

- $2⅜ ($237.50 per contract) for a January call with a strike price of $40.
- $2⅜ ($237.50 per contract) for a January put with a strike price of $40.

The total cost of this straddle is $475.00 ($237.50 + $237.50) plus commissions, which means that the greatest potential loss is limited to this cost if Exxon stock does not rise above $44¾ or below $35¼ per share in the next six months before expiration. If the price of oil goes up, oil stocks could jump in price. Assume that Exxon stock goes up to $48 per share. The call option could be sold at around $800 ($8 × 100 shares), resulting in a profit for the investor. If, on the other hand, Iraqi oil comes back into the worldwide supply, causing a glut of oil, oil stock prices could fall. If Exxon stock falls to $33 per share, the put option could be sold for around $7 per share, resulting in a profit from selling this option.

If Exxon stock trades above $44.75 or below $35.25, the investor profits from selling the call or put options, respectively. If Exxon trades within the $35.25 to $44.75 range, the investor loses money on the straddle. The amount of the loss depends on the price of Exxon stock. For example, if the investor sold the call option when Exxon stock was trading at $43.50, the option could be sold at around $3.50, or $350 per contract. The loss then would be $125 (the cost of the straddle options, $475, minus the proceeds received from the sale of the option, $350). Commissions increase the loss further.

To profit from this straddle, the price of the underlying stock has to move considerably in either direction, upward or downward.

Using a Spread

An investor can use a spread strategy, which is the purchase and sale of different options with different strike prices and expiration dates. For example, an investor could take both a long and a short position in two different options on the same stock. Consider the following information in Table 10-8.

There are a number of different spreads that can be used to hedge positions, and limit potential losses and potential profits. You can use the Internet to obtain information on option prices to test your straddle and spread strategies before you invest. Table 10-9 illustrates how to obtain information using Yahoo's Web site.

TABLE 10-8

Use of a Spread

Stock price of a company $43

Six-month call option with a strike price of $40 with a premium cost of $4 per share ($400 per contract)

Three-month call option with a strike price of $45 with a premium cost of $2 per share ($200 per contract)

Strategy

Buy the call option with a strike price of $40 per share	Cost	($400)
Write (sell) the call option with a strike price of $45 per share	Premium receipt	200
	Net outlay	$200

The maximum profit if the stock rises above $45 is $300 from this combination. The investor exercises the call and pays $40 per share and then tenders the shares, receiving $45 per share when the call option with the strike price of $45 is exercised. This results in a profit of $300 ($500 minus the $200 net outlay for option premium). The maximum loss is $200 if the stock price falls below $45 per share.

TABLE 10-9

Web Exercise

Go to www.yahoo.com. Click on "Finance", and enter stock symbols that you are interested in following. Pull up a detailed view of these stocks. Click on "options", found beneath the chart. Use the options quotes to test your straddle and spread strategies.

How to Use Stock Index Options

Stock index options allow investors to take long and short positions in the market without having to buy or sell short the stocks that make up the index. A stock index option is a put or call written on a market index. Options are offered on most of the major stock market indices, namely, the Standard and Poors (S&P) 500 Index, the Dow Jones Industrial Average, the Nasdaq 100 Index, and the Russell 2000 Index. Settlement for stock index options is in cash rather than stocks. For example, if a call option for the S&P 500 Index has a strike price of $1,050, the holder has the option of buying the index for cash for $105,000 (100 × 1,050) at expiration. If the S&P 500 Index increases above the strike price plus the cost of the option, the holder will make some money. If you think that the market is going to decline, you can buy a put option.

With stock index options you can track the markets without having to buy or sell the stocks. The Dow Jones Industrial Average consists of 30 blue chip stocks, the S&P 500 Index consists of 500 large-capitalization stocks, the Nasdaq 100 tracks the 100 largest stocks on the Nasdaq, and the Russell 2000 consists of 2,000 small-capitalized stocks. These broad-based stock index options are traded actively primarily on the Chicago Board Options Exchange. Options on stock indices are valued and trade in the same way as options on individual stocks, with the notable exceptions that settlement is made in cash for the former.

The use of stock index options can assist individual investors with large stock portfolios to hedge against potential losses. If the investor does not want to sell holdings of appreciated stocks in the portfolio, the investor can protect these gains by buying stock index put options. If the market declines, the stock index puts will rise in value, which will offset the losses on the individual stocks. Instead, if the investor wrote call options on the stock index resembling the portfolio, the value of the options would decline if the market declined. The stocks in the portfolio would lose value, but this loss would be offset by the premiums received from writing the call options.

CHAPTER 11

Futures

KEY CONCEPTS

- Futures contracts
- The mechanics of investing in futures contracts and stocks
- Returns from investing in futures contracts
- Speculating or hedging using futures contracts
- Analysis of the futures markets
- Financial futures

Futures contracts are complex investments that should not feature in the portfolios of most investors owing to their higher risk of loss than other securities such as stocks and bonds. The higher risk is due in part to the leverage obtained from futures contracts. Investors in futures contracts are required to pay only a small percentage (2 to 10 percent) of the total value of the contract. If the value of the contracts decline significantly, investors are required to pay in additional amounts. Failure to remit these additional funds results in losses and a liquidation of investors' positions.

FUTURES CONTRACTS

The *futures market* is an organized market in which futures contracts on commodities and financial futures are traded. Some of the commodities include agricultural products, such as corn, soybeans, barley, orange juice, cattle, pork bellies, coffee, cotton, and lumber, and metals, such as gold, platinum, silver, and copper. There are a number of financial futures that include trading in contracts on U.S. Treasury notes and bonds, the stock market indices, such as the Dow Jones Industrial Average and the Standard & Poor's (S&P) 500 Index, the Municipal Bond Index, and foreign currencies such as the euro, Japanese yen, Swiss franc, and British pound.

Trading in the futures markets can provide an adult with the same exhilaration that a rollercoaster ride provides a child. There are overnight profits and losses of a far greater magnitude than those offered by other financial investments such as stocks and bonds. Consequently, investing in the futures market is also among the riskier investments.

THE MECHANICS OF INVESTING IN FUTURES CONTRACTS

A *futures contract* is an agreement between a buyer and a seller to take or make delivery of a commodity or financial security on a particular date in the future at an agreed-on price. The futures exchanges are where futures contracts are bid and offered by traders. A commodity or financial future can be purchased for current or future delivery. A futures contract is a binding contract that is standardized. A commodity contract specifies the type of commodity, grade, and size. For example, a Chicago Board of Trade corn contract is traded in 5,000 bushels of number 2 yellow corn. The delivery month is the specified month within which the delivery is made. The month defines the life of the contract in the same manner as an option. For corn contracts, the delivery months are March, May, July, September, and December. The exchanges also have their own trading hours, unlike those of stocks, which begin trading on the New York Stock Exchange (NYSE) at 9.30 A.M. Eastern time and close at 4 P.M. U.S. Treasury bond futures, for example, trade from 7.20 A.M. to 2.00 P.M., whereas S&P 500 Index futures contracts trade between 8.30 A.M. and 3.15 P.M. Commodities contracts also trade at different times. Table 11-1 presents an example of the quantities and values of a cross section of commodity and financial futures contracts.

The exchanges listed are the Chicago Board of Trade (CBT), Chicago Mercantile Exchange (CME), Commodities Exchange (CMX), and the New York Mercantile Exchange (NYM). Table 11-2 illustrates how to obtain futures contract information using the Chicago Board of Trade Web site.

TABLE 11-1

Selected Information on Futures Contracts

Contract	Size	Exchange	Market Value per Contract*
5-Year Treasury	$100,000	CBT	$108,005
Eurodollars	$1 million	CME	$970,000
Nasdaq 100 Index	$100 × Index	CME	$153,200
Gold	100 troy oz.	CMX	$ 44,300
Light sweet crude	1,000 bbl.	NYM	$ 54,590
Soybean meal	100 tons	CBT	$ 18,100

* Market value is as of the settlement price on March 8, 2005.

TABLE 11-2

How to Obtain Information on Futures Contracts Using the Web

Use the Internet to gather information on different futures contracts. On the Chicago Board of Trade Web site, www.cbot.com, you can determine contract specifications for various commodities, margin requirements, and trade quotes. In addition, explore the links on the Web site to provide additional information on futures trading: Knowledge Center, Glossary of Terms, and Frequently Asked Questions.

How to Read Futures Quotations.

Prices of futures contracts are reported daily in the financial section of the newspapers in the same way as stock and bond quotes. Intraday prices of commodities and financial futures contracts can be obtained by logging onto the Web sites of the futures exchanges. Table 11-3 shows the information on gold futures quotes found in the Futures section of the newspaper.

Gold is traded at the COMEX, a division of the New York Mercantile Exchange, and the unit for trading in each gold futures contract is 100 troy ounces. The price quotes are in dollars per troy ounce. The first column indicates the month of expiration (delivery) of each contract. For the April-delivery gold contract, the opening price was $435.80, the high price for the day was $441.30, and the low price for the day was $435.20. The *settle price* is the closing price for the day ($441.10), which was $5.30 higher than the previous

TABLE 11-3

Financial Futures Quotations

Gold (CMX) 100 troy oz; $ per troy oz.						Lifetime		Open
	Open	High	Low	Settle	Chg.	High	Low	Int.
Apr	435.80	441.30	435.20	441.10	5.30	460.50	380.00	186,586
Dec	447.00	452.00	447.00	451.80	5.30	471.00	298.40	21,808
Fb06	451.40	451.40	451.40	454.80	5.40	469.00	415.00	3,181

Prices as of March 8, 2005.

day's closing price. The lifetime high and low prices indicate the range of prices for each contract. *Open interest* is the number of contracts outstanding, 186,586 for April delivery. A large number of open contracts indicate greater liquidity and activity, such as for April gold delivery. A small number of delivery contracts is not unusual for contracts nearing their expiration dates. This is so because many positions are closed out before delivery. Less than 2 percent of all futures positions are delivered. Thus, over the life of a contract, the open interest increases after the contract comes into existence and then declines as the delivery date approaches.

The following example illustrates how futures trading works. Assume that you decide to buy a December gold contract (delivery in three months) at the current price of $448.00 because you think that the price of gold will rise in the future. If in three months time gold goes up in price and the contract now trades at $478.80, you either could sell the contract at $478.80 per ounce or could wait until expiration and receive delivery of 100 troy ounces, paying $448.00 per ounce. You then could sell the 100 troy ounces of gold immediately at the spot price to make your profit. Assume that the cash price is $478.60 per ounce.

Trade the futures contract

Buy the gold futures contract at $448.00

Sell the futures contract at $478.80

Profit per ounce $30.80

Profit per contract = 30.80 × 100 ounces = $3,080

Buy futures contract and take delivery

Buy the gold contract at $448.00
and take delivery of 100 ounces   Total cost $44,800

Sell 100 ounces of gold at the
cash price $478.60   Proceeds   <u>47,860</u>

      Profit $3,060, or $30.60 per ounce

If gold declines in price after you buy the contract, the price of your futures contract will decline. If you sell the contract when the price declines to $430.00, you will have lost $18.00 per ounce or $1,800 per contract ($18.00 × 100 troy ounces).

Buying a futures contract is referred to as *taking a long position. A long position* is established when futures contracts are bought because the buyer expects the price to increase. The preceding example illustrates a long position. When selling futures contracts, the seller expects prices to decline and therefore *takes a short position. A short position* is established when contracts are sold in expectation of future price declines in the commodity/financial security. The following example illustrates a short position.

Example: Sell Short a Futures Contract

If you expect gold prices to decline in the future, you could sell short gold futures contracts. Suppose that you sell short the December-delivery gold futures contract at $448.00. This represents a contract value of $44,800 ($448.00 × 100).

If gold declines $5 per ounce, you could buy a December contract to close out your position, and your profit would be $500 per contract. Of course, if gold goes up $5, you would lose $500 per contract.

What Makes Trading Futures Different from Trading Stocks?

Futures contracts are bought on margin. *Margin* is the minimum amount of funds required on deposit to purchase or sell short a futures contract. The difference between the margin requirements for stocks and futures is considerable. The margin requirements for purchasing stock is 50 percent of the purchase price, whereas the margin required to purchase futures contracts varies from about 2 to 10 percent of the purchase price. Margin is defined as the amount of equity that must be deposited when purchasing securities.

Consequently, using margin to trade futures contracts plays an even larger role than in the purchase of stocks and bonds.

An *initial margin requirement* is the amount of money that must be deposited when initiating a position in a futures contract. These minimum amounts are set for each commodity or financial futures contract by the exchange, but the brokerage firm has the right to increase this minimum requirement. For example, the initial margin requirements for a corn futures contract was $506, a wheat contract $810, and a minisized soybean contract $365 effective as of March 4, 2005, according to the Chicago Board of Trade.

The market values of futures contracts fluctuate with changes in the price of the underlying commodity/security. Consequently, brokerage firms require a *maintenance margin*, which is a minimum amount of funds that must be deposited to hold the position in the account. When the amount of funds in the account falls below this minimum amount it triggers a margin call. For example, if $506 is the initial margin required on deposit for a corn contract, an amount of $375 may be required as a maintenance margin. Generally, the amount of the maintenance margin is less than the initial margin requirement. If the amount of the futures contract falls below the maintenance margin level, the investor will need to invest more funds to bring the level back up to the additional maintenance level or the position will be liquidated by the brokerage firm. The request for additional funds is referred to as a *margin call*. A margin call is a request from the brokerage firm for additional funds in order to maintain the position when the account drops below the maintenance margin amount. The following example illustrates the use of the margin process.

Example of How Margins Work

Assume that an investor buys a gold futures contract with an initial margin requirement of $1,350. Assume that the maintenance margin is $1,000 and that the investor buys one futures contract at $400 per ounce. The investor deposits $1,350 in an account with the brokerage firm to place the order.

If gold closes down $1 per ounce the next day, the investor's margin account is debited (deducted) $100 for the loss on the contract. A $1 move results in a $100 change because each contract size is 100 troy ounces. The balance in the account is now $1,250 ($1,350 – $100).

If gold declines by $3 on the next day, the account balance drops to $950 ($1250 – 300). This is below the margin maintenance of $1,000 per contract. The investor receives a margin call for additional funds. The investor must either deposit more funds to keep the gold futures contract or liquidate the position. If the investor decides to deposit more funds, a deposit of $400 will be required to bring the balance back to initial margin requirement of $1,350.

There are several points to be noted in trading futures contracts that differ from trading stocks.

1. Because margins are a small fraction of the value of a futures contract, these transactions are highly leveraged (the ability to control a large account value with a small investment). A small change in the price of the commodity results in large changes in the total value of the contract. This means that the investor can rack up large potential gains or losses from small moves in the underlying commodity or financial security.

2. Gains and losses on futures accounts are recognized on a daily basis. This process is referred to as *marking to the market* in which futures accounts are valued at the close of each trading day. Marking to the market is the process of adjusting futures contract accounts to reflect their market values at the end of the trading day. When the account level falls below the margin maintenance amount, a margin call is issued. If additional funds are not added to the account to restore the margin requirement, the futures position is liquidated.

3. Only a small percentage of futures contracts are held to maturity. Most futures positions are closed out before maturity. To close out a position, the investor reverses the position. For example, if the investor is short a corn futures contract, the broker is instructed by the investor to go long a corn futures contract, which cancels the position.

4. Exchanges impose daily limits on the amount of price changes allowed for futures contracts in a day. The *daily limit* is the maximum price increase or decrease allowed for a commodity futures' price from the preceding day's settle price. If a commodity futures contract falls by the allowable daily limit, further price decreases are not allowed for the rest of the day. The same applies to price increases to the allowable daily limit price. Trading in these contracts still can take place at the limit prices or within the daily trading range for that day. For example, the daily allowable limit for pork belly contracts is currently 3 cents per pound up or down

from the previous day's closing price. Thus, if pork belly contracts decline by 3 cents from the previous day's closing price and there is further weakness in pork belly pricing, the price would not fall below the 3 cent limit. If there are no buyers at the limit price, no trades take place. The reasons for setting these daily limits are to limit the potentially disruptive financial effects of large moves in commodity futures prices and to maintain orderly markets.

RETURNS FROM INVESTING IN FUTURES CONTRACTS

The only type of return received from investing in futures contracts is in the form of a capital gain or loss. Holders of futures contracts receive no income. Investors in futures contracts put up a small fraction of the total cost of the contract, which is the margin requirement. Consequently, if there are wide swings in price of the underlying commodity or financial security, an investor's margin requirement can double or be eliminated within a short period of time. The following equation illustrates how to determine the return on an investment in a futures contract. The return is based on the amount invested (margin deposit) and not the total value of the contract. It is this use of leverage that magnifies the potential returns or losses on these contracts.

$$\text{Return on investment} = \frac{\text{selling price of futures contract} - \text{purchase price of futures contract}}{\text{margin deposit}}$$

Assume that you bought two gold futures contracts at \$400 (\$400 per troy ounce), requiring an initial margin of \$2,700 (\$1,350 per contract). These two contracts control 200 troy ounces of gold worth \$80,000 ($2 \times 100 \times \$400$). If you closed out your contracts when they rise in price to \$412, your return on invested capital would be 89 percent:

$$\text{Return on investment} = \frac{\text{selling price of futures contract} - \text{purchase price of futures contract}}{\text{margin deposit}}$$

$$= \frac{\$82,400 - \$80,000}{2,700}$$

$$= 89 \text{ percent}$$

This return of 89 percent is mainly due to leverage. The amount of the initial margin requirement that was invested was only 3.38 percent of the total value of the contract at purchase, whereas the price of the gold contract only rose by 3 percent ($12/$400). If the price of the commodity falls below the purchase price, leverage works as a double-edged sword in that the losses also would be magnified. Assume that you closed out your position in the two gold contracts when the price decreased to $393 rather than depositing additional funds as requested by a margin call. Your loss would be 52 percent:

$$\text{Return on investment} = \frac{\text{selling price of futures contract} - \text{purchase price of futures contract}}{\text{margin deposit}}$$

$$= \frac{\$78,600 - \$80,000}{2,700}$$

$$= -52 \text{ percent}$$

SPECULATING OR HEDGING USING FUTURES CONTRACTS

There are two basic types of participants in the futures markets: speculators and hedgers. *Speculators* are traders who buy and sell futures contracts without intending to take delivery of a commodity or financial security. In other words, they are short-term traders of futures contracts (taking long or short positions) based on their assessment of the direction of futures prices. The large speculators usually consist of fund managers, and small speculators are individual traders, which account for most of the trading volume.

Hedgers are traders who seek to protect themselves from price fluctuations by taking opposite positions. In other words, traders seek to reduce the risk of loss from price fluctuations in commodities and financial securities by simultaneously taking a long and short position. Some examples of hedgers are farmers, jewelers, importers, exporters, and stock portfolio managers who seek to protect themselves from price fluctuations in their respective positions in underlying commodities and financial securities. For example, corn farmers are aware of their costs to grow corn and would like to profit from their efforts. If it costs $2.25 to grow a bushel of corn for delivery in March and a corn futures contract is trading at $2.40 per bushel, a corn farmer can lock in a profit of $0.15 per bushel. The farmer would sell a March futures contract for $2.40 per bushel, and the buyer would take delivery of 5,000 bushels (the contract size) in March. If the price of corn falls to $2.20 per bushel, the farmer would have locked in a profit of $0.15 per bushel because the buyer of the contract pays $2.40 per bushel. However, if the price of corn increases to $2.50 per bushel, the corn farmer would receive only $2.40 per bushel. In this case it is the buyer who profits when the corn futures price rises above $2.40. The buyer pays the contract price of $2.40 per bushel and then can turn around and sell the corn in the cash market for $2.50 per bushel, realizing a $0.10 per bushel profit. Thus users of a commodity can profit by hedging their positions in the opposite direction.

If a jeweler needs 100 ounces of gold in three months time, the jeweler could wait for three months and then buy the gold in the cash market at the prevailing price. Another option is to hedge against rising prices by using a futures contract. If a gold futures contract for delivery in three months time is trading at $440 per ounce, the jeweler buys the contract, locking in that price per ounce. If gold rises above $440 per ounce, the jeweler has hedged his or her position successfully and would not be out of pocket by the additional rise in the gold price above $440 per ounce. However, if gold falls below $440 per ounce, the jeweler would lose money. For example, if the price falls to $430 and he or she sells the contract losing $10 per ounce, the jeweler can then buy the gold in the cash market for $430 per ounce. Thus hedgers are also involved in the *cash* market.

The *cash price* of a commodity or financial security is the price for current delivery. This is also referred to as the *spot price*. The cash price is different from the futures price, which is the price of a contract for future delivery of a commodity or financial security. The difference between the cash and future prices is known as the *basis*. Generally, futures prices are higher than cash prices, reflecting the time until delivery, the storage costs of the commodity, and interest rates (opportunity cost). The differences between futures and cash prices diminish as the delivery time approaches.

Table 11-4 shows the difference in price between cash and futures for selected commodities. Corn has a positive basis in that the futures price of corn for July delivery is trading at $2.3525 per bushel, whereas the cash price is $1.98 per bushel. If you bought 5,000 bushels of corn in the cash market for $1.98 per bushel and sold short a July-delivery contract at $2.3525 per bushel, you would lock in a $0.3725 profit per bushel before expenses. The expenses incurred would be the storage costs of the 5,000 bushels of corn, the insurance

TABLE 11-4

Selected Cash and Futures Prices as of March 15, 2005

	Cash	July Delivery	September Delivery
Corn no. 2 yellow per bushel	$1.98	$2.3525	$2.535
Soybeans no. 1 yellow per bushel	$6.29	$6.8475	$6.60
Cocoa, $ metric ton	$2.002	$1.801	$1.815

Source: Financial newspapers and the Internet.

costs, and the financing costs and opportunity costs of tying up your cash to buy the corn in the cash market. These costs eat into your profits, and if they are greater than $0.3725 per bushel, you would incur a loss.

In some cases, the cash price is greater than the futures price, such as for the cocoa example in Table 11-4. In this case, an arbitrageur might profit by selling short 10 metric tons of cocoa at $2.002 per metric ton and simultaneously buying the July cocoa futures contract at $1.801 per bushel, resulting in a $0.2010 profit per ton. These actions by arbitrageurs close the gaps in these price discrepancies. Cocoa futures prices would increase as more traders buy them, and the cash price of cocoa would fall when traders sell short the commodity.

ANALYSIS OF THE FUTURES MARKETS

The two basic methods for analyzing the futures markets are fundamental analysis and technical analysis. These bear some similarities to the methods used in the selection of stocks.

Fundamental analysis refers to factors that affect the physical supply and demand of commodities, which then affect their prices. The physical supply of a commodity consists of current production plus the carryover from the prior year plus any imports. For example, the supply of gold includes the gold mined in the United States and Canada plus gold stored in vaults and any additional gold imports from South Africa, Australia, and Russia. For some commodities, information on supply is hard to come by. Information on the grain supply, for example, is released to the public during the growing season. The current supply relative to the demand of a commodity influences future prices.

Demand is the quantity that buyers are willing to buy at a specific price. When the price is high, there would be less demand for a commodity than when the price is low when demand increases. Similarly, an increase in the supply of a commodity has the effect of lowering the price, and a decrease in supply generally has the opposite effect (increasing the price). Speculators anticipate price changes and react as follows: When prices of commodities are expected to rise, futures contracts are purchased, and when prices are expected to decline, contracts are sold. However, if it were this easy to predict future prices of commodities, there would be many more millionaires, and this would by the only game in town. There are many other unanticipated factors that affect the supply and demand for a commodity, which prevent clairvoyance into the future directions of prices of commodities.

Technical analysis uses past volume and price movements to determine future prices and is based on the premise that history repeats itself (past prices determine future prices) and that there are trends to price movements. Fundamental factors are already incorporated into prices, so the technical analyst looks to spot trends in the movement of prices and moves along with the trend based on the previous patterns of price movements.

Regardless of whether fundamental or technical analysis is used, investors in futures contracts should have a strategy. One such strategy is to limit losses and allow profits to run. Owing to the leverage obtained from investing in futures contracts, if prices decline to the point of having to meet margin calls, investors then are committing additional funds in the hopes of recovering some of the losses instead of limiting their losses by getting out of their positions. When prices rise, investors should allow their profits to grow, while monitoring carefully the price to take a profit.

FINANCIAL FUTURES

A growing segment of the futures markets has been in financial futures. *Financial futures contracts* are obligations to buy or sell positions in financial securities. Financial futures are traded on Treasury bonds, Treasury notes, Treasury bills, S&P 500 Index, Mini S&P 500 Index, Dow Jones Industrial Average, British pound, euro currency, and Japanese yen. Financial futures contracts include trading in interest-rate futures, index futures, and currency trading futures.

Interest Rate Futures

Interest-rate futures are contracts on the future delivery of interest-bearing securities (debt). Interest-rate futures allow speculators and hedgers to buy and sell these contracts by locking in prices of these securities for future delivery. Interest rate futures include the following securities:

- Treasury bonds
- Treasury notes
- Treasury bills
- 10-year Agency notes
- 10-year Muni Note Index
- 30-day federal funds
- Eurodollar deposits
- Selected foreign government bonds

Changes in interest rates affect bond prices. Speculators buy or sell interest-rate futures based on their projections of the direction of future interest rates in an attempt to make large returns. Investors with large bond portfolios can reduce their risks of loss owing to changes in interest rates by hedging their positions using interest-rate futures.

Suppose that a speculator expects interest rates to decline in the near future. The speculator would take a long position by buying a futures contract for the delivery of Treasury bonds. If interest rates fall, the price of Treasury bonds would rise and the value of the Treasury bond futures contract also would increase. The speculator then can profit from selling the Treasury bond futures contract at a higher price. If, however, interest rates rise, the speculator would lose money, because Treasury bond prices would fall, resulting in a decline in the bond futures contract price.

The opposite occurs when a speculator anticipates a rise in interest rates. The speculator would sell short a Treasury bond futures contract, and if interest rates increase, the value of the Treasury bond futures contract would decline. The speculator then can buy back the contract at a lower price, closing out his or her position at a profit.

Bond portfolio managers and individuals with large bond portfolios can hedge against increases in interest rates by selling short Treasury bond or other bond index futures that resemble the makeup of the types of bonds held in the portfolio. The difference between

TABLE 11-5

Mini-Futures Contracts

Besides futures contracts offered on commodities, currencies, and stock indices, there are also mini-futures contracts offered on individual stocks and stock indices. Instead of having to put up the entire amount to purchase individual stocks or stock indices, investors can participate in mini stock futures on specified stocks or indices by putting up the minimum margin requirements (a small fraction of the total amount). These mini-futures contracts trade in the same way as regular futures contracts. A mini-futures S&P 500 Index contract has a value of 50 times the S&P 500 Index, whereas a regular futures contract on the S&P 500 Index has a contract value of 250 times the S&P 500 Index. These minicontracts are actively traded on the exchanges. For example, the mini-S&P 500 Index trades roughly 700,000 contracts a day. The margin requirements for minicontracts are less than those required for regular contracts.

Investors can buy or sell short these minicontracts at the current contract price. If the contract price rises, a long position would be profitable, and a short position would lose money. Although investing in options on individual stocks offers the advantage of leverage similar to an investment in mini-futures contracts, the differences between the two types of investments are as follows:

1. With options, the holder/seller has the right but not the obligation to exercise the contract, whereas at expiration of a futures contract, the parties are obligated to make delivery or accept delivery of the underlying asset or cash.

2. With mini-futures contracts, the investor's accounts are settled daily (marking to the market), which may require additional deposits of funds.

Additional information on mini-futures contracts may be obtained from the Chicago Mercantile Exchange, www.cme.com and the Chicago Board of Trade www.cbot.com.

hedgers and speculators is that hedgers actually hold the financial securities and deal in them. Table 11–5 discusses mini-futures contracts, which are offered on individual stocks and stock indices.

Currency Futures

Currency futures are contracts on the future delivery of foreign currencies. Participants in the currency futures markets are hedgers and speculators who trade them in the same way as commodities. Currency futures are quoted in U.S. dollars and cents. For example, if the settlement price for an Australian dollar futures contract is $0.7168, then this contract is worth $71,680. (The contract size is $100,000 multiplied by the settlement price $0.7168). Currency futures include the following:

- Japanese yen
- Canadian dollar
- British pound
- Swiss franc
- Australian dollar
- Mexican peso
- Euro/U.S. dollar
- Euro/Japanese yen
- Euro/British pound

As with interest-rate futures, the difference between hedgers and speculators in currency futures is that hedgers participate in the cash markets as well to deal in the currency. Multinational companies use currency futures to hedge their currency positions by locking in a rate so as to preserve their profits in international trade. For example, suppose that a company does a significant amount of trade with Australian companies, and the Australian dollar fluctuates daily against the U.S. dollar. If the company expects the Australian dollar to rise against the U.S. dollar, the company would buy a futures contract to lock in the price. If the company is correct and the U.S. dollar falls against the value of the Australian dollar, the price of the futures contract would increase. The company then would have locked in a lower price for future delivery of the contract. Similarly, if the company anticipates a fall in the Australian dollar, the company would sell short Australian dollar futures contracts for future delivery. If correct and the Australian dollar does decline, the company would profit. The company would buy Australian dollars in the cash market for the lower price and deliver them as required by the contract, which was sold short at a higher price.

Stock Index Futures

Stock index futures are contracts based on stock market indices, such as the Dow Jones Industrial Average, Standard & Poor's 500 Index, and the New York Stock Exchange Composite Index. Futures contracts are written on most of the major stock market indices:

- The Dow Jones Industrial Average
- The S&P 500 Index
- The S&P 400 Mid-Cap Index

Point of Interest: Triple-Witch Friday and Double-Witch Friday

The phrase *triple-witch Friday* sounds more like it belongs in a gothic novel with three witches crowding around a cauldron on a fire casting spells than a term used on Wall Street. *Triple-witch Friday* is the third Friday in March, June, September, and December, when stock options contracts, stock index options contracts, and stock index futures contracts all expire. The expiration of these contracts can cause unusual volatility in the markets on those four days during the year. The expiration of stock index futures results in the buying and selling of large blocks of stocks to settle contract positions. Imbalances in the buy and sell orders result in large price swings and account for the volatility

Arbitrageurs exploit any price discrepancies between cash prices of stocks and stock index futures by the simultaneous buying and selling of stocks against futures contracts. By locking in their profits, they settle their positions on the day of expiration.

Double-witch Friday occurs on the third Friday in months when there are no futures expirations and only stock options and stock index options expire. Investors who have sold put options would have to buy the stocks back if the stocks pass the exercise price. Similarly, those who sell call options on stocks that have passed the exercise price would have to buy the stocks. Consequently, larger blocks of buy orders than sell orders would cause stock prices to increase, and stock prices would decrease if there are more large blocks of sell orders than buy orders. There is less volatility in the stock market on double-witch Fridays than on triple-witch Fridays.

Paul Cherney studied the performance of the S&P 500 Index on triple-witch Fridays in the month of September only from 1986 to 2002. He found that only on 20 percent of the Fridays did the S&P 500 increase or decrease by more than 1 percent. The rest of the Fridays, the S&P 500 closed up or down by less than 1 percent. Part of the reason for this lessened volatility is that in 1988 the Chicago Mercantile Exchange staggered the expiration of futures and options contracts. Stock index futures contracts are settled at the opening prices of stocks on triple-witch Friday mornings rather than using closing prices at the end of the day. This lessens volatility by allowing stock specialists on the NYSE to find balancing bids and offers on these stocks. However, this move also accounts for some of the delayed openings of stocks for trade on the NYSE on triple-witch Fridays.

Source: Paul Cherney. "Downside Remains Limited," *Business Week Online*, September 15, 2003.

- The NYSE Composite Index
- The Nasdaq 100 Index
- The Russell 2000 Index
- Nikkei 225 Stock Average
- Other foreign stock market indices.

Stock index *futures* are similar to other financial futures except for the fact that with stock index futures, delivery is not in stocks but in cash at expiration. Thus, if the Dow Jones Industrial Average has a price of $9,843, the futures contract is worth the contract size multiplied by the price ($10 \times 9,843 = \$98,430$). Delivery for this contract would not be in the 30 stocks of the Dow Jones Industrial Average but in cash. Both speculators and hedgers use stock index futures contracts.

Speculators profit from taking long positions in stock index futures when the markets rise and lose money if the markets decline in price. Sellers of contracts profit when the stock markets fall and lose money when the markets rise in price. Portfolio managers hedge their positions against adverse price swings in the market by buying or selling short stock index futures contracts that match the make-up of their portfolios.

Real Estate, Precious Metals, and Collectibles

KEY CONCEPTS

- Investing in real estate
- Types of mortgages
- Investing in unimproved land and improved land
- Passive methods of investing in real estate
- Investing in precious metals
- Investing in collectibles

Investing in real assets (i.e., real estate, precious metals, and collectibles) is essentially the same as investing in financial assets in that investors expect returns through either income and/or capital appreciation. The major differences from investing in financial assets and real assets are the requirement of specialized knowledge and the lack of centralized markets. Specialized knowledge of real estate and collectibles is essential in order to obtain profits in these investments. Investors in financial assets can get by with less specialized knowledge by investing in mutual funds and exchange-traded funds and relying on financial professionals.

Expertise in real estate, art, precious metals, coins, and antiques is essential to enable you to make the right purchases and sales at the right prices. There is very little pricing transparency in real assets because there are no formal markets such as the stock exchanges for stocks. Prices of real assets can be obtained from specialized magazines and publications, but it also can be difficult to compare prices of real assets because of differences in features, characteristics, and quality. Consequently, price comparisons are not readily available, so specialized knowledge of the particular real asset class protects the investor from overpaying or selling below the value of the asset.

The major advantages of investing in real assets are that they generally outperform financial assets during periods of high inflation and together with financial assets offer greater portfolio diversification. The major disadvantages of real assets are that they are not marketable like stocks and some bonds that can be sold within minutes, as well as not being liquid. An investor might never obtain the asked price and in order to sell the real asset might have to incur significant price concessions.

INVESTING IN REAL ESTATE

The types of real estate investments include home ownership, rental properties, land, and indirect investments in real estate through limited partnerships and real estate investment trusts (REITs). The most common type of real estate investment is home ownership, which generally also accounts for the largest single investment made by many families.

Home Ownership

The purchase of a home might be the largest single expenditure that you make, but this expenditure differs from other expenditures that you make. Few people have enough cash to pay the entire cost of the home. Instead, they make a down payment and borrow the balance from a financial institution using the home as collateral on the mortgage loan. Securing a mortgage loan from a financial lender requires that the borrower has the financial means to be able to repay monthly amounts of interest and principal, as well as to be able to cover insurance, real estate taxes, and maintenance on the property.

Home ownership offers significant tax benefits and opportunities to increase wealth and capital appreciation. Over long periods, most homes appreciate in value, and prices tend to keep up with inflation. Tax benefits come from being able to deduct both interest expenses on the home mortgage and real estate taxes from taxable income at the federal level. These deductions result in lowering taxable income and taxes paid to the federal government. In addition, interest expense on a home mortgage is not subject to inclusion in the computation of the alternative minimum tax (AMT). Because a portion of each monthly mortgage payment is applied to the repayment of the mortgage loan, the home owner is reducing the mortgage balance with each monthly payment and increasing his or her equity position, which is another form of saving.

The disadvantage of home ownership is that if house prices decline and you have to sell your house when the property market is depressed, you could end up losing money. Home ownership also can decrease your mobility in that it might not be easy to sell your home and move to another location in a short period of time.

Income Tax Benefits

Interest paid on a home mortgage loan is a tax-deductible expense, that reduces taxable income at the federal level, thereby resulting in savings on taxes paid. For example, in the taxable year, if interest on a home loan mortgage is $12,000, taxable income is reduced by this amount. Consequently, the effective rate of the cost of the home loan is reduced by the tax saving:

Effective interest cost = mortgage rate $\times$ (1 – marginal tax rate)

For example, an investor in the 35 percent marginal tax bracket with a 6 percent mortgage loan has an effective (after tax) rate of 3.9 percent on the mortgage loan.

$$\text{Effective interest cost} = 0.06 \times (1 - 0.35)$$

$$= 0.039$$

The second tax benefit to home ownership is the deductibility of property taxes on the home, which reduces taxable income and taxes paid.

The third tax benefit from home ownership occurs when the home is sold. The profit on the sale of a principal residence is not taxable if the gain is less than $250,000 for a tax payer filing a single return and $500,000 for a taxpayer filing a joint return. To qualify for this exclusion from capital gains taxes, the homeowner must have lived in the home for at least two of the five years, and the exclusion applies to only one sale every two years. Home prices have risen over the past 50 years. Consequently, this exclusion from capital gains tax results in an increased return on after-tax profits from the sale of a principal residence when compared with the sale of other investments such as stocks and bonds.

These tax benefits generally make it advantageous to buy a home rather than rent. There are times, however, when it becomes advantageous to rent rather than buy. See Table 12-1 for a discussion of the cost gap of renting versus buying.

TABLE 12-1

When Renting a Home Becomes Less Costly than Buying

Renting or buying a home (condominium) depends on many factors. The more obvious financial advantages of purchasing a home are the tax advantages, the building of equity, and the potential for capital appreciation. The major disadvantages of home ownership are that you bear the risk of loss if property values fall, and home owner-ship decreases your mobility in that it might not be easy to sell a house in a short period of time. It is this latter disadvantage that gives renters mobility over home-owners, as well as not having to face unpredictable expenditures on maintenance and repairs of a home.

When determining the costs of renting versus the costs of ownership, the advantages for many years were with homeownership. With appreciating prices and low interest rates, many renters have turned to home ownership, thereby driving house prices up even more. These actions have weakened the rental market, prompting landlords to lower rents or raise them modestly by lower increments than in the past. In some cities in the United States, renting has become less costly than buying. For example, the cost gap of renting versus buying was 40 percent in San Diego and 45 percent in San Francisco in 2004, as measured by Torto Wheaton Research (Simon and Smith, pp. D1 and D2). The advantage of the lower costs of renting over buying is not limited to the major cities but prevails in small towns such as Plano, Texas, as well (Simon and Smith, p. D2.).

This cost gap between renting and buying is also related to the Housing Affordability Index, which is a measure of demand for housing by comparing an individual's median income with required levels of mortgage debt. When the Housing Affordability Index is less than 1, most families cannot afford the cost of median priced housing. When the index is above 1, most families have sufficient income to purchase median-priced houses. Even though the index is above 1 (2004) owing to the lowest levels of mortgage interest rates in 50 years, making larger mortgages more affordable, the anomaly is presented in the form of higher house prices. Not only have house prices risen significantly throughout major cities in the United States, but also the rate of home ownership has risen from 67.5 percent in 2000 to 69.2 percent in the fourth quarter of 2004 (Simon and Smith, p. D2). In 2005, the Federal Reserve has raised short-term interest rates and has indicated future rises in interest rates, indicating that with more costly mortgages owing to higher mortgage rates, housing prices might level off and begin to decline.

Source: Simon, Ruth, and Ray A. Smith. "In the Hottest Markets, Renting is the Real Bargain," *Wall Street Journal*, March 22, 2005, pp. D1 and D2.

TYPES OF MORTGAGES

Banks, savings and loan associations, and financial institutions provide two basic types of mortgages: *conventional mortgages* and *mortgages with federal agency backing*. A conventional mortgage has a fixed interest rate over the term of the loan, and the real estate serves as collateral for the loan. The borrower retires the loan by making fixed monthly payments that include both interest and the reduction of principal through the life of the loan.

For example, a person buys a house for $240,000, makes a down payment of $40,000, and accepts a mortgage loan of $200,000 from the bank at 7 percent for 30 years. The monthly payment of $1,330.60 can be determined using Microsoft's Excel software, as shown in Table 12-2.

How a Conventional Mortgage Works

Mortgages and installment loans encompass the same financial principles and are essentially the same except for the length of their terms. Mortgages have terms of 15 to 30 years, whereas installment loans have shorter maturities. The difference in maturities occurs because the amount borrowed to finance the purchase of a house is invariably so large that it requires a long period of time to pay it back.

TABLE 12-2

Using Microsoft's Excel to Calculate the Mortgage Payment

Calculate the monthly payment for a $200,000, 30-year, 7 percent mortgage.

Click on "f*" in the toolbar row of Microsoft's Excel spreadsheet program. Highlight "financial" in the left-hand box and "pmt" in the right-hand box, and then click "ok." Enter your data:

Rate	0.07/12
Nper	360
PV	200,000
FV	0
Type	0
Formula result =	−1330.60

The formula result (monthly payment) is $1,330.60.

The equal payments are made on a monthly basis, with a portion of the payment going toward principal reduction and the balance going toward covering the interest expense charged by the lender. In the early years of the mortgage, the greatest amount of the payment goes toward interest expense, as shown in the amortization schedule in Table 12-3. As the loan balance declines, the portion of the payment applied to interest expense declines, and the portion applied to loan reduction increases. Toward the end of the term of the mortgage, most of the payment is applied to reducing the loan balance.

There are many software programs for personal computers that will print an amortization schedule such as the one in Table 12-3, which presents the first 20 payments on a $200,000, 7 percent, 30-year mortgage. Some financial calculators also can determine mortgage

TABLE 12-3

Amortization Schedule for a $200,000, 7 Percent, 30-Year Mortgage

Payment No.	Payment Amount	Principal	Interest	Balance
—	—	—	—	200,000.00
1	$1,330.60	163.93	1,167.67	199,836.07
2	1,330.60	164.89	1,165.71	199,671.18
3	1,330.60	165.89	1,164.75	199,505.33
4	1,330.60	166.82	1,163.78	199,338.51
5	1,330.60	167.79	1,162.81	199,170.72
6	1,330.60	168.77	1,161.83	199,001.95
7	1,330.60	169.76	1,160.84	198,832.19
8	1,330.60	170.75	1,159.85	198,661.44
9	1,330.60	171.74	1,158.86	198,489.70
10	1,330.60	172.74	1,157.86	198,316.96
11	1,330.60	173.75	1,156.85	198,143.21
12	1,330.60	174.76	1,155.84	197,968.45
13	1,330.60	175.78	1,154.82	197,792.67
14	1,330.60	176.81	1,153.79	197,615.86
15	1,330.60	177.84	1,152.76	197,438.02
16	1,330.60	178.88	1,151.72	197,259.14
17	1,330.60	179.92	1,150.68	197,079.22
18	1,330.60	180.97	1,149.63	196,898.25
19	1,330.60	182.03	1,148.57	196,716.22
20	1,330.60	183.09	1,147.51	196,533.13

balances. However, if you have neither a computer nor a financial calculator, you can compute an amortization schedule quite easily using a pen and paper.

How to Calculate an Amortization Schedule Using Pen and Paper

Using the example of a $200,000, 7 percent, 30-year term mortgage with equal monthly payments of $1,330.60, the first step is to determine how much of each payment is applied to interest and how much goes toward reducing the loan balance. Assume that in this example the mortgage for $200,000 is taken out on January 1. The first payment of $1,330.60 is made on January 31. The interest expense is the interest rate per month, which is 0.00583333 (0.07/12). Multiply the loan balance outstanding at the beginning of the month by this monthly rate to get the interest expense for the month (200,000 × 0.00583333 = 1,166.67). Thus, from the payment of $1,330.60, $1,166.67 is applied to interest, and the balance (1,330.60 − 1,166.67) of $163.93 goes toward repaying the loan. The new loan balance becomes the old balance minus the principal reduction, which is $199,836.07 ($200,000.00 − 163.93). Repeating this procedure gives February's figures, and by continuing the procedure, the entire amortization schedule can be determined. Table 12-4 shows the first few months of the schedule.

One variant of the conventional mortgage is an adjustable rate mortgage (ARM). A conventional mortgage has a fixed interest rate over the term of the mortgage, but with an adjustable-rate mortgage, the interest rate fluctuates over the life of the loan. With an ARM, the borrower bears the risk of changing interest rates, whereas with a conventional fixed rate mortgage the lender bears the risk of changing interest rates in the economy. When interest rates rise, the lender of a conventional mortgage is stuck holding a lower-interest-rate mortgage. On the other hand, if interest rates decline, the borrower is stuck holding a higher-rate mortgage, but the borrower has the option of refinancing the mortgage with a lower-rate loan.

With an adjustable rate mortgage (ARM), the interest rate changes according to some index selected by the lender. The adjustment period varies, on a quarter, semiannual, or annual basis or for longer periods of time. Some indices are more volatile than others, so you should take care in selecting your ARM by investigating the index tied to the mortgage. ARMs are offered at lower rates than

TABLE 12-4

Determination of an Amortization Schedule

Date	Payment (a)	Interest Expense (b)	Principal (c)	Loan Balance (d)
Jan 1	—	—	—	$200,000.00
Jan 31	$1,330.60	1,166.67	163.93	199,836.07
Feb 28	1,330.60	1,165.71*	164.89[†]	199,671.18[‡]

Interest = rate per month multiplied by the loan balance at the beginning of the month
$$= 0.00583333 \times 200,000$$
$$= \$1,166.67$$

Principal reduction = payment minus interest expense (a) − (b)
$$= 1,330.60 - 1166.67$$
$$= 163.93$$

New loan balance = old balance minus principal reduction (d) − (c)
$$= 200,000 - 163.93$$
$$= 199,836.07$$

February Interest = *0.00583333 × 199,836.07
$$= 1,165.71$$

Principal reduction = [†]1,330.60 − 1,165.71 (a) − (b)
$$= 164.89$$

New loan balance = [‡]199,836.07 − 164.89 (d) − (c)
$$= 199,671.18$$

conventional mortgages. The differential could be 1 to 3 percent lower than conventional mortgages. Some ARMs are offered at very low rates, known as *teaser rates,* to encourage borrowers. However, after a short period of time, generally a year, the rate reverts back to normal rates.

Mortgage lenders have introduced new mortgage variations to entice borrowers who might not be able to afford the higher payments of conventional fixed-rate mortgages owing due to both rising interest rates and higher house prices. One such variation is an interest-only ARM, which makes it easier for borrowers to be able to afford lower mortgage payments. How an interest-only ARM works is illustrated as follows.

A conventional $200,000, 30-year, 7 percent fixed-rate mortgage has a monthly payment cost of $1,330.60. An ARM of $200,000 for 30 years with a 5 percent interest rate for the first year has a monthly cost of $1,073.64. However, an interest-only ARM of $200,000 for 30 years with a 5.125 percent interest rate for the first five years would cost $854.17 per month. A comparison of these three mortgages shows that the interest-only ARM saves the borrower $219.47 per month over the ARM and $476.43 per month over the conventional fixed-rate mortgage. Table 12-5 presents a comparison of these three types of mortgages.

Even though the interest rate for the interest-only ARM is one-eighth of a point higher than the ARM, the interest-only payments are less because the borrower does not make any principal payments. Consequently, the loan balance remains at $200,000 after one year, whereas with the ARM and the conventional mortgage, the loan balances decline by the amount of the principal reduction payments.

If interest rates increase in the second year to 6 percent for the ARM and 6.25 for the interest-only ARM, the monthly cost rises to $1,196.10 for the ARM and $1,041.67 for the interest-only ARM. With each interest rate increase in ARMs, there is an increase to the monthly payment amounts, which typically can make ARMs more expensive than locking into a fixed-rate mortgage should the adjustable rate exceed the fixed rate. Consequently, borrowers always should work out their worst-case scenario to make sure that they can cover those larger payments.

With an ARM, a decline in the interest rate results in a drop in the monthly payment, and conversely, an increase in interest rates

TABLE 12-5

Comparison of the Three Types of Mortgages for a $200,000, 30-Year Term Loan

		End First Year		
Type of Mortgage	Rate	Monthly Payment	Principal Reduction	Loan Balance
Conventional fixed rate	7%	$1,330.60	$2,031.55	$197,968.45
Adjustable rate	5%	1,073.64	2,950.69	197,049.31
Interest-only ARM	5.125%	854.17	0	200,000
		End of Second Year		
Conventional fixed rate	7%	$1,330.60	2,178.42	195,790.03
Adjustable rate	6%	1,196.10	2,600.99	194,448.32
Interest-only ARM	6.25%	1,041.67	0	200,000

results in an increase in the monthly payments. The disadvantages of an interest-only mortgage are that interest rates could rise, negating the advantage of the initial lower monthly payments at the inception of the loan, and after the five-year period of interest only payments, the loan balance has not been reduced. The borrower then faces higher monthly payments to include the reduction of principal.

Another variation of the conventional mortgage is a graduated-payment mortgage. With a graduated payment mortgage, the payment amount is not fixed over the life of the loan. The monthly payments are lower during the early years of the mortgage and then rise later in the life of the loan. Borrowers of this type of loan need to be able to cover these increased monthly payments. Consequently, this type of mortgage is suitable for borrowers whose incomes are anticipated to increase in order to be able to cover the future additional payment amounts.

The federal government encourages mortgage lending through a number of its agencies. The Federal Housing Loan Administration (FHA) encourages financial institutions to lend to low-income home buyers by insuring the loans. If a borrower defaults on a loan, then the FHA will stand by the loan. Similarly, the Veterans Administration guarantees mortgage loans to veterans to reduce the risk of loss to financial lenders.

INVESTING IN UNIMPROVED LAND AND IMPROVED LAND

You can invest in real estate through purchasing land and or improved land. *Unimproved land* is in its natural state with no improvements, which without improvements generates no income. Unimproved land is purchased either to develop (improve) or to hold for potential capital appreciation.

The disadvantages of investing in unimproved land are as follows:

- Unimproved land is taxed by state and possibly local governments.
- The investment might be neither liquid nor marketable. It could take time to sell unimproved land, and the price would have to appreciate considerably to cover the real estate commissions, legal fees, and any other fees incurred in the purchase and sale of the land.

Consequently, any appreciation on unimproved land would have to be greater than the total costs incurred to buy, hold, and then sell unimproved land in order to make a profit.

Improved land includes improvements to the property, such as curbs and gutters, and can be classified into different types:

- Residential that has single-family or multifamily housing
- Commercial that includes shopping centers, stores, theaters, hotels, office space, and parking lots
- Industrial that includes warehouses, industrial districts, and factories
- Special-purpose properties that include schools, cemeteries, churches, and government held lands
- Agricultural land that includes farms, ranches, timberland, and orchards

Each of these real estate markets has different characteristics that determine the price of the real estate. Investing in these markets requires specialized knowledge about the geography and the improvements on the land (zoning and other land-use laws) and a business analysis of the improvements (for income-producing properties).

Business Analysis of Investing in Rental Properties

Investing in improved land requires a long time horizon in order to realize the potential financial benefits, as well as for many of the reasons stated earlier in the chapter (difficulty in selling real estate quickly without losing a significant part of the investor's principal). The following example illustrates some of the financial difficulties of not holding investment real estate long enough to realize the financial benefits.

Assume that a rental property is purchased for $200,000. A conventional fixed-rate mortgage of $170,000 is taken out at 7 percent for 15 years. The property is rented at $26,000 per year, with an assumption that the rent will increase by 2 percent every year. For simplification purposes, the mortgage is paid back in 15 equal annual payments of $18,665.08. Table 12-6 shows a breakdown of the interest and principal-reduction payments for the life of the mortgage.

TABLE 1 2 - 6

Amortization Schedule of a Mortgage for $170,000 at 7 Percent for 15 Years

Payment No.	Payment Amount	Interest	Principal Reduction	Loan Balance
—	—	—	—	$170,000.00
1	$18,665.08	$11,900.00	$6,765.08	163,234.92
2	18,665.08	11,426.44	7,238.64	155,996.28
3	18,665.08	10,919.74	7,745.34	148,250.94
4	18,665.08	10,377.57	8,287.51	139,963.43
5	18,665.08	9,797.44	8,867.64	131,095.79
6	18,665.08	9,176.71	9,488.37	121,607.41
7	18,665.08	8,512.52	10,152.56	111,454.85
8	18,665.08	7,801.84	10,863.24	100,591.61
9	18,665.08	7,041.41	11,623.67	88,967.94
10	18,665.08	6,227.76	12,437.32	76,530.62
11	18,665.08	5,357.14	13,307.94	63,222.68
12	18,665.08	4,425.59	14,239.49	48,983.19
13	18,665.08	3,428.82	15,236.26	33,746.93
14	18,665.08	2,362.29	16,302.79	17,444.14
15	18,665.08	1,220.94	17,444.14	0

Table 12-7 presents the net income (loss) for this rental property. The first column shows the annual rental income with the 2 percent increments every year. Column 2 shows the depreciation expense, which in this example for simplification purposes is using the straight-line method over 15 years. The value of the building is $150,000, and the land is valued at $50,000. Only the building is depreciated. The yearly depreciation expense is $10,000 ($150,000/15). In reality, under the current tax code (2004), residential rental property is depreciated over 27.5 years and nonresidential rental property over 39 years. Other expenses incurred are maintenance and insurance on the property and interest expense on the mortgage and real estate taxes (columns 3, 4, and 5). Maintenance and insurance are expected to increase by 3 percent per year. All expenses are deducted from rental income to equal income (loss) before taxes, shown in column 6. This investor has to wait 7 years to receive positive income before taxes.

Taxes are paid on earnings at the taxpayer's marginal tax rate. Losses, however, are used to offset income from other properties

TABLE 1 2 - 7

Income Statement for the Rental Property

Year	(1) Rental Income	(2) Depreciation Expense	(3) Maintenance & Insurance	(4) Interest Expense	(5) Real Estate Taxes	(6) Income (Loss) before Taxes
1	$26,000	$10,000	$4,000	$11,900	$4,200	(4,100)
2	26,520	10,000	4,120	11,426	4,400	(3,426)
3	27,050	10,000	4,244	10,919	4,600	(2,713)
4	27,591	10,000	4,371	10,338	4,900	(2,018)
5	28,143	10,000	4,502	9,797	5,200	(1,356)
6	28,706	10,000	4,637	9,177	5,400	(508)
7	29,280	10,000	4,776	8,513	5,700	291
8	30,463	10,000	4,919	7,802	5,900	1,842
9	31,072	10,000	5,067	7,041	6,300	2,664
10	31,693	10,000	5,219	6,228	6,700	3,546
11	32,327	10,000	5,376	5,357	7,000	4,594
12	32,974	10,000	5,537	4,426	7,350	5,661
13	33,633	10,000	5,703	3,429	7,600	6,901
14	34,306	10,000	5,874	2,362	7,900	8,170
15	34,992	10,000	6,050	1,221	8,200	9,521

and also might be used as a tax shelter to reduce total tax liability, provided the investor fulfills all the complex requirements in the tax code. Assuming that the investor in this property is in the 35 percent marginal tax bracket and qualifies in terms of the regulations in the tax code to offset losses from income, Table 12-8 shows the tax benefits on the losses (years 1 through 6) and the tax liability on income earned (years 7 through 15). Income before taxes only becomes positive in year 7. However, investors in rental properties are more concerned with cash flow than with net income or net loss because a large portion of the expenses deducted consists of depreciation, which is a noncash charge. Consequently, depreciation is added back to net income (loss), and the principal-reduction payment is deducted from net income to equal the cash flow for each year as shown in Table 12-8. Cash flow is positive for the first 9 years in this example, whereas net income is only positive from years 8 through 15. This is attributable mainly to the principal repayments that increase each year. These repayments are not taxdeductible like interest, but they also

TABLE 12-8

Cash Flow for the Rental Property

	(1) Income (Loss) before Taxes	(2) Taxes	(3) Net Income	(4) Depreciation	(5) Principal Reduction	(6) Cash Flow (3 + 4 − 5)	(7) Cumulative Cash Flow
1	$(4,100)	$1,435	$(2,665)	$ 10,000	$ 6,765	$ 570	$ 570
2	(3,426)	1,199	(2,227)	10,000	7,239	534	1,104
3	(2,713)	949	(1,764)	10,000	7,745	491	1,595
4	(2,018)	706	(1,312)	10,000	8,288	400	1,995
5	(1,356)	475	(881)	10,000	8,868	251	2,246
6	(508)	178	(330)	10,000	9,488	182	2,428
7	291	(102)	189	10,000	10,153	36	2,464
8	1,842	(645)	1,197	10,000	10,863	334	2,798
9	2,664	(932)	1,732	10,000	11,624	108	2,906
10	3,546	(1,241)	2,305	10,000	12,437	(132)	2,774
11	4,594	(1,608)	2,986	10,000	13,308	(322)	2,452
12	5,661	(1,981)	3,680	10,000	14,239	(559)	1,893
13	6,901	(2,415)	4,486	10,000	15,236	(750)	1,143
14	8,170	(2,859)	5,311	10,000	16,303	(992)	151
15	9,521	(3,332)	6,189	10,000	17,444	(1,255)	(1,104)

decrease cash every time that they are paid. Even though principal repayments reduce cash flow, the investor's equity increases with each principal repayment.

Cash flows are invested to earn a return, which is added to the appreciation of the property value as illustrated in Table 12-9. The property value is assumed to appreciate by 3 percent per year, and cash-flow rate of return is also assumed to be 3 percent.

If the investor retains the rental property for 15 years, the cash flow invested at 3 percent plus the appreciated value is worth $111,607 before taxes ($311,593 minus the $200,000 cost of the property), assuming that the property appreciates at around 3 percent a year.

Risks of Investing in Rental Properties

Although many assumptions were made in the preceding illustration, which if they do not materialize would change actual revenues and

TABLE 12-9

Return on Investment

	Value of Property $200,000 (3% Appreciation)	Cash Flow (Cumulative)	+ 3% Interest	Total = Cash Flow	+ Appreciation	= Total Value
1	$206,000*	$ 570	$ 17	$ 587[†]	$ 6,000[§]	$ 6,587
2	212,180	1,121[‡]	33	1,154	12,180	13,334
3	218,545	1,645	49	1,694	18,545	20,239
4	225,101	2,094	62	2,156	25,101	27,257
5	231,854	2,407	72	2,479	31,854	34,333
6	238,810	2,661	80	2,741	38,810	41,551
7	245,974	2,777	83	2,860	45,974	48,834
8	253,354	3,194	96	3,290	53,354	56,664
9	260,954	3,398	102	3,500	60,954	64,454
10	268,783	3,368	101	3,469	68,783	72,252
11	276,846	3,147	94	3,241	76,846	80,087
12	285,152	2,682	80	2,762	85,152	87,914
13	293,706	2,012	60	2,072	93,706	95,776
14	302,517	1,080	32	1,112	102,517	103,629
15	311,593	(143)	0	(143)	111,593	111,450

*$200,000 × 1.03
[†]$570 + $17
[‡]$587 + $534
[§]$206,000 − $200,000

expenses in this project and consequently alter income and cash flow projections, it is important for potential investors to go through with this type of analysis. Four major points come to mind from this analysis.

The first is that an assumption is made that the property would be rented for the entire 15-year period and that the rent would increase by 2 percent per year. In reality, rental increases vary, as do occupancy rates, and you would be fortunate indeed to have a 100 percent occupancy rate. Rental increases generally do not occur evenly on an annual basis.

The second point is similar to the first in that increases in expenses also occur on an erratic and unpredictable basis. A large increase in expenses could cause cash flows to turn negative, thereby having an impact on the investor's bank balance.

Third, if the property is not rented, the investor might have to incur capital expenditures to improve the property in order to attract potential renters.

The fourth major point involves the rate of appreciation, which is determined by the geographic location. Some geographic areas are more prosperous than other areas, thereby appreciating more than the average for that type of land improvement. Consequently, average appreciation percentages quoted for geographic regions could vary considerably.

When evaluating the business analysis of rental property projects, use conservative assumptions and be aware that many changes to your model could occur, affecting income and cash flows.

PASSIVE METHODS OF INVESTING IN REAL ESTATE

An investor might invest in real estate as an individual or with a partner to form a partnership. These forms involve the individual's active participation. However, there are passive forms of investment in real estate that do not involve the investor in management of the real estate. These passive forms of investment in real estate are limited partnerships and real estate investment trusts. Real estate investment trusts (REITs) are discussed in Chapter 4.

Limited Partnerships

Investors who either do not have the time or the inclination to actively manage their real estate investments might consider investing in limited partnerships. A *limited partnership* is a business entity owned and managed by general partners who sell shares to limited partners to raise capital for the purchase of real estate properties. General partners have unlimited liability, whereas limited partners have limited liability. In other words, the most that a limited partner can lose is the amount of his or her investment.

Changes to the tax code in 1986 removed the tax shelter benefits of owning real estate limited partnerships for limited partners. Real estate limited partnerships generally incur net losses owing to large depreciation expenses (for tax purposes, accelerated depreciation methods are used, which generate larger deductions in the early years of the asset than straight line depreciation). Because of changes to the tax code in 1986, passive investors in real estate limited partnerships can no longer offset their losses against income. Losses can only be offset against other passive income. Losses generated could be large owing to depreciation expenses, but these losses do not require the use of cash, thereby generating positive cash flows, which are then paid out to limited partners as a return of capital (not taxable). When the properties in the real estate partnership are sold, appreciation in value is treated as a capital gain. Income taxes on limited partnerships are complex, and investors interested in passive real estate investments should explore REITs, where tax rules are not as complex.

Another disadvantage of real estate partnerships is the high up-front fees and commissions charged by the partnership. The range of these fees can be anywhere from 5 to 20 percent.

Investors should be cautious when investing in blind pool limited partnerships, in which the real estate properties have not been purchased when limited partners invest their funds. Limited partners invest their capital, and then the general partners use the capital to purchase the real estate known as a *blind pool*. Potential investors should be given some guidelines as to the specific real estate projects the general partners intend to purchase. Another caveat for potential investors is to investigate the historical records of the performance of the general partners and whether the general partners have lawsuits on file against them.

INVESTING IN PRECIOUS METALS

Investors invest in precious metals primarily for the potential price appreciation. Price appreciation is realized when the net selling price is greater than the net purchase price, and this appreciation is taxed as a capital gain. Commissions to buy and sell precious metals and transaction costs that are charged to store metals reduce potential returns. Of the precious metals, gold has been the most popular investment as a store of value. Although this discussion is limited to gold, the same information can be applied to silver and other precious metals.

Gold

Advocates of gold investments believe that gold is the best hedge against inflation and stock market declines. Historically, gold has performed well during periods of high rates of inflation, but since 1979–1980 when both inflation and gold were at high levels, both inflation and the price of gold have declined in the first four years of the twenty-first century. Figure 12-1 shows the decline in the price of gold from 1987 through 2003, which emphasizes the potential risk of loss from investing in gold. When the price of gold rises above the purchase price, investors realize capital gains when selling. The opposite is a capital loss when investors sell when the purchase price is greater than the selling price. Gold is classified as a collectible by the Internal Revenue Service, so long-term (held more than one year) capital gains are taxed at the higher 28 percent rate. Investors in gold are dependent on market prices to earn positive returns on their investments owing to the fact that they do not receive interest or dividend payments.

There are different forms of gold ownership, namely, gold bullion, gold coins, gold mining stocks, gold mutual funds, gold options, and gold futures.

Gold bullion or *gold bars* are bought and sold through brokerage firms and gold dealers. Gold bars trade at a premium (varies from 1 to 7 percent) to the market price of gold. After purchase, gold bullion generally remains in the custody of the brokerage firm or dealers, thereby incurring storage and insurance costs. If you take possession of the gold bars to avoid these additional costs, there are a number of other factors that must be considered. First, you must store the gold bars in a safe place. Second, when you purchase the gold bars, the broker or dealer should issue you with a numbered certificate that correlates with the numbers on the bars. When you come to sell the bars, the certificate is presented along with the gold bars, which does not always prevent you from having to assay the gold to guarantee the quality. The assay costs are borne by the seller.

FIGURE 12-1

Historical Price of Gold

You can avoid the storage and assay costs by investing in *gold coins* instead of gold bullion. Although gold coins also trade at a premium to the price of gold, this form is more cost-effective for small investors in gold. Two primary considerations of investing in gold coins are the numismatic value of the coins and the gold content of the coins. The numismatic value of the coin is related to its value as a collector's item. For example, South Africa's Krugerrand and Canada's Maple Leaf are widely traded gold coins, whereas older, rarer coins such as the French Napoleon trade at many multiples of their gold content. Gold content is the second consideration. The Canadian Maple Leaf consists of 1 troy ounce of fine gold, making it more marketable than a gold coin that consists of less than 1 troy ounce of fine gold.

An indirect way of investing in gold is through the purchase of *stocks of gold mining companies.* You should be aware that the prices of gold mining stocks do not always move in the same direction as the price of gold. This is due to a number of factors, both related to gold and not related to gold. The costs to mine gold vary among gold mining companies. For example, the length of the mine life is an indication of the costs to extract gold: A long life implies that the mining company does not have to go deeper into the mineshaft to extract gold, whereas a short mine life implies a deeper, more costly process to extract gold. The largest mining companies are in South Africa, Canada, and the United States. South African mining companies have had costly labor strikes in the past, raising their mining costs.

Gold mining stock prices tend to be more volatile than the price movements of gold, which explains why some gold mining company stocks decline when the price of gold rises and the opposite (gold company stock prices rise when the price of gold falls). One reason for this phenomenon is that some gold mining companies hedge their future output using gold futures contracts. Despite the overall short-term volatility, gold stock prices generally do keep in step with the longer-term price trend of gold bullion. When investing in stocks of gold mining companies, look for mining companies with long lives and low extraction costs.

If you would like to invest in gold without having to pay the high costs of storage and insurance and without having to deliberate over the strengths and weaknesses of different mining companies, you can invest in gold through *gold mutual funds* and *gold ETFs.* Gold mutual funds offer you a diversified portfolio of gold mining stocks. There are several open-end and closed-end funds to choose from. American Century Global Gold Fund and Vanguard's Precious Metals and Mining Fund both outperformed the stock market in 2003. Both these funds have low expense ratios, which is one of the major factors to look for when choosing a mutual fund.

Gold ETFs (exchange-traded funds) offer you a convenient way to own gold bullion without having to worry about storage and insurance costs. Shares of ETFs trade on the stock exchanges. The first gold ETF, offered by State Street in 2004, trades on the New York Stock Exchange under the ticker symbol GLD. State Street serves as a custodian for the gold bullion, and the expenses for storing, insuring, and transporting the gold bullion are paid by the selling of fractional amounts of gold held in the fund. This form of payment decreases the life of the fund. Mutual funds and ETFs are discussed in detail in Chapter 4 of this book.

You also can use *gold options* either to insure existing investments in gold or to speculate on changes in gold prices. If you expect gold prices to rise, you would buy call options on gold, and if you expect the price of gold to decline, you would buy put options on gold. Refer to the discussion on options in Chapter 11.

Gold futures contracts also allow you to speculate or hedge your positions on gold. You can hedge your positions in gold bullion in the following way: If you expect gold prices to decline, you would sell short a gold futures contract. If gold does fall in price, you can trade out of your futures contract at a profit that offsets some of the losses in the price of your gold bullion held. The opposite position is a long position. If you expect gold to increase in price, you buy a gold futures contract, and if gold does increase in price, you can trade out of the contract at a profit. Gold speculators do not hold gold bullion, and they take positions in futures contracts in an attempt to profit from their positions in these contracts. The overriding feature is the leverage that gold futures contracts offer. For example, if the price of gold is $400 per ounce and you buy a gold futures contract, which consists of 100 troy ounces, the contract value is $40,000. If the margin requirement for a gold futures contract is $4,000, you can control the $40,000 contract value with a small investment. If gold increases in price by $1 per ounce, your contract value would increase by $1,000 for a total worth of $41,000. The opposite is also true with leverage. If gold decreases in price by $1 per ounce, your contract value would decrease by $1,000 to $39,000. The volatility of the price of gold lends itself to making great profits and also substantial losses by investing in gold futures contracts. Commodity futures contracts are discussed in detail in Chapter 11.

INVESTING IN COLLECTIBLES

Collectibles include art, antiques, vintage cars, rare books, Persian rugs, coins, stamps, baseball cards and other items that offer the potential for appreciation. There are several characteristics that distinguish investing in collectibles from investing in financial securities.

- Specialized knowledge is required to be able to determine the value of the specific collectible, whether it is art, a rare book, or a vintage car. It is easy to pay too much for a collectible if you do not have the expertise and knowledge of that collectible item. You should be knowledgeable about the factors that determine the value of the specific collectible.

- Supply and demand often determine the value for collectibles. For example, the supply of paintings of the truly great masters is limited, and therefore, it requires a very large amount of money to invest in these paintings. By comparison, the works by unknown artists are vast, thereby selling for relatively small sums of money.

- The markets for collectibles are informal and unregulated. When buying or selling a collectible item, you should have an idea of the worth of the item because you are dealing with individual buyers or sellers. There are no listed current prices as with stocks. Similarly, there is no governmental body such as the Securities and Exchange Commission that regulates companies that list their financial securities on the financial markets. You can easily pay too much or sell your collectible for too little without being able to seek recourse from a governmental regulator. Many collectibles are bought and sold at auctions, where prices can vary.

- Investing in collectibles does not bring overnight profits. Returns are realized when collectibles appreciate in value and are sold at a higher price than the purchase price. This might take a few years at the least.

- Investing in a collectible is characterized as an illiquid asset with high transaction costs.

Yet, for many collectors, investing in collectibles provides a sense of pleasure and enjoyment. Many specialized magazines, books, and Internet Web sites provide specialized knowledge on the different collectibles for interested investors.

INDEX

A

Accrued interest, 182–184, 201, 230–231, 234, 235, 236, 238
American depository receipts (ADRs), 153
American Stock Exchange (AMEX), 40, 41, 47, 49–63, 61, 80, 81, 91, 93, 155, 182, 204
American Stock Exchange Index, 40, 41
Arbitrage, 224–225, 226
Arbitrageurs, 220, 225, 273, 278
Ask price, 48, 61, 63, 64, 127, 182, 190, 198, 205, 206, 247
Asset allocation, 11–12, 27, 42–45
Assets, 8–10, 22, 58, 85, 86, 91, 138, 141, 142, 143, 154, 157–158, 166, 225

B

Balance Sheet, 8–9, 21, 22, 58, 140, 141–142, 144, 169, 207
Bankers' acceptances, 16, 119, 120, 121, 122, 133, 136
Bankruptcy, 21, 138, 156, 157, 158, 166–167, 169, 207, 225, 229
Bear market, 137, 147
Beta coefficient, 110
Bid and ask spread, 48–49, 51–52, 60, 61, 64, 172, 182, 190, 198, 206, 210, 212, 213–214, 224
Bid price, 48, 61, 63, 64, 127, 182, 190, 198, 205, 206, 247
Block trade, 65–66, 94
Bond market, 48, 120, 217
Bond(s), 12, 14, 16, 21, 26–28, 29, 32, 34, 42, 44, 45, 53–54, 55, 60, 138, 156, 158, 161–184, 185–215, 216–240, 263
    Collateral trust, 166
    Debenture, 167, 203, 217
    Equipment trust, 166
    Flat, 184
    Floating rate, 171, 204
    Foreign, 53
    Income, 167
    Indenture, 165, 167–168
    Intermediate-term, 162, 187
    Investment–grade, 115, 170, 203
    Ladder, 205
    Listed, 205, 206

Bond(s) (*Cont.*):
    Long-term, 162, 187, 202
    Mortgage-backed, 115, 166, 203
    Prices, 48–49, 98, 163–164, 170, 171, 172, 173, 178, 179, 180–184, 191, 198, 275
    Risks of, 168–172
    Secured, 166–167
    Subordinated debenture, 167, 223, 229
    Unsecured, 166–167, 203
    Valuation of, 178–179
Broker, 54, 60, 61, 63, 69–70, 71, 76, 88, 91, 94, 106, 125, 198
Broker-dealer, 54

C

Call premium, 165
Call price, 159, 165, 176, 206
Call provision, 155, 157, 159–160, 164–165, 166, 168, 171, 175, 204, 206, 210, 214–215, 220, 223, 225, 235, 236
    Deferred, 165
    Freely callable, 165
    Non callable, 164–165
Capital gains, 17, 2732, 33, 83, 86, 96, 103, 104, 108, 109–110, 123, 140, 146, 147, 159, 199, 212–213, 219, 224, 269, 270, 281, 282, 283, 289
Capital growth, 10–11, 42, 45, 97, 100, 216
Capital market, 16, 17
Capital loss, 3386, 103, 104, 108, 123, 134, 146, 199, 253, 269, 270
Capital preservation, 10–11, 31, 43, 45, 95, 100, 120, 213, 216
Cash account, 73, 75, 140–141, 144
Cash flow, 58, 147, 172, 173, 195, 197, 202, 292–294
    Negative, 190, 230, 231, 238
Certificate of deposit (CD), 16, 119, 121, 122, 131–132, 136, 161–162
    Negotiable, 131–132, 162
Cheat sheet, 57
Chicago Board of Trade, (CBT), 264, 265, 268, 276
Chicago Board Options Exchange, 242, 262
Chicago Mercantile Exchange, (CME), 264, 276

Churning, 76
Closed-end funds, 84–85, 87–88, 89, 94, 117
Collateralized mortgage obligation, (CMO), 200, 201–203
Collectibles, 300
Commercial paper, 16, 119, 120, 121, 122, 132, 136
Commission broker, 67
Commodities, 29, 242, 263
Commodities Exchange, (CMX), 264
Common stock, 17, 29, 42, 55, 137–154, 155, 218–220
Compounding, 3, 6, 11
Contingent convertible bonds, 238–240
Convertible bond, 16, 203, 216–228, 229, 239–240
    Advantages of, 224–225
Conversion discount, 227–228
Conversion feature, 217, 218–223
Conversion premium, 227–228
Conversion price, 158, 217, 218, 219–221, 224, 229
Conversion ratio, 158–159, 217, 218
Conversion value, 217–221, 225, 227
    Disadvantages of, 225
    Risks of, 223
Corporate bonds, 67, 169, 177, 179, 182.186, 187, 193, 200, 203–207, 223.224
    Risks of, 203–204
Coupon rate, 163, 164, 165, 168, 171–172, 179, 180–181, 190, 191, 201, 203, 204, 205, 206, 207, 217, 218, 220, 221, 223, 237
Coupon yield, 172–173, 175, 199
Coverage ratio, 22
Creditors, 162, 169
Credit rating 169–171, 220
Credit quality, 110, 220
Current yield, 173, 175, 180, 228
Cusip number, 188

D
Day order, 67, 68
Debt ratio, 22
Debt securities, 15
Debt level, 91, 155, 203, 207
Debt-to-equity ratio, 21, 91
Debt-to-total assets ratio, 207
Dealer (market maker), 49, 51, 53, 54, 60, 63, 192, 198, 212
Derivative securities, 15, 17–18, 95, 233, 241–242

Discount, 124, 125, 132, 163, 166, 173, 178, 180, 181, 190, 212–213, 228
Discount brokerage firm, 70–71
Discretionary account, 95
Diversification, 13, 22–25, 92, 94, 101, 115, 116, 117, 170–171, 205, 207
Dividends, 17, 21, 27, 32, 33, 34, 83, 86, 89, 90, 91, 93, 96, 103, 104, 109–110, 123, 138, 139–149, 155, 156, 157–158, 159, 213, 224
    Arrears, 158
    Cash, 140–141
    Date of declaration, 139
    Date of record, 139
    Ex-dividend, date, 139–140
    Extra, 141, 144
    Payment date, 140
    Property, 143
    Reinvestment plan (DRIP), 145, 146
    Special, 143–145
    Stock dividends, 141–142
Dogs of the Dow, 38
Double witch Friday, 278
Dow Jones Composite Average, 38
Dow Jones Industrial Average (DJIA), 37, 92, 93, 137, 146, 153, 262, 264, 274, 277
Dow Jones Transportation Average, 38
Dow Jones Utility Average, 38
Dutch auction method, 130, 191

E
EAFE Index, 41
Earnings, 59, 139, 140, 141, 142, 146, 147–150, 152, 153, 154, 161
Earnings per share, 218, 239
Economy:
    Expansion, 151
    Recession, 151
Efficient market hypothesis, 13,
Electronic Communications Networks, (ECNs), 48, 50, 52–53, 64
Emergency fund, 6, 14, 16
Equity, 58, 142, 154–155, 156, 221
Equity securities, 12, 15, 17
Eurodollars, 121, 295
Exchange traded funds (ETFs), 83, 84, 91–94, 117
Exit fees (back-load), 105
Expenses, 104
Expiration date, 241, 242, 243, 247, 249, 252, 266

F

Face value, *see* Par value.
Federal Deposit Insurance Corp (FDIC), 95, 122
Federal funds rate, 133
Federal Home Loan Mortgage Corporation, 192, 196, 199–201, 202
  Guaranteed mortgage certificate 200
  Participation certificate, 199–200
Federal National Mortgage Association (FNMA) securities, 53–54, 192, 196, 200–202
Federal Reserve bank(s), 53, 54, 125, 126, 127, 131, 132, 187–188
Fees, 70, 73, 83, 85, 88, 92, 94, 120–121, 146, 223, 296
Financial investments, 14–17
Financial life cycle, 9–11
Financial objectives, 7–8
Financial planners. 69, 106
Financial statements, 58
Floor broker, 61, 62
Foreign currencies, 264, 274
Futures, 17–18, 52, 54, 241, 242, 263–279
  Basis, 272, 273
  Commodity, 264, 265
  Currency, 276–277
  Daily limit, 269–270
  Financial, 263–264, 265, 274–279
  Fundamental analysis, 273–274
  Interest rate, 274, 275–276
  Market, 263–264
  Mini contracts, 276
  Open interest, 266
  Price quotes, 265–267
  Settle, 265–266
  Spot market, 266–267, 272–273
  Stock index, 277–279
  Technical analysis, 274

G

Gold, 296–299
  Bullion, 297–298
  Coins, 298
  ETFs, 298, 299
  Futures, 299
  Mining stocks, 298
  Mutual funds, 298–299
  Options, 299
Government agency bonds, 53, 60, 115, 177, 185, 186, 187, 192–203, 207, 275

Government National Mortgage Association (GNMA) bonds, 53–54, 99, 107, 196–201, 202
Good till canceled order, 67, 68
Gross profit margin, 148

H

Hedge funds, 96, 99, 100
Hedgers, 271–272, 275, 276, 277

I

Income generation, 100, 120, 156, 188, 213, 216
Income statement, 58–59, 169, 207
Inflation, 29, 30, 89, 134, 171, 185, 190–192, 204, 224, 281, 297–299
Initial Public Offering (IPO), 55–59, 60, 89, 145
Interest, 86, 103, 131, 133, 139, 161, 163, 164, 166, 167, 187, 189, 190, 193, 194–195, 197, 198, 199, 200, 201
Interest rates, 28, 30, 44, 45, 90, 95, 98, 99, 115, 156, 159, 163, 164, 165, 177, 178, 180–181, 198, 199, 204, 205, 216, 220, 223, 224, 225, 226, 232, 275, 286
Investing, 1–3
Reasons for, 3–5
Investment plan, 6, 69
Investment process, 5–14
Investment strategy, 12–13
  Active, 12–13, 98
  Passive, 12–13

J

Junk bond(s). 30, 32, 99, 170, 185, 186, 203

L

Level 1 quotes, 63
Level 2 quotes, 52, 63, 64, 72
Level 3 quotes, 63, 64
Leverage, 78, 245, 249, 252, 253, 263, 269, 270–271, 274
Liabilities, 8–10, 22, 58, 85, 86, 91, 141, 142, 143
Limited partnerships, 100
Limit order, 66, 67–68, 182
Liquid investments, 6, 14, 16, 30, 49, 119–136
Lock-up period, 56
Long position, 77, 100, 267, 271, 275, 276

M
Maintenance margin, 74, 76, 268, 269
Management fees, 89, 106–107
Margin, 267–269
Margin account, 74–76, 77, 78, 79
Margin call, 74, 76, 268–269, 271, 274
Margin deposit, 270
Margin requirement, 74, 267, 269, 270, 276
    Initial, 268–269, 271
Markdown, 54
Market capitalization, 153
Market order(s), 56, 66–67, 68, 69, 182
Marketable securities, 30, 119–136
Market maker, 51, 54, 60, 63, 64, 72
Marking to market, 114, 269
Markup, 54, 60, 187, 210, 214, 223–224
Maturity, 110, 162, 176, 177, 178, 179, 180,
    181, 190, 191, 196, 197, 201–202, 205,
    206, 220, 228
Maturity date, 162–163, 164, 166, 167, 168
Moody's, 169, 203, 232
Money market, 15, 16, 73, 119
    Caveats of, 124
    General purpose, 121
    Risks of, 122–123
    Tax–exempt, 122
    U.S. Government, 121
    Securities, 12, 15, 16, 28, 29, 42, 44, 45, 95,
        119–135
Mortgage, 193–195, 198, 199, 200, 281,
    284–289
    Adjustable rate (ARM), 286, 287, 288, 289
    Conventional, 284–289
    Federal agency backed, 284, 289
    Graduated payment, 289
    Interest, 281–282, 283, 284–289, 290–291
    Interest only ARM, 287–288, 289
    Principal, 281–282, 283, 284–289, 290–291
Mortgage-backed (Pass through) securities,
    186, 192–203
    Average life, 196–197
    Half life, 197
    Mortgage pools, 193–199, 200, 202
Municipal bond(s), 53, 60, 83, 99, 185, 186,
    207–215, 224
    General obligation, 207–208
    Revenue, 207–208, 210
    Risks of, 208–211
    Serial, 213
Mutual funds, 40, 41, 57, 82–117, 280
    Aggressive growth, 96, 98
    Balanced, 96, 98

Mutual funds (*Cont.*):
    Bond, 96, 98–99
    Convertible, 115
    Corporate bond, 96
    Emerging market, 96
    Equity, 96, 97–98, 114
    Expenses, 101, 115, 117, 123
    Global equity, 96
    GNMA, 97
    Growth, 96
    Growth and Income, 96
    High yield bond, 96
    Income equity, 96
    Index, 94, 96, 98, 109
    International equity, 96
    Load, 104–107, 121, 124
    Money market, 16, 95, 119, 120–124, 132,
        136
    Municipal bond 88, 96
    No-load, 104–107, 115, 121
    Objectives, 83, 84, 87, 97, 100, 101, 123
    Portfolio turnover, 109
    Professional management, 115, 117
    Prospectus, 98, 99, 101, 104, 107, 122, 123
    Risks of, 113–114, 132
    Short-term bond, 121, 123, 124
    Strategies, 100–101
    Style box, 110
    Value, 109
    Zero-coupon 115

N
Nasdaq Composite Index, 36, 40, 41, 92,
    262, 278
Nasdaq market, 40, 48, 49–53, 63, 80, 81, 155
Net asset value (NAV), 84, 85–87, 88, 89, 93,
    94, 95, 99, 103, 104, 105, 108–110, 113, 115
New issue, 55, 59, 60, 207
New York Mercantile Exchange, (NYM) 264
New York Stock Exchange (NYSE), 38, 40,
    41, 47, 48, 49–53, 61, 62, 67, 80, 81,
    153, 155, 157, 182, 199, 200, 204, 205,
    242, 264
New York Stock Exchange Composite
    Index, 40, 277
Net worth, 9, 10, 100
Non financial investments, 14–16

O
Odd lot, 64–65
Offer price, 104, 105
Online brokerage firm, 71, 72

Online trading, 71
Open-end funds, 84–87, 94, 100
Options, 17–18, 50, 52, 54, 241–262, 276
    At the money, 249, 255
    Call, 242, 246–252, 255, 259–262
    Covered call, 255–256
    Covered put, 257
    Index, 262
    In the money, 249, 255
    Intrinsic value, 248, 254–255
    LEAPS, 245, 258
    Naked call, 256–257
    Naked put, 257–258
    Open interest, 247
    Out of the money, 249, 255
    Price (premium), 244, 245–247, 252
    Put, 242, 246–247, 252–255, 259–262
    Spread, 259–261
    Straddle, 259–260
    Uncovered, 74
    Writing, 255–258
Options Clearing Corporation (OCC), 245
Option holder, 242–243
Option writer, 242–243
OTC market, 40, 41, 47, 49, 51, 53–54, 63,
    85, 87, 153, 182, 190, 204, 205, 206,
    223, 242

P
Pacific Exchange, 242
Par value, 34, 124, 125, 126, 156, 161, 162,
    163, 165, 173, 178, 199, 205, 218, 219,
    228
Philadelphia Exchange, 242
Poison put, 204, 206
Precious metals, 296–299
Preferred stock, 17, 28, 55, 138, 154–160,
    239–240
    Adjustable rate, 156, 160
    Classes of, 157
    Convertible, 158–159
    Cumulative preferred, 157, 158
    Noncumulative, 158
    Trust, 156–157
Premium, 113, 163, 164, 166, 171, 178, 180,
    181, 190, 199, 206, 212–213, 221–222
Price-to-book value, 91
Price-to-earnings (P/E) ratio, 97, 101, 110,
    148, 149, 155
Price transparency, 48, 49, 54, 60, 210–211,
    224, 280–281
Primary market, 55–59, 125

Principal, 161, 162, 166, 167, 168, 190, 191,
    194–195, 198, 199, 200, 201, 208
Prospectus, 55, 57, 58, 59, 206
Put provision, 165, 204, 205, 236

R
Rate of return, 3, 5, 33–36, 74, 75, 83, 115,
    173–174, 229–230
Redemption charge, 104, 107, 124
Real return, 32, 124
Real estate, 14, 15, 26, 28.29, 31, 45, 89,
    280–296
    Home ownership, 281–289
    Land, 281, 289–290
    Limited partnerships, 281, 295–296
        Blind pool, 296
    Rental properties, 281, 290–295
    Taxes, 281, 282
Real Estate Investment Trust (REIT), 89–91,
    147–148, 281, 295, 296
    Equity, 89–90
    Finite life (FREIT) 90
    Hybrid, 89–90
    Mortgage, 89–90
Refunding provision, 164, 168, 206, 210
Repurchase agreements, 16, 119, 120, 121,
    133–134, 136
Required rate of return, 172, 178
Retained earnings, 53, 140, 142, 144
Retirement fund(s), 3, 10
Return, 20, 26–28, 29, 36, 45, 55–56, 101–102,
    103–104, 105, 107, 108–110, 119, 120,
    134, 138, 153, 154, 185, 192, 198, 212,
    217, 223, 270–271
Reverse stock split, 143
Risk, 2, 5, 7–11, 19–31, 45, 74, 90, 93, 101,
    110, 120, 134, 152, 154, 177, 202
    Business, 20–25, 169
    Call risk, 171, 210, 223, 237
    Credit, 21, 95, 98, 166–167, 168, 169, 170,
        185, 186, 193, 196, 200, 202, 203, 208,
        232
    Default, 21, 95, 98, 119, 122, 125, 165, 166,
        167–168, 169, 179, 185, 186, 203,
        208–209, 223, 231–232
    Event, 22, 29, 203, 206
    Exchange rate, 22, 29–30
    Financial, 21–25
    Fraud, 113–114
    Insolvency, 113
    Interest rate, 22, 28, 113, 115, 168–169,
        191, 204, 205, 209, 223, 236–237

Risk (*Cont.*):
  Liquidity, 22, 30–31, 172
  Market, 22, 25–28, 41, 42, 113
  Operating, 21
  Purchasing power, 29, 168, 171, 204
  Reinvestment rate, 168, 171–172,
      197–198, 237
  Systematic, 22, 41
  Unsystematic, 21, 25, 41
Risk and return, 31–33, 41–42, 45
Risk-free rate, 32
Risk of loss, 2, 5, 12, 18, 25, 32, 57, 58–59, 72,
    101, 113, 134, 154, 242, 244, 253, 256, 263,
    271, 275, 289
Round lot, 64, 131–132
Routing number, 126, 188
Russell 2000, 262
Russell 3000 Index, 41

S
Saving, 1–2, 3, 5, 8
Secondary market, 53, 55, 56, 59–69, 125,
    131, 162, 190, 191, 198, 199, 211, 223
Separate Trading of Registered Interest and
    Principal Securities (STRIPS), 191,
    233–234
Serial bond, 163
Settlement date, 73
Shareholders' equity, 58
Shelf registration, 59
Short interest, 81
Short selling, 74, 76–81, 93, 224–225, 252, 253,
    257, 267, 271, 275, 276, 277
  Risks of, 79–80.
Sinking fund provision, 166, 168, 206
Specialist(s), 48, 50, 61–62, 67
Speculating, 1–2
Speculators, 271, 275, 276, 277
Spin off, 144–145
Split off 145
Standard & Poor's, 169
Standard & Poor's 500 Index, 38–40, 41, 45,
    92, 93, 98, 153, 262, 264, 274, 276, 277
Stock market, 48, 85, 97, 91, 137, 217
Stock market indices, 36–41, 91
Stocks, 14, 26–28, 34, 36–46.47–53, 60, 69,
    137–154, 155, 185, 206, 216, 217–228,
    241–262, 263
  Blue chip, 32, 38, 44, 98, 140, 146–147, 153,
      154, 182
  Cabinet, 64
  Classes of, 145

Stocks (*Cont.*):
  Cyclical, 20, 150–151
  Defensive, 151, 154
  Emerging market, 98, 113
  Foreign, 44, 152–153
  Growth, 32, 40, 44, 83, 97, 110, 140, 146,
      147, 148–149, 150, 151, 153, 154
  Income, 32, 140, 147–148
  Indices, 242
  Large-cap, 26–28, 110, 153–154
  Mid-cap 98, 110, 153–154
  Penny, 64
  Small-cap, 26–28, 101, 110, 113, 153–154
  Speculative, 32, 51, 98, 151–152
  Stable, 21
  Value, 40, 44, 97, 110, 149, 150, 151, 153
Stock split, 141–143
Stop order, 68–69, 80
Stop out yield, 130, 189
Street name, 71–73, 74, 77
Strike (exercise) price, 241, 242, 243, 245–249,
    252, 259
Systematic withdrawal plan, (SWP), 124

T
12(b)-1 fees, 104, 106, 107
Taxable equivalent yield, 214–215
Tax deferred accounts, 231, 235
Tax exempt interest, 185, 186, 187, 193, 207,
    213–215, 234
Taxes, 86, 89, 96, 99, 123, 186, 191, 202–215,
    230, 231, 235, 238, 281–283, 296
Term bond, 162–163
Thinly traded securities, 30, 51210
Time horizon, 3–5, 7–11, 12, 14, 26, 30, 41,
    45, 110
Time value of money, 4, 6, 34, 174, 178
Trade date, 73
Tranches, 201–203
Transaction costs, 48–49, 65–66, 70, 94,
    104–107, 131, 186, 188, 190–192
Treasury bills, 16, 26, 30, 32, 45, 60, 119, 120,
    122, 124–131, 133, 136, 274, 275
  Auction, 125–127
  Commercial book entry system, 127
  Competitive bid, 125, 127, 130, 131
  Noncompetitive bid, 125, 127, 130–131
  Prices, 125–127
Treasury Inflation Protection Securities,
    (TIPS), 171
Treasury notes and bonds, 99, 179, 185,
    187–190, 191, 197, 233, 274, 275

Treasury notes and bonds (*Cont.*):
  Auction, 187–190, 191
  Competitive bid, 189
  Non-competitive bid, 189
  Risks of, 190
  Treasury Receipts, 233
  Treasury securities, 14, 53, 54, 60, 95, 116,
    122, 169, 176, 177186–192, 193, 203,
    207
  Triple witch Friday, 278

U
Underwriter(s), 55, 57, 58, 91, 223
U.S. government securities, 133
Unit investment trust (UIT), 84–85, 88–89
Uptick, 79, 80

V
Value Line Composite Index, 41
Voting rights, 138

W
Wilshire 5000 Index, 41

Y
Yield(s), 88, 90.91, 95, 98, 101, 103, 104, 107,
    110, 113, 125–126, 130, 133, 156, 164,
    172–178, 180, 186, 187, 189, 191.192,
    193, 197, 199, 200, 202, 213–215, 225,
    229.230, 232, 235
  After tax dividend yield, 215
  Bank discount, 126
Yield curve, 172, 176–178
Yield to call, 175–76
Yield to maturity, 173–176, 181

Z
Zero-coupon bonds, 16, 84, 172, 201–203,
    216–217, 228–240
  Advantages and disadvantages of,
    237–238
  Corporate convertible, 235–236
  Federal agency, 234
  Mortgage backed, 234
  Municipal, 234–235
  Risks of, 236–237
Zero-tick, 80

ABOUT THE AUTHOR

Esmé Faerber, M.B.A., C.P.A., is professor of business and accounting a Rosemont College. She is the author of numerous books on investments and finance, including *All about Stocks, All about Bonds and Bond Mutual Funds, Fundamentals of the Bond Market,* and *the Personal Finance Calculator.*